Metropolitan Resilience in a Time of Economic Turmoil

THE URBAN AGENDA

Series Editor, Michael A. Pagano

Metropolitan Resilience in a Time of Economic Turmoil

EDITED BY MICHAEL A. PAGANO

University of Illinois at Chicago

PUBLISHED FOR THE
COLLEGE OF URBAN PLANNING
AND PUBLIC AFFAIRS,
UNIVERSITY OF ILLINOIS AT CHICAGO,
BY THE UNIVERSITY OF ILLINOIS PRESS
Urbana, Chicago, and Springfield

The College of Urban Planning and Public Affairs of the University of Illinois at Chicago and the University of Illinois Press gratefully acknowledge that publication of this book was assisted by a grant from the John D. and Catherine T. MacArthur Foundation.

Manufactured in the United States of America
1 2 3 4 5 C P 5 4 3 2 1

∞ This book is printed on acid-free paper.

Library of Congress Control Number: 2013952709

Contents

Preface and Acknowledgments

The University of Illinois at Chicago (UIC) has hosted a forum on urban issues since 1995, when the first forum was convened under the auspices of the Great Cities Institute at UIC. The "Winter Forum" met annually until 2005, convening scholars, public intellectuals, policy makers, and elected officials from the Chicago region as well as from other parts of the country. Starting in 2005, UIC in partnership with the city of Chicago hosted the Richard J. Daley Urban Forum annually for six years. This forum was designed from its beginnings as a collaboration aimed at convening key public, private, and nonprofit leaders in an academic arena to discuss, analyze, and propose pragmatic and innovative solutions to enhance the lives of city dwellers around the globe.

In 2012, UIC Chancellor Paula Allen-Meares revitalized the UIC annual conference on urban issues, titling it the UIC Urban Forum and charging it with the responsibility of bringing together policy makers, academics, public intellectuals, students, community activists, and citizens to discuss, debate, and recommend policy action to the pressing and intractable challenges of cities and metropolitan regions. The activities of the UIC Urban Forum are directed toward two major goals: staging a major annual event to advance a national and global dialogue about the urban future; and disseminating policy options, recommendations, and best practices.

PARTNERSHIP AND COLLABORATION

The UIC Urban Forum works in collaboration with a multiplicity of partners, including foundations, the nonprofit community, governments, the corporate sector, and the media. The partners of the 2012 UIC Urban Forum included the Chicago Community Trust, BMO Harris, the John D. and Catherine T. MacArthur Foundation, Abbott, ITW, Baxter, Walgreen's, UIC's College of Urban Planning and Public Affairs, and UIC's Institute for Policy and Civic Engagement, whose financial support was instrumental in the success of the forum. I am particularly grateful to the MacArthur Foundation and its vice president, Julia Stasch, for providing a subvention that covered some publishing costs for this monograph.

The forum's partnership with the public radio station in Chicago, Chicago Public Media (WBEZ), is also gratefully acknowledged. WBEZ not only supplied moderators for the morning panels, which included elected and appointed policy officials, but also recorded and archived the entire event. The audio from each panel can be found at WBEZ's Chicago Amplified website, wbez.org/amplified, or at wbez.org/urbanforum. Breeze Richardson of WBEZ was instrumental in ensuring the success of the partnership, and her energy and vision are deeply appreciated. Torey Malatia, the general manager of WBEZ, helped bring the collaboration to fruition. WBEZ's engagement with the UIC Urban Forum, and with UIC more generally, speaks to the understanding and recognition by both parties of the critical importance of bringing academic research to the public square for deliberation, reflection, and action.

The UIC Urban Forum partnered with the University of Illinois Press to disseminate the Urban Forum White Papers, whose purpose is to provide an intellectual underpinning to the conference's theme, and a synopsis of the "Conversations with Local Policy Officials" panel at the conference. The Urban Agenda series established by the press will publish the proceedings from the annual conference. This volume is the first installment of the partnership. Collaboration with the director of the University of Illinois Press, Willis Regier, has been and will no doubt continue to be delightful and educational. His gracious and gentle guidance of that project, and his insightful proposal to title the series The Urban Agenda, have made the partnership an important element of the UIC Urban Forum.

Finally, the UIC Urban Forum's primary internal partner is the UIC College of Urban Planning and Public Affairs (CUPPA). The project director of the UIC Urban Forum is the dean of the college, and the executive committee consists of CUPPA's director of the Great Cities Institute and a delegate from the chancellor's office.

THE 2012 UIC URBAN FORUM

The theme of the 2012 UIC Urban Forum was metropolitan resilience in a time of economic turmoil, and the forum was cochaired by Illinois governor

Pat Quinn, Chicago mayor Rahm Emanuel, Cook County Board president Toni Preckwinkle, and UIC chancellor Paula Allen-Meares. Held on December 6, 2012, the daylong event began with two panels that included appointed and elected policy officials. The afternoon panels were organized around the themes of the four white papers. At the conclusion of the afternoon session's panels, U.S. Secretary of Transportation Ray LaHood engaged in a lively conversation with the executive director of UIC's Urban Transportation Center, Steven Schlickman, on the role, vitality, and vision of transportation for the United States and U.S. metropolitan regions.

The 2012 UIC Urban Forum was organized by an executive committee that chose the theme of the conference; a committee of UIC scholars that identified the white papers and the authors; an external advisory board that recommended participants for the morning panels; and an operations committee that organized and planned the conference. The executive committee, which I chaired, included the interim director of UIC's Great Cities Institute, Dennis Judd, and UIC's dean of education, Vicki Chou. The UIC Urban Forum Committee of Academic Advisors included David Perry, Dick Simpson, Rachel Weber, David Merriman, Nathan Anderson, and Rebecca Hendrick.

The external board of advisors included Bruce Katz (vice president of the Brookings Institution), Henry Cisneros (former HUD secretary and mayor of San Antonio), Lee Fisher (president and CEO of CEOs for Cities), Donald Borut (executive director of the National League of Cities), Terry Mazany (president of the Chicago Community Trust), MarySue Barrett (president of the Metropolitan Planning Council), Randy Blankenhorn (executive director of the Chicago Metropolitan Agency for Planning), Rita Athas (president of World Business Chicago), Karen Freeman-Wilson (mayor of Gary), Rahm Emanuel (mayor of Chicago), Luke Ravenstahl (mayor of Pittsburgh), and Michael Coleman (mayor of Columbus).

Participants on the panels included the following, to whom a deep debt of gratitude is owed: Philip Ashton, MarySue Barrett, Randy Blankenhorn, Niala Boodhoo, Raphael Bostic, Forrest Claypool, Teresa L. Córdova, Richard Feiock, Karen Freeman-Wilson, Rachel Gordon, Rebecca Hendrick, Geoffrey Hewings, Terry Mazany, David Merriman, Natalie Moore, Laurence Msall, Richard Nathan, Lance Pressl, Julia Stasch, Annette Steinacker, Nik Theodore, Rachel Weber, and Margaret Weir. Public officials who were panelists in the morning sessions included Cristal Thomas (deputy governor of Illinois), Steve Koch (deputy mayor, city of Chicago), Neil Khare (deputy chief of staff to the Cook County Board), Michael Coleman (mayor of Columbus), Betsy Fretwell (city manager of Las Vegas), and Luke Ravenstahl (mayor of Pittsburgh).

Finally, I wish to acknowledge the people who met weekly for six months and ensured the smooth operating success of the 2012 UIC Urban Forum. In particular, I offer my grateful appreciation to the support, advice, and dedicated effort of Jenny Sweeny, who was responsible for planning and organizing the event. Also instrumental in the success of the event were the help provided by Jennifer Woodard and Mark Rosati in the UIC Office of External Affairs; the development work of Darcy Evon and Rona Heifetz; the spectacular contribution of graduate assistants Emma Heemskerk, Sarah Falconer, and Sarah Acosta; and the flawless performance of the staff of Jasculca-Terman Associates, especially Maureen Meehan, Carly Olsman, Kristi Sebestyen, Bill Strong, Jessica Thunberg, and Bailey Vance, in planning and organizing the UIC Urban Forum.

Emma Heemskerk and Sarah Falconer, without whose editorial assistance and manuscript supervision the book-production process would have been severely handicapped, deserve a heartfelt "thank you."

The eight hundred registrants of the one-day conference were challenged to ensure that we, as active citizens and participants of the democratic experiment, continue to prod our communities, dream about a better future, and experiment with policy options that will enhance the quality of life and human condition of cities and metropolitan regions. The annual UIC Urban Forum offers thoughtful conferences on critical urban issues in a venue to which all the world's citizens are invited.

Michael A. Pagano
Project Director, 2012 UIC Urban Forum
Dean, UIC College of Urban Planning and Public Affairs
Chicago, February 2013

PART ONE
OVERVIEW

Cities and the Great Recession

Lessons in Dynamic Change and Adaptation

MICHAEL A. PAGANO

UNIVERSITY OF ILLINOIS AT CHICAGO

The Great Recession has had a powerful effect on metropolitan regions and on local governments. The real-estate bubble burst in 2007, putting many owners under water (the mortgage exceeded the market value of the home) and the stock markets plummeted in 2008, wiping out hundreds of billions of dollars in investments. Consequently, the unemployment rate in the nation soared quickly to over 9 percent and has declined ever-so-slightly over the last several years and appears stuck at around 7–8 percent, well above the pre–Great Recession levels of 4–5 percent. Job loss in 2008 and 2009 wracked cities and urbanized regions as nearly all of the loss was in the private sector, down by some 8 million jobs; since then, nearly 5 million private-sector jobs have been created, benefiting the nation's metropolitan regions. At the same time, however, job loss in the local government sector has worsened. The U.S. Bureau of Labor Statistics indicated that local government employment at the end of 2012 shrank by 577,000 employees from the peak of 14,610,000 reached in 2008.[1] Local governments, including school districts, cities, and counties—which generated 75 percent of their total tax revenue from a tax on real-estate values—in particular are hard-pressed to recoup the losses of the last five years as the real-estate market is only recently showing signs of recovery.[2] Fortunately, the real-estate sector may be stabilizing—and mortgage rates remain at historically low rates, benefiting the housing market—but property tax collections by cities, counties, school districts, and townships lag the "real-time" market by two to three years and sometimes longer. Consequently, cities' capacities to provide a level of service that citizens enjoyed in, say, 2006, may not be reached for several more years, if ever.[3]

To complicate the growth challenges of metropolitan regions, estimates of basic infrastructure needs total in the trillions of dollars and pension obligations for local governments, as well as health benefits for retired municipal employees, reach unfathomable heights.[4] A recent study on the unfunded liability of the municipal pension systems and the unfunded portion of "other post-employment benefits" (typically including health care costs) estimated that the unfunded liability for 61 cities reached a staggering $217 billion.[5] In other words, cities labor under a creaky tax regimen today and for the foreseeable future just at the same time that pension obligations, health costs for city retirees, and the "life" of infrastructure assets are reaching critical needs.

The quality of life in urban regions depends on the capacity of cities and metropolitan regions to respond to the environmental, infrastructural, organizational, and human challenges of the global era. Cities and urban regions that are resilient enough to cope with the challenges posed both by unexpected shocks and longer-term trends will be positioned to provide adequately for the health, safety, and well-being of their citizens. These challenges require the application of human and financial capital, innovation and entrepreneurship, a vibrant private sector, and the involvement of government and nonprofit institutions in governance and service delivery. When natural disasters strike (e.g., Hurricane Katrina, Super Storm Sandy, and the Blizzard of 2011, all in a series of "storms of the century") or when the economic swings of the business cycle hit cities' foundations (e.g., the Great Recession, the dot-com bust), the preponderance of cities are resilient enough to survive and even thrive. Cities "come back," they "rebound" and "adapt."[6] They age and they also reinvent themselves, and a very few do indeed become ghost towns and die.

Metropolitan regions and cities, the engines of the national and global economies, are straining under the confluence of these critical factors. Private-sector employment, the growth of private-firm formation, the training of an appropriately skilled work force, and the linking of the component parts of a sustainability economy require an adequate delivery of municipal services. The health and welfare of the nation depends on the strength and resilience of its cities.[7]

IT HASN'T BEEN THIS BAD SINCE . . .

"Not since the Great Depression" is the opening line to many contemporary analyses of unemployment, the fiscal position of cities and counties, the fraying of social safety nets, increased poverty levels, declining housing markets, and crushing personal and commercial bankruptcies. In truth, the

Great Recession that raised its ugly head with the bursting of the real-estate bubble in 2007, and its acceleration with the stock market crash of September 2008, does not truly equate to the disastrous economic collapse of the 1930s. The great lessons of the Great Depression were found in the broad regulatory and social institutions created during that era for the purpose of averting, or at least softening, the catastrophic human and commercial effects of failed systems.[8] Regulation at a national scale was created through New Deal legislation, including a national system of Social Security, recognition of collective bargaining rights, establishment of minimum wages and work regulations, banking and stock market regulations, among a host of other regulations over the national economy. These regulations have been effectively coupled with the fiscal powers of the federal government and, with the monetary powers of the Federal Reserve system over the supply of currency, they constitute a powerful and profound influence over the economy, the distribution of wealth, and the quality of life. These regulatory institutions were certainly called on after the onset of the Great Recession to perform what they were designed to do, namely, to ease the human suffering caused by drastic shifts in the national and global economies.

In its time, the Great Depression spawned numerous regulatory agencies and interventions designed to ensure efficient and safe markets as well as to provide a social safety net for those suffering both short- and long-term employment dislocations. The comparison, therefore, between the effects and impacts of the Great Depression on the economy, social fabric, and livelihood of the nation differ markedly from those of the Great Recession. A few illustrations highlight the stark differences.[9]

- Unemployment. At the peak of the Great Recession, unemployment reached nearly 10 percent by 2009, while at the peak of the Great Depression, unemployment approached 25 percent.
- Stock market. The Dow Jones Industrial Average plummeted by 89 percent between 1929 and 1933, while it dropped some 20–30 percent between 2008 and 2010.
- Prices. The prices of goods and services declined nearly 25 percent between 1929 and 1933—hence the term "depression"—while prices remained stable during the Great Recession.
- Bank foreclosures. Bank foreclosures reached nearly 50 percent of all banks by 1933, but only 10 percent by 2012.
- Municipal bankruptcies. During the Great Depression, 4,770 local governments defaulted on their debts; during the Great Recession, only a handful defaulted.[10]

- Social disruptions. Urban and rural riots during the 1930s were abundant, while the most notable disturbances related to the Great Recession in the United States were the Occupy Wall Street movement and the Wisconsin teachers' actions in reaction to Governor Scott Walker's proposal to disallow collective bargaining for state employees (the federal Wagner Act protects the collective bargaining rights of private-sector employees, except in agriculture, but not those of state and local government employees).[11]

Since the Great Depression of the 1930s, the nation has continued its move from an agrarian economy to an industrial and service economy to a metropolitan-centered economy. By the end of World War I, the nation's urban population and rural population were nearly identical. By 1930 and the start of the Great Depression, 56.1 percent of the nation's population resided in urbanized areas; by 2010, the census numbers indicated that 80.7 percent resided in urban areas.

The economic drivers of the twenty-first century are the nation's metropolitan regions. Fully 85 percent of the nation's GDP can be tied directly to the economic activity of the nation's cities and metropolitan regions. As the nation's cities attract an ever-growing share of the U.S. population, the capacity of local governments to honor service commitments, build and maintain necessary infrastructure, and meet their financial obligations will have a profound effect on local and regional economies, public safety, education, and overall quality of life for hundreds of millions of Americans.

It is not a stretch to say that the ability of U.S. cities and metropolitan regions to address challenges from transportation and economic development to health care in the years ahead will determine the kind of country we become. Unfunded pension liabilities, the gaping infrastructure deficit, the promises of "other post-employment benefits" to retired municipal employees, and the continued strain of delivering basic city services as the tax base of cities stagnates, all combine to threaten the fiscal foundation of cities and their citizens in a way that we have experienced "not since the Great Depression."

Metropolitan regions—and the individuals, households, and firms that link together to form networks of social, political, and economic life within the metropolitan region—are challenged by changes and shifts in systemic linkages to other metropolitan regions, international markets, migratory patterns, social disturbances, and other shocks to their welfare. Metropolitan regions and cities, just like other social organizations, adapt and change to these shifting systems and either survive and grow in new and different ways or stagnate and decline. Municipal governments, like other social organizations, engage in problem-solving activities in order to maintain an equilibrium between the city government and its internal and external environments.[12] A city's external environment consists primarily of citizens who receive local governmental services and of taxpayers who provide revenues for such services. The city searches for an equilibrium or steady state in its relationship with this external environment. This equilibrium can be explained in Tieboutian terms as the "bundle of services" that residents receive for a given tax price.[13] Taxpayers can and do "vote with their feet" in search of municipalities with good public services for which they are willing to pay the taxes and fees. Local governments, then, are in a continuous game of competition with neighbors to be efficient and effective service providers.

While the challenges that cities and metropolitan regions face today are not new, investment in the economic development potential of metro regions is tied directly to the nation's capacity to survive the Great Recession and rebound. The underlying premise of this volume is that cities and metropolitan regions are and can be resilient, they can successfully adapt to changing circumstances, and they can survive in a brave new world that they might not have anticipated only a few years earlier.

The Fiscal Effects of the Great Recession on Cities

The early years of the Great Recession were certainly painful to the economy and civil society, but its impacts cannot be compared with the devastating impacts of the Great Depression on society. The Great Recession has taken a toll on the fiscal health of cities as well as on the nation's employment and income. Although municipal defaults during the Great Depression amounted to 4,770, such defaults were few and far between in the late 2000s, except for those considered "newsworthy" (none of which was related to the Great Recession, e.g., the inability of Harrisburg, Pa., to pay borrowing costs for an incinerator; the inability of Jefferson County, Ala., to retire its debt for its massive sewer system; Vallejo, Calif.). Since the start of the Great Recession, only a few city governments (e.g., Stockton, Calif.), have petitioned the federal courts through Chapter 9, the federal bankruptcy legislation for local government protection.[14] Indeed, because the part of the federal bankruptcy code that applies to cities requires that state law specifically authorize the municipality to be a debtor, the number of states that permit their municipalities to file for Chapter 9 bankruptcy protection is small. Twelve states allow cities to file in federal bankruptcy courts, another twelve authorize a "contingent filing," three grant limited authorization, and "two states prohibit filing. . . . The remaining 21 [states] are either unclear or do not have specific authorization."[15] Few cities contemplate filing for Chapter 9, even if their states permit it, because cities have the authority to adjust their spending and taxing responsibilities.

For the most part, city officials have approached their elected offices responsibly and have managed to balance their resources with their service delivery responsibilities, as challenging as that has been during the Great Recession. In fact, an annual survey of the nation's cities' chief financial officers on city fiscal conditions indicates that cities are quite active in ensuring that their revenue-raising and spending responsibilities stay in alignment. Since 1987, nearly half of all responding cities in National League of Cities surveys have increased fees and charges each year, and another one-quarter have identified new activities for which to charge fees. In contrast, just one in four cities has raised the property tax rate annually since at least 1992.[16] Due to the cities' powers to adjust spending levels and levy taxes and fees, and due to their balanced budget requirement, few municipal governments, then, actually declare bankruptcy.

The case of Columbus, Ohio, is instructive. During the depths of the Great Recession, the city, under Mayor Michael Coleman, proposed raising the municipal income tax by half a percent. At the time, a 2 percent municipal income tax rate was levied on wages and salaries of residents and of nonresidents who worked within the city limits, as well as on the net profits of businesses. The proposed 0.5 percent increase would raise income tax receipts to the city by $90–$100 million. The city had already eliminated over a hundred positions and closed one-third of the city parks because of the recession, which resulted in a nearly $80 million decline in city revenue. Yet, on August 4, 2009, the city voters approved raising taxes rather than continue to reduce service levels and city government employment.

Is a Federal Bailout Possible?

Cities' financial capacity to remain solvent does not rely on bailouts from the federal government. Historically, the federal government's intervention in the affairs of municipalities was quite modest until the 1960s. The public works projects funded and administered by the Works Progress Administration, the Public Works Administration, and the Civilian Conservation Corps during the Great Depression were cooperative projects with state and local governments.[17] Yet, as the Great Depression wound down with the escalation of the global military conflicts culminating in World War II, the federal government retreated from its broad entanglements with municipalities of the 1930s and settled into cooperative agreements in areas of public housing and social welfare, policy arenas that were principally linkages with the states. With the rise of a political coalition that pushed for broader federal-city collaboration, starting in the Great Society years of the 1960s, the federal government stepped up its aid to cities as a means of fighting poverty, creating jobs, and promoting urban economic development.[18] When President Lyndon B. Johnson signed the law creating the U.S. Department of Housing and Urban Development in 1965, he opened the curtain on a decade that would see a vast increase in U.S. attention to (and spending on) cities. Among the subsequent laws that made significant new federal funds available to municipalities were the State and Local Fiscal Assistance Act (also known as General Revenue Sharing) in 1972 and the Housing and Community Development Act of 1974, which initiated the Community Development Block Grant (CDBG) program.

As figure 1 shows, federal aid to municipalities reached $25 billion (in constant dollars) in fiscal year 1978, amounting to nearly 15 percent of general municipal revenue. This high-water mark coincided with the release under the Carter administration of the National Urban Policy Report of 1978, which outlined a series of measures aimed at stimulating jobs and investments in the nation's inner cities. Within a year of the release of the report, however, rampant inflation wracked the economy with increasing joblessness ("stagflation"), and the electorate wanted the government to reduce taxes and deficits. In response, the Carter administration furiously backpedaled away from a "national urban policy" and from further financial entanglements with cities.

The 1980 election of President Ronald Reagan represented the first time a sitting president had been defeated since Herbert Hoover in 1932. Reagan implemented his policy of the three Ds—decentralization, decongestion, and devolution—which resulted in more Ds, namely a rapid de-escalation in direct federal aid.[19] "Decongestion" would ease the effects of, or eliminate, four hundred mandates on state and local governments; and "decentralization" and consolidation would affect five hundred state-local grants. Devolution and the attendant policy conversations about "sorting out" functions by an appropriate and constitutional level of government meant that the financial bonds between the federal government and local governments would be severely weakened.

By fiscal year 1987, federal aid as a percentage of municipal revenues had retreated to 6.4 percent from the 15 percent high achieved in 1978. Measured in constant dollars, the aid flowing from Washington to municipalities had declined by half in the previous ten years. After the decline in federal aid under President Reagan, city revenues stabilized to a level with 73 percent derived from own-source revenues, 22 percent from state aid, and 5 percent from federal aid. Federal aid to municipalities has remained at or near the 5 percent mark for a quarter century. Cities' financial fortunes, then, are only weakly linked to the direct flows of federal funds.

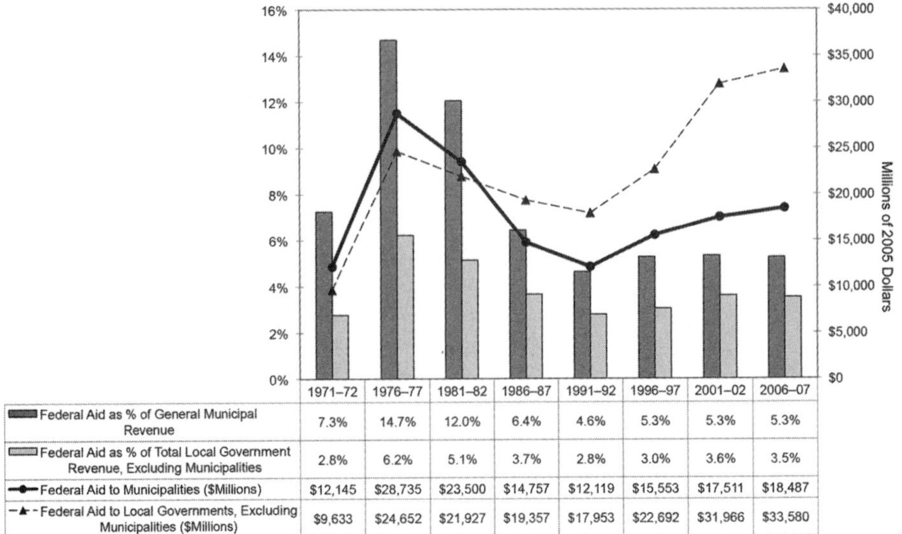

	1971–72	1976–77	1981–82	1986–87	1991–92	1996–97	2001–02	2006–07
Federal Aid as % of General Municipal Revenue	7.3%	14.7%	12.0%	6.4%	4.6%	5.3%	5.3%	5.3%
Federal Aid as % of Total Local Government Revenue, Excluding Municipalities	2.8%	6.2%	5.1%	3.7%	2.8%	3.0%	3.6%	3.5%
Federal Aid to Municipalities ($Millions)	$12,145	$28,735	$23,500	$14,757	$12,119	$15,553	$17,511	$18,487
Federal Aid to Local Governments, Excluding Municipalities ($Millions)	$9,633	$24,652	$21,927	$19,357	$17,953	$22,692	$31,966	$33,580

Figure 1. Federal Aid to Municipalities and to Other Local Governments, 1972–2007. Source: US Bureau of the Census, *Government Finances* (various years).

Cities' Fiscal Positions

One way that cities prepare for future fiscal challenges is to maintain adequate levels of general-fund ending balances. Ending balances are similar to reserves, or what might be thought of as cities' equivalents to "rainy-day funds," in that they provide a financial cushion for cities in the event of a fiscal downturn or the need for an unexpected outlay. Unlike states' reserves, or "rainy-day funds," there is no trigger mechanism—such as an increase in unemployment—to force release of the funds; instead, reserves are available for spending at any time or for saving for a specific purpose. City ending balances, which are transferred forward to the next fiscal year in most cases, are maintained for many reasons. For example, cities build up healthy balances in anticipation of unpredictable events, such as natural disasters and economic downturns. But ending balances are also built up deliberately, much like a personal savings account, to set aside funds for planned events such as the construction of capital projects.[20] Because bond underwriters see reserves as an indicator of fiscal responsibility, these can increase credit ratings and decrease the costs of city debt, thereby saving the city money in

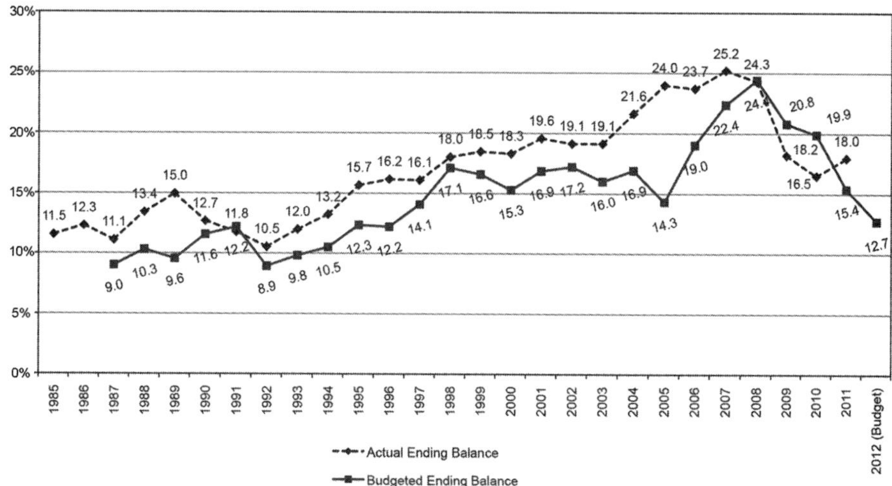

Figure 2. Ending Balances as a Percentage of Expenditures (General Fund). Source: Christopher Hoene, Michael Pagano, and Christy McFarland, *City Fiscal Conditions in 2012* (Washington, DC: National League of Cities, 2012).

annual debt service costs. Finally, as federal and state aid to cities has become a smaller proportion of city revenues, cities have become more self-reliant and are more likely to set aside funds for emergencies and other purposes.

Prior to the Great Recession, as city finances experienced sustained growth, city ending balances as a percentage of general fund expenditures reached a historical high for the survey of 25 percent. However, as economic conditions made balancing city budgets more difficult in recent years, ending balances have been increasingly utilized to fill the gap. In 2011, cities reduced their ending balances to 18 percent of expenditures (compared to a projected 15.4 percent). In 2012, city finance officers projected ending balances at 12.7 percent of expenditures, a decline of nearly 50 percent in five years. (See fig. 2.)

The Effects of Housing on Cities

The burst in the housing market bubble reverberated around the national economy, dropping the value of residential real estate more than at any time since the Great Depression. Although local housing markets varied in the severity of the impact, it was clear that the 2007 real-estate recession began to turn around only in late 2012. The metropolitan effects of the decline, however, varied markedly. According to the Case-Shiller index, housing prices in Dallas and Denver fell by approximately 10 percent from the peak year to the worst (through November 2012), while housing prices in Las Vegas, Miami, and Phoenix plummeted by over 50 percent (see fig. 3).

The data on the twenty cities depicted in figure 3 illustrate vividly both the severity of the real-estate market decline since 2007 and the variation. Note that housing prices have not yet returned to precollapse levels six years after the housing bubble burst. Although housing prices tend to moderate during recessions, the severity of the decline has not been felt for decades. As a consequence, the construction trades sector and ancillary industries that rely on a robust housing market quickly lost employment.

Las Vegas provides a case in point. In the downtown area alone, which is home to older casinos, vintage hotels, and government offices, between 2008 and 2010 the assessed value of land and buildings dropped by $1 billion from its peak, according to City Manager Betsy Fretwell. In all, Las Vegas faced a 20 percent decline in revenues in the span of just two years. Fretwell saw no alternative other than cutting 615 positions in city government, which amounted to one in five workers. Local government also moved to a more economical city hall, while slashing funds for everything from parks and recreation to streets and maintenance.

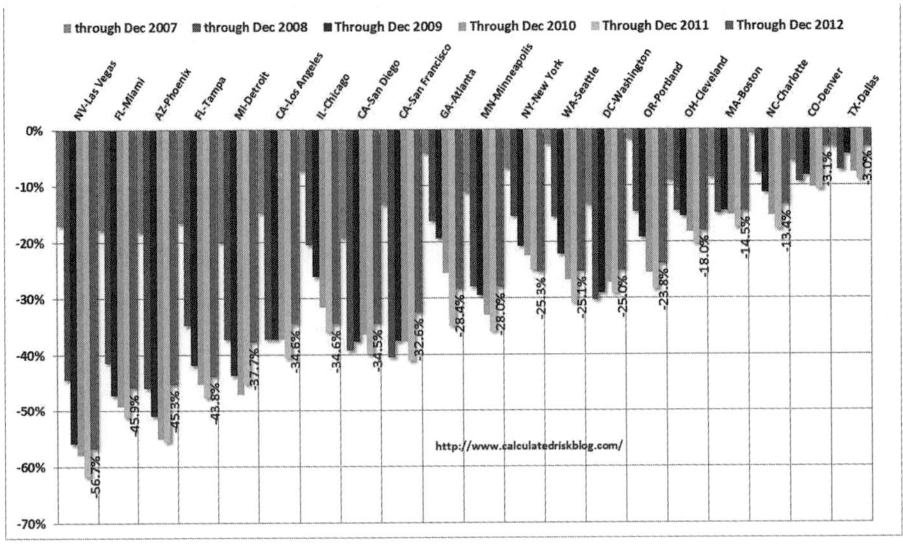

Figure 3. Case-Shiller Price Cumulative Declines from Peak.

OVERVIEW OF THE BOOK

The confluence of the fiscal and economic effects of the Great Recession has created challenges for cities, metropolitan regions, and their governments. Cities and metropolitan regions adjust, adapt, right-size, react, and respond to their environments. Some are more successful than others, but all have survived and will likely continue to survive. The challenges confronting cities in this post–Great Recession era are daunting. To begin raising both the concerns based on analyses of the urban situation and the possibilities based on assessments of practices and experiments, four preeminent scholars and observers of the urban condition prepared white papers for the 2012 UIC Urban Forum. A discussion of each white paper was prepared by two scholars who not only critiqued the papers but also offered commentary and observations. Their discussants' comments were presented at the conference at panels around which each white paper was convened. The authors of the white papers were asked to address four broad sets of issues that policy makers and academics, as well as public intellectuals, neighborhoods and communities, citizens, and taxpayer-voters, need to examine:

- the fraying of the social safety net
- the metropolises' concerns for promoting economic development and growth and for improving employment and income prospects for households
- the economic and financial instincts and behaviors of local governments to both cooperate and compete with their neighbors, and
- the crushing contemporary and future costs of policy decisions in prior years (especially pensions, health care costs, and infrastructure disinvestment).

Margaret Weir argues in her chapter in this book, "Building the Local Social Safety Net in an Era of Fiscal Constraint," that local governments approach their responsibility to provide for the health, safety, and welfare of their residents with conflicting impulses. On the one hand, as Weir notes, "local governments . . . possess strong political and economic incentives to ensure a high quality of life that will attract and retain prosperous residents and businesses." While acknowledging that the Great Recession has severely hampered local governments' financial support in providing a social safety net to residents, Weir discusses the critical roles of the federal government and states, which supply the lion's share of funding for redistributive programs. Local governments have adopted strategies for building and securing the social safety nets for residents. One of those strategies is serving as "connectors" to federal and state benefits and resources. Local governments connect program recipients to federal and state programs, ensuring that residents have access to existing programs and maximizing resource transfers to those populations who rely on the safety net. A second strategy is to be "system builders" in which local governments build networking relationships among diverse public and private organizations that administer policy. Local governments can also think outside the box by innovating with program services and delivery or becoming what Weir calls "program innovators." In this role, they seek new strategies for program delivery and can become role models for other governments. Finally, local governments often adopt the role of "advocates" to the federal government for more comprehensive and better targeted programs to assist those in need. In this role, local governments use their political leverage to secure resources for program recipients.

Raphael Bostic contends in "Resilient Economic Development: Challenges and Opportunities" that the depth and intensity of the Great Recession will create conditions for a "new normal" of greater economic volatility than the nation has experience since the Great Depression of the 1930s. This "new normal" will require coherent and effective local strategies to promote economic growth and development. After identifying characteristics of successful economic development, Bostic then addresses the numerous forces that affect development and how those forces will manifest themselves differently in different places. He recommends approaches to economic development that, in his words, "allow policy makers to maximize resilience and ensure that efforts seeking to promote enduring change and growth are not hampered by disruptions to resource provision."

Richard Feiock argues in "How Cities Collaborate While Competing in the New Economy" that the Great Recession unleashed forces that are reshaping the way that metropolitan regions are governed. In particular, local governments and metropolitan regions are pursuing competitive and collaborative strategies simultaneously. His approach to understanding urban resilience is based on institutional collective action theory in which he argues that intergovernmental collaboration can indeed be a rational behavior for providing efficient local government services. Feiock explores theories of public goods and regionalism within a context of local urban problems. He concludes that "self-organizing network governance can mediate competition and collaboration for local development."

Richard Nathan identifies four financial "legacy" strategies in his chapter, "Legacy Costs of Earlier Decisions." The first—and by far the most discussed—legacy cost is that the pension systems of many state and local governments have been damaged by poor market performance due to the Great Recession and, in some cases, by government officials' short-sighted and poor policy decisions. A second legacy is underfunded and inadequate infrastructure. Even as elected officials find the photo ops of ribbon-cutting ceremonies politically exhilarating, maintaining and repairing infrastructure is less visible and, often, neglected. Nathan also introduces a legacy cost that we often overlook, namely, the imposition of federal and state mandates on local governments. It is not uncommon for states governments, in particular, to impose mandates during fiscally challenging times. A fourth type of legacy cost, according to Nathan, is "permanent appropriations to aid individuals and groups, and special tax provisions with similar purposes." These policies have few immediate consequences for local governments, but out-year financial problems often result when estimates of appropriations and tax expenditures are unrealistic. As he notes, "the temptation is to promise something without recognizing and taking into account the anticipated future costs."

The "Conversations with Policy Officials" chapter is written by Breeze Richardson, who summarizes the broad themes and ideas discussed by panelists at the morning session of the 2012 UIC Urban Forum. The first panel included policy officials from Chicago (Steve Koch, deputy mayor), Cook County (Neil Khare, deputy chief of staff to the Cook County Board), and the state of Illinois (Cristal Thomas, deputy governor). The moderator, Niala Boodhoo of WBEZ, engaged in a wide-ranging conversation about the situation in which cities and local governments find themselves during and after the Great Recession. Cities, indeed all levels of government, now find themselves at an inflection point, a point that will symbolize a break from previous eras, a new starting line against which future fiscal action will be measured—a new normal. The features of the New Normal refer to nonincremental adjustments that will need to be made to right-size governments in the future. The panelists agreed that earlier administrations' "kicking the can down the road" has now landed at their feet. Pension liabilities for the state of Illinois, for example, now reach nearly $100 billion, while the city of Chicago's approaches $25 billion, and must be dealt with immediately. Unbalanced budgets at the levels of the city of Chicago (which faced a $400 million shortfall in 2011, Mayor Emanuel's first year in office) and Cook County (which faced a $500 million shortfall in 2012, Cook County president Preckwinkle's first year in office) cannot be easily balanced with quick fixes, Band-Aids, or asset sales. They must be addressed immediately. And the soft housing market, due to the real-estate bubble's bursting, means that property tax receipts are not going to be as robust as they were prior to the

Great Recession. New ideas that speak to the Chicago metropolitan region and its position in the global economy will need to be entertained. Collaboration and repositioning are the buzzwords for metropolitan regions. The 1,400 local governments in the Chicago metropolitan region must work together to adapt to the new economic reality, from education and workforce development to infrastructure and economic development activities and to social welfare and healthcare.

Cities have demonstrated that they do adapt and adjust to the New Normal, as the second set of panelists attested. Mayor Michael Coleman (Columbus, Ohio), Mayor Luke Ravenstahl (Pittsburgh, Pa.), and City Manager Betsy Fretwell (Las Vegas, Nev.) explored their cities' trials and tribulations in coping with the Great Recession in a panel moderated by WBEZ's Natalie Moore. Because Columbus relies heavily on the income tax to support its basic operations and services, the impact of the Great Recession was felt quickly and immediately. Income tax receipts in 2008 were lower than in 2007, and the mayor was forced to make cuts of up to $100 million, which pushed the city toward its fiscal cliff sooner than most U.S. cities. The city administration worked with stakeholders and designed a "job development and business growth" approach to its activities.

Las Vegas, which relies heavily on the property tax, felt the effects of the housing bubble burst more than any other city. Unemployment soared to 14.5 percent (July 2010), significantly higher than the highest national average of 10.2 percent (October 2009), housing foreclosures affected over 130,000 homes, and city revenues plummeted by $80 million. The city made draconian reductions in service and employment levels, repositioning itself for the New Normal. Las Vegas engaged in participatory budgeting and public strategic planning sessions, thereby rebuilding confidence in city government. A smaller city government was planned for.

Pittsburgh, which had been suffering from city financial challenges since 2003, when it was placed in the Commonwealth of Pennsylvania's Act 47 status, allowing the state to intervene in its budgetary affairs, has been actively adjusting to its New Normal. The decline of the steel industry that began in earnest in the 1980s, when employment reached nearly 18 percent, and accelerated by the early 2000s, pushed the city to reconsider its future and its economic base. The city chose to invest in the educational and healthcare industries, financial services and high-tech companies, life sciences companies and the energy sector. The third "renaissance" in Pittsburgh portends a different city of the future, a city that has shed the Steel City moniker.

The last few pages of the book list in bullet form a few of the recommendations, ideas, and suggestions that emerged during the 2012 UIC Urban

Forum. The policy officials, academics, and stakeholders discussed the future of metropolitan regions and identified a host of policy experiments that cities ought to consider.

The broad narrative presented by the local policy officials from around the nation speaks to the resilience and dynamism of cities and metropolitan regions. The chapters that follow raise important issues and describe various approaches to the changing urban landscape and the future of metropolitan regions.

Notes

1. U.S. Bureau of Labor Statistics, http://www.bls.gov/home.htm, accessed February 1, 2013.

2. The 75 percent figure is from U.S. Census Bureau, State and Local Government Finances 2010, by Jeffrey L. Barnett and Phillip M. Vidal, http://www2.census.gov/govs/estimate/summary_report.pdf, accessed June 7, 2013. The reliance of municipalities on the property tax is much less than the combined "local government" average of 75 percent. Municipalities generate approximately half of their total tax revenues (excluding fees and charges) from the property tax.

3. See, e.g., Christopher Hoene, Michael A. Pagano, and Christy McFarland, *City Fiscal Conditions in 2012* (Washington, D.C.: National League of Cities, 2012).

4. The American Society of Civil Engineers periodically estimates the backlog in infrastructure spending in the United States. The latest report card estimated infrastructure needs at over $3.6 trillion. See ASCE, Report Card for America's Infrastructure, http://www.infrastructurereportcard.org, accessed June 7, 2013.

5. Pew Center on the States, *A Widening Gap in Cities: Shortfall in Funding for Pensions and Retiree Health Care*, January 2013, http://www.pewstates.org/uploadedFiles/PCS_Assets/2013/Pew_city_pensions_report.pdf, accessed February 1, 2013.

6. On comeback cities, see Paul Grogan, *Comeback Cities: A Blueprint for Urban Neighborhood Revival* (New York: Basic Books, 2000). On cities that rebound, see, e.g., Allan Mallach, ed., *Rebuilding America's Legacy Cities: New Directions for the Industrial Heartland* (New York: American Assembly, Columbia University, 2012); Susan Clarke and Gary Gaile, *The Work of Cities* (Minneapolis: University of Minnesota Press, 1998); Richard Florida, *The Rise of the Creative Class* (New York: Basic Books, 2002).

7. See, e.g., Edward Glaeser, *Triumph of the City: How Our Greatest Invention Makes Us Richer, Smarter, Greener, Healthier, and Happier* (London: Penguin Press, 2011); William R. Barnes and Larry C. Ledebur, *The New Regional Economies* (Thousand Oaks, Calif.: Sage Publications, 1998); Jane Jacobs, *Cities and the Wealth of Nations* (New York: Random House, 1984); Nancy Pindus, Margaret Weir, Howard Wial, and Harold Wolman, eds., *Urban and Regional Policy and Its Effects*: Building Resilient Regions, vol. 4 (Washington, D.C.: Brookings Institution Press, 2012); Brookings Institution, *MetroNation: How U.S. Metropolitan Areas Fuel American Prosperity* (Wash-

ington, D.C.: Brookings Institution, 2007), http://www.brookings.edu/~/media/research/files/reports/2007/11/06%20metronation%20berube/metronationbp.pdf, accessed 7 June 2013.

8. See, e.g., William Leuchtenburg, ed., *The New Deal: A Documentary History* (New York: Harper and Row, 1968); Joseph E. Stiglitz, *The Price of Inequality* (New York: W. W. Norton, 2012).

9. See, e.g., Herbert Stein, *The Fiscal Revolution in America* (Chicago: University of Chicago Press, 1969).

10. Natalie R. Cohen, "Municipal Default Patterns: An Historical Study," *Public Budgeting and Finance*, (winter 1989): 55–65.

11. On the riots of the 1930s, see, e.g., Paul Keith Conkin, *Tomorrow a New World: The New Deal Community Program* (Ithaca, N.Y.: Cornell University Press, 1959).

12. See, e.g., Harold Wolman, "Understanding Local Government Responses to Fiscal Pressure," *Journal of Public Policy* 3 (August 1983): 245–64; James March and Herbert Simon, *Organizations* (New York: John Wiley, 1958); Richard Cyert and James March, *A Behavioral Theory of the Firm*, 2nd ed. (Englewood Cliffs, N.J.: Prentice-Hall, 1963); Michael A. Pagano and Ann O'M. Bowman, *Cityscapes and Capital* (Baltimore, Md.: Johns Hopkins University Press, 1995).

13. Charles Tiebout, "A Pure Theory of Local Public Expenditures," *Journal of Political Economy* 64 (October 1956): 416–24.

14. James E. Spiotto, Anne E. Acker, and Laura E. Appleby, *Municipalities in Distress? How States and Investors Deal with Local Government Financial Emergencies* (Chicago: Chapman and Cutler, 2012).

15. Ibid., 51n93.

16. Author's data derived from raw data (unpublished) in the annual survey of cities since 1992, National League of Cities.

17. See, e.g., Howard Zinn, *New Deal Thought* (Indianapolis, Ind.: Bobbs-Merrill, 1966); Robert D. Leighninger Jr., *Long-Range Public Investment: The Forgotten Legacy of the New Deal* (Columbia: University of South Carolina Press, 2007).

18. See, e.g., Marshall Kaplan and Peggy Cuciti, eds., *The Great Society and Its Legacy* (Durham, N.C.: Duke University Press, 1986); James Sundquist, *Politics and Policy: The Eisenhower, Kennedy, and Johnson Years* (Washington, D.C.: Brookings Institution, 1968).

19. See, e.g., Paul Peterson, Barry Rabe, and Kenneth Wong, *When Federalism Works* (Washington, D.C.: Brookings Institution Press, 1986); George Peterson and Carol W. Lewis, eds., *Reagan and the Cities* (Washington, D.C.: Urban Institute Press, 1986); Richard P. Nathan, Fred C. Doolittle, and Associates, *Reagan and the States* (Princeton, N.J.: Princeton University Press, 1987).

20. Michael A. Pagano and Jocelyn Johnston, "Life at the Bottom of the Fiscal Food Chain: Examining City and County Revenue Decisions," *Publius: The Journal of Federalism* 30:1–2 (winter 2000): 159–70.

PART TWO
WHITE PAPERS

Building the Local Social Safety Net in an Era of Fiscal Constraint

MARGARET WEIR

UNIVERSITY OF CALIFORNIA, BERKELEY

Despite the complex funding responsibilities and administrative arrangements for the social safety net, municipal government engagement with that net is crucial to the health and well-being of all residents. This chapter introduces the strategies local governments use to build safety nets for their residents. They construct such nets by serving as 1) *connectors* to federal and state benefits and resources; 2) *system builders* among the diverse public and private local organizations that administer policy; 3) *program innovators*; and 4) *advocates* in state and national politics for a stronger safety net. By building effective public bureaucracies to administer social programs and by supporting outreach, local governments can ensure high take-up rates for federal benefits. When local governments act as system builders, they maximize their role as key implementers of federal programs, influencing the quality and reach of the safety net. As program innovators, local governments initiate new strategies that can provide models for other localities. Finally, when local governments act as advocates, they use their political connections to secure federal and state resources for programs serving low-income residents.

Yet, not all local governments are willing or able to strengthen the social safety net. The chapter distinguishes among *engaged local governments*, which seek to implement the strategies described above; *weak local governments*, which have little public capacity and struggle to implement any strategy to assist low-income residents; and *avoiders*, local governments that shun responsibility for the social safety net, often placing additional burdens on neighboring localities that provide services. In areas where the public sector is unwilling or unable to address the needs of low-income residents, advocates must turn to nonprofits and philanthropic organizations to create a social safety net.

Strategies for strengthening the social safety net include improving take-up of federal social benefits, especially in immigrant communities; building coherent regional systems for delivering services, strengthening the role of metropolitan planning organizations and community development financial institutions in creating regional systems for services; devising new federal programs to work with regional nonprofits and philanthropy to address the special problems of highly distressed suburbs and cities; and reengaging local governments as advocates for federal programs that support low-income residents, such as the Temporary Assistance for Needy Families (TANF) Emergency Fund, which allowed states to create subsidized jobs for TANF recipients.

Local governments approach their responsibility to provide for the health, safety, and welfare of their residents with conflicting impulses. On the one hand, they possess strong political and economic incentives to ensure a high quality of life that will attract and retain prosperous residents and businesses. Moreover, as research on fiscal federalism has posited for decades, local governments have little fiscal incentive to support redistribution to lower-income residents, even when politically pressured to do so. Yet, fiscal pressures are only one factor shaping local engagement with the social safety net. The federal government and the states—not local government—supply most of the funds for redistributive policies; moreover, key safety net programs—such as the TANF program, Supplemental Nutrition Assistance Program (SNAP, formerly called food stamps), housing programs, and child care—are administered by a diverse array of entities, including the federal government, state governments, county governments, local governments, and nonprofit organizations.

Federal and state funding and the engagement of multiple administrative channels present local governments with a menu of choices to ensure a high quality of life and build a strong social safety net. Local governments can seek to minimize pressures to engage in redistribution by limiting the population that relies on the social safety net. Localities choosing this route may seek to reduce demand for safety net services, or they may simply leave the safety net to nonprofits and other governments (such as the state, county, or township), thereby freeing local government to focus exclusively on improving the quality of life for its more affluent residents and businesses. Alternatively, local governments can use their limited fiscal resources, their political leadership, and their administrative capabilities to enhance the safety net, by taking up one of the four strategies mentioned above. The Great Recession reduced local government choices as it tightened the local fiscal noose; but at the same time it made substantial new resources temporarily available through the American Recovery and Reinvestment Act (ARRA).

This chapter examines how local governments with distinct demographic profiles and resource bases have approached these challenges and how the worst fiscal crisis—and the sharpest increases in need—since the Great Depression have altered their perspectives. Although the term *local safety net* evokes images of cities, the rise in suburban poverty—by 2008, more than half the poor lived in suburbs—necessitates that any consideration of the local safety net also examine suburbs.[1] While an array of special districts, townships, and counties comprise local government, this chapter focuses on the strategies of general-purpose municipal governments, remaining attentive to the ways they intersect with other local governments and nonprofit organizations. The chapter first briefly presents the fiscal federalism argument and sketches the diverse financial flows and organizational responsibilities for the social safety net. The second section examines the strategies of three types of local governments: the engaged, cities and suburbs that deploy one or more strategy to strengthen the safety net even as they prioritize quality of life for the middle-class and affluent residents; the weak, very poor cities and suburbs that have limited public resources for building the social safety net; the avoiders, mainly affluent suburbs that shun the strategies described above and focus primarily on the quality of life for the middle class. The final section considers policy actions for the future, attentive to the resource constraints that accompany the end of the federal stimulus.

LOCAL GOVERNMENTS, REDISTRIBUTION, AND THE SOCIAL SAFETY NET

The classic arguments of fiscal federalism posit that local governments will shun redistributive programs but may have strong incentives to improve the quality of life.[2] Competition forces local governments to emphasize economic development and activities that attract and retain tax-paying residents and businesses. By diverting resources and imposing burdens on the affluent, redistribution jeopardizes these goals, leaving localities disadvantaged in interlocal competition. Improving the quality of life, on the other hand, can help attract and retain businesses and taxpayers.[3]

The stark claims of the fiscal federalism model have fueled a long and contentious debate about how much room local governments have to maneuver when supporting redistribution and whether redistributive goals and economic development can be made compatible. Empirical studies show that, indeed, the model overstates local economic constraints.[4] Big cities with large needy populations and electoral coalitions connected to low-income populations have historically found the fiscal slack to support some level of redistribution. For example, in 1999, Glaeser and Kahn found that large cities spent 2.5 percent of their budgets on local welfare expenditures compared with 0.7 percent in smaller cities. Large cities spent even more on public housing and health—7.4 percent of the budget compared with only 3.6 for smaller cities.[5] But big-city redistributive spending has fallen significantly since the 1970s, when cities first began to experience fiscal crisis and again in the 1980s when federal aid to local governments dropped sharply. Faced with restricted budgets and competition from edge cities, cities began to focus on improving the quality of life, aiming to attract tourists, retain residents, and in the 2000s to lure "the creative class."[6] As figure 1 indicates, city revenues received a severe blow from the Great Recession, which had come on the heels of a difficult decade for city finances.

As the small proportion of city budgets dedicated to redistribution suggests, even at the height of local spending on redistributive programs, the bulk of funding for social policy came from the states and, especially, from Washington. The federal government directly funds key safety net programs such as the Supplemental Nutrition Assistance Program (SNAP), Supplemental Security Income (SSI), and housing choice vouchers; it offers other programs, such as the Social Services Block Grant (SSBG), the Community Development Block Grant (CDBG), Low-Income Home Energy Assistance, and the Child Care and Development Fund, as grants that go directly to cities, counties, and states. Washington also supplies a host of other grants, such as the Choice Neighborhoods Act, and competitive housing and education grants for which local governments must apply. The other key safety net programs—TANF and Medicaid—receive joint federal-state funding. The trend to rely on Washington accelerated during the 2000s, when state and local funding for the safety net declined, with the exception of Medicaid. In 2006, 61 percent of social-welfare spending came from the federal government; state and local governments funded the rest.[7] The Great Recession has reinforced the dominant federal role in financing the social safety net as ARRA offered supplemental funding for a range of safety net programs.[8]

Despite their relatively small role in funding social programs, local governments play a critical role in ensuring a strong social safety net. Four roles stand out: that of connector, system builder, program innovator, and advo-

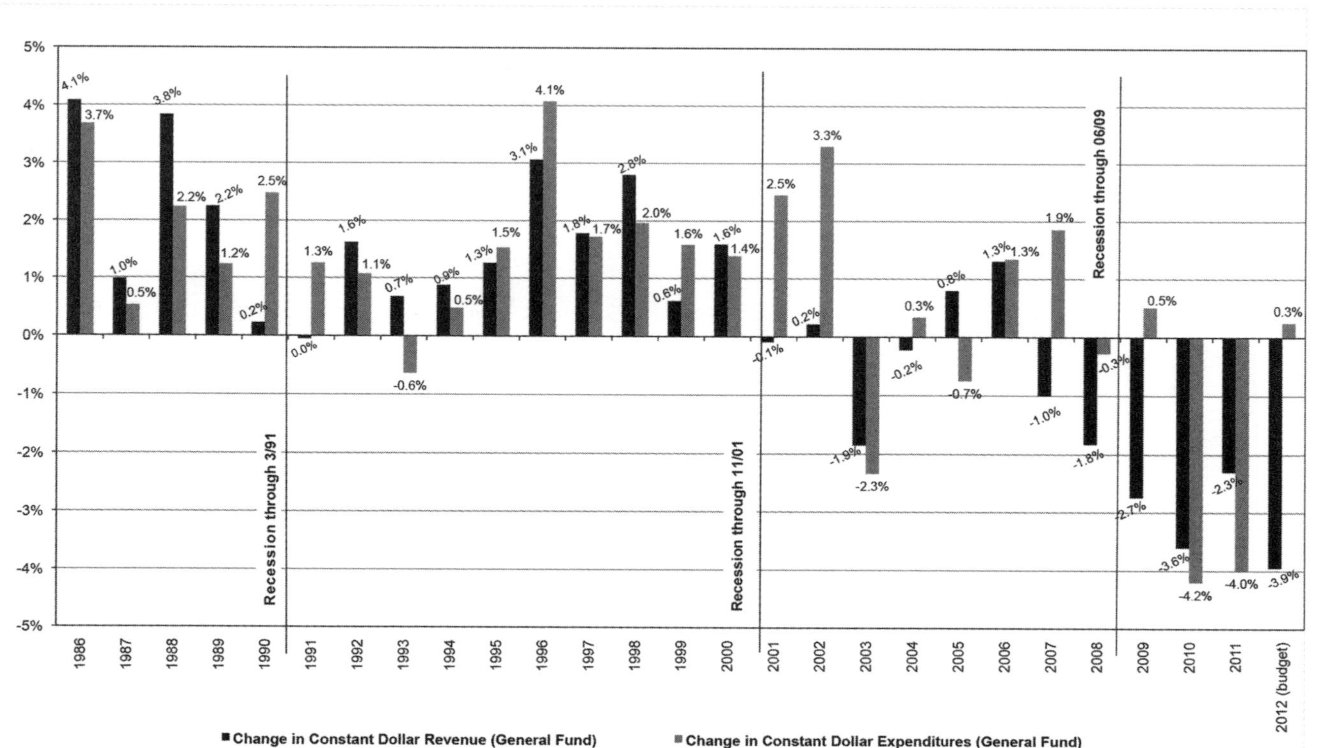

Figure 1. Year-to-Year Change in General Fund Revenues and Expenditures (Constant Dollars). Source: Christopher Hoene, Michael Pagano, and Christy McFarland, *City Fiscal Conditions in 2012* (Washington, DC: National League of Cities, 2012).

cate. A brief review of how these strategies have evolved lays the groundwork for considering the local safety net prior to and during the Great Recession. (Table 1 summarizes these strategies; examples are presented later in the chapter.)

In their role as connector, local governments can influence access to benefits. By building strong local public bureaucracies to administer social programs and by supporting outreach, local governments can ensure high take-up rates for federal benefits. On the other hand, by having unresponsive bureaucracies and discouraging rules, local governments can make the safety net difficult for residents to access.[9] Even in fully federal programs, such as SNAP, local governments play a key role because they pay part of the costs of administering the program, thus shaping access to benefits.

When local governments act as system builders, they maximize their role as implementers of federal programs. Local government influence over implementation determines much about the quality and reach of the safety net. For example, contrasts between the fate of post–World War II public housing in New York and Chicago highlight the role of local administration in weakening Chicago's public housing and strengthening New York's.[10] Yet, local governments rarely administer safety net programs alone. In most cases, they are one actor among many, including nonprofit organizations and other governments. The outsourcing of the safety net to nonprofits, which can be traced to the reliance of the Johnson administration's War on Poverty on nonprofit community action agencies, accelerated during the 1980s.

After the 1996 welfare reform, which substantially reduced the number of families qualifying for cash assistance, nonprofit services—such as child care and job training—became essential components of the work-oriented system of assistance.[11] As a result, the infrastructure for delivering safety net benefits has aptly been called a "policy field," which varies by policy and from community to community, depending on governmental arrangements and the strength of the nonprofit sector.[12] Within this array of diverse actors, local governments often play a pivotal role. They can assist nonprofit providers in finding and renovating space or they can reinforce "not-in-my-back-yard" (NIMBY) sentiments of local residents.[13] Local governments make important decisions about the distribution of block grants such as CDBG and SSBG. They can determine whether CDBG funds are closely targeted on the needs of low-income residents and select which agencies receive SSBG funds and for what purposes. Mayoral leadership is especially important in coordinating initiatives that require the engagement of multiple agencies and programs.[14]

Table 1. Local Government Strategies for Strengthening the Social Safety Net

Strategy	Actions	Policy Examples
Connector	Connect low-income residents to existing state and federal assistance	Chicago's campaign to expand EITC take-up rate
System Builder	Oversee new connections among local organizations to promote more effective service programs; combine state and federal income streams in new ways	New York City's EarlyLearn NYC merged child care, Head Start, and universal prekindergarten funds to support system redesign
		Chicago's Regional Housing Choice Initiative
Program Innovator	Launch new programs to support security and opportunity for low-income residents	San Francisco's health care access program Healthy San Francisco
		New York City's Social Impact Bonds
Advocate	Support nonprofit efforts to secure federal, state, and local funds; may require matching grants	San Antonio's support for Choice and Promise Neighborhoods program
	Lobby to secure additional state and federal funds for low-income residents or to change federal, state, and local programs to support more effective local action	Mobilization to increase Community Development Block Grant Funds
	Support coalitions of nonprofits advocating for low-income residents	

Local governments can also act as program innovators. During the Great Depression, New York's mayor Fiorella LaGuardia set the pace for introducing innovations to support poor New Yorkers.[15] After the 1970s, however, limited city resources and the political invisibility of low-income residents in many localities meant that only the wealthiest cities—or those with strong political support for the poor—introduced innovations that required significant spending. But even localities with limited resources can introduce smaller-scale innovations.

Finally, local officials can also act as advocates for their low-income communities. They can decide whether to apply for competitive state and federal grants, and they can use their political connections to secure additional federal, state, and local the resources for programs that serve low-income residents. Local governments can support nonprofits with matching funds, which are often required for federal grants. Such engagement signals to federal granting agencies a level of commitment and organization that makes successful implementation more likely.

Local governments have also used their political connections to lobby for increasing the pool of resources to assist low-income residents. During the Great Depression of the 1930s, local governments—especially big cities—pressed Washington for assistance to the poor, advocating for work and relief programs. Banded together in the U.S. Conference of Mayors, big cities constituted a powerful intergovernmental lobby. Although concerns about the safety net never topped the agenda of such organizations, the urban lobby could be counted on at that time to keep concerns about poverty and opportunity on the national agenda. However, as big cities lost population and responsibility for urban social programs devolved to the states beginning in the 1980s, cities lost much of their political clout in national politics.[16] Today local governments—even big cities—have become a much weaker force in national politics and are much less likely to prioritize the needs of low-income residents in their interactions with state and federal officials. As table 2 shows, most discretionary low-income block grants programs, which are most vulnerable to cuts and erosion in value, have declined substantially since 2001.

There is little systematic research detailing what local governments do to strengthen the local safety net or identifying which governments are more likely to launch particular kinds of initiatives. Many local governments are content to leave full responsibility for the social safety net to the state, counties, and in some states the townships, all of which already bear formal financial and administrative responsibilities for some aspects of the net. Others may decide to take leadership roles in addressing poverty. In 2007, the National League of Cities surveyed its members to chart local antipoverty initiatives. Although the survey's very low response rate (fewer than a hundred responses from the 1,600 local NLC members) limits its representativeness, more than half of the respondents reported having no antipoverty initiatives in place and no plans to devise such initiatives. Of those that reported launching an antipoverty scheme, typical plans included creating a coordinating agency; setting a target for action (such as Earned Income Tax Credit outreach); focusing on particular neighborhoods or groups; or other policy-specific initiatives, such as efforts to reach the unbanked.[17]

Just as there is no representative portrait of local antipoverty initiatives, there are no broad assessments that evaluate which types of local interventions are most effective at reducing poverty. Local economic development activities have been criticized as ineffective because they are "swimming against the tide" of policy incentives that leave some places poorer than others.[18] Yet, many local government initiatives promote access to federally supported benefits that directly reduce poverty, such as affordable housing, medical care, food assistance, and cash benefits. Even though local governments devote a small proportion of their budgets to redistribution, their critical roles as connectors, system builders, innovators, and advocates make them essential partners in building a strong social safety net.

Table 2. Funding History of Major Discretionary Low-Income Block Grant Programs

Program	Year of inception	Funding in FY 2011 (millions)	Change in funding since 2001*	Change in funding since inception*
Preventive Health and Health Services Block Grant	1982	$80	-64%	-57%
Public Housing Capital Fund	1998	$2,040	-46%	-40%
Community Development Block Grants	1982	$3,336	-39%	-57%
Training and Employment. Services Block Grants	1982	$2,884	-38%	-55%
Home Investment Partnership Program	1992	$1,607	-29%	-32%
Maternal and Child Health Block Giant	1982	$661	-27%	-22%
Native American Housing Block Grant	1998	$649	-21%	-21%
Mental Health and Substance Abuse Block Grants	1992	$2,102	-20%	-5%
Child Care and Development Block Grant	1991	$2,223	-12%	89%
Community Services Block Grant	1982	$678	-11%	-18%
Education for the Disadvantaged (Title 1)	1981	$15,567	35%	128%
Low income Heating and Energy Assistance	1982	$4,701	86%	12%

* Adjusted for inflation

Source: Douglas Rice and Will Fischer, "Proposal to Greatly Expand 'Moving to Work' Initiative Risks Deep Cuts in Housing Assistance Over Time" (Washington, D.C.: Center on Budget and Policy Priorities, January 10, 2012), http://www.cbpp.org/files/1-10-12hous.pdf, accessed June 6, 2013; Office of Management and Budget documents, House Conference Report 112 331; and other sources.

LOCAL GOVERNMENTS AND THE GREAT RECESSION

The Great Recession presented local governments with a set of contradictory pressures. As local and state funds plummeted, the recession strained city budgets and the nonprofit sector at the same time that poverty rates soared.[19] The poverty rate grew from 12.3 percent of the population in 2006 to 15.0 in 2011.[20] Even so, between 2009 and 2011, federal stimulus funds shielded local governments from the full impact of the recession and offered opportunities to launch new programs and collaborations. Local governments responded in different ways to this conflicting set of pressures. The Great Recession confronted each of these localities with new strains that have tested traditional local responses and engendered experimentation. The engaged, the weak, and the avoiders all confronted the recession with different experiences, resources, and political will for implementing strategies to assist low-income communities.

Engaged Local Governments

Localities—and especially big- to medium-sized cities and some affluent suburbs—approach their responsibilities for enhancing the quality of life and addressing safety net issues with a mix of preferences and resources. For economic and political reasons, they may prioritize enhancing the quality of life for business, the middle class, and affluent residents; but they also are pressured politically to strengthen the safety net. Cities are likely to have significant numbers of low-income residents and especially be home to populations with incomes well below the poverty line. These localities experience strained financial resources but often possess a well-established public and nonprofit organizational infrastructure for assisting low-income residents. The recession has enhanced the fiscal strain and resulted in cutbacks of key services, diminishing the quality of life in the vast majority of these places. But, at the same time that the recession has battered the finances of these cities, federal ARRA funds have made possible some new initiatives. This combination of stress and new resources prompted many local governments to engage as connectors, system builders, innovators, and advocates for the safety net, even as others have taken actions that may undermine the net in the future.

CONNECTORS Cities have long played the role of connector, linking beneficiaries to federal and state benefits through local public bureaucracies. Some cities extended this role in the 1990s by initiating campaigns to encourage take-up of the Earned Income Tax Credit.[21] Initially brought together by the Center for Budget and Policy Priorities, a Washington-based nonprofit organization, some cities developed strategies for reaching constituencies eligible for the expanded benefits. In 2000, Milwaukee and Chicago launched outreach campaigns that became models for other cities. These campaigns typically engage a broad spectrum of organizations, including nonprofits and businesses, but the leadership of city officials is essential for their success. As urban outreach campaigns developed over time, they built a system of free tax preparation, the community Volunteer Income Tax Assistance (VITA) program (supported by the Internal Revenue Service), which helps protect low-income filers from being pressured to accept high-interest "instant-refund" loans offered by commercial preparers.

Cities have also launched outreach campaigns to encourage take-up of SNAP benefits, which vary widely across localities. For example, in 2011, the Food Research and Action Center estimated that in Detroit 97 percent of those eligible received benefits, compared with only 56 percent in Los Angeles and 40 percent in San Diego.[22] The relatively low take-up rates in cities with high immigrant populations points to the need for targeted outreach among immigrants. Yet cities also enact regulations that limit the take-up of SNAP benefits. Although in 2007 New York State ended the requirement that applicants for food stamps be fingerprinted, New York City continued to require fingerprinting as part of its effort to combat fraud. In 2012, the state ended the fingerprinting requirement in New York City, opening the door for increasing the take-up of benefits.[23] The expansion of the SNAP benefits as part of the ARRA made SNAP the most important safety net program during the Great Recession.

SYSTEM BUILDERS A host of local actors administer the local safety net. When local governments step into the role of system builder, they make it much more likely that these local actors can cooperate effectively toward the same goals. The well-established antipoverty organizations in many cities first appeared during the War on Poverty. Many urban community action agencies and community development corporations have had decades to build their organizational capacities and political credibility. Some community-based organizations, which Nicole Marwell calls machine-CBOs (community-based organizations), have nurtured close ties to state legislators that allow them to tap significant funding streams.[24] Big cities are also home to philanthropic institutions, many of which trace their origins to the Progressive Era. Large community foundations, such as the Chicago Community Trust, which focus on geographic communities, rarely have robust counterparts in the suburbs.[25]

Although federal and state government programs provide most of the funding for nonprofits, philanthropic dollars provide critical support for organization building and new initiatives, both of which are essential for effective safety net systems. Public institutions that serve the poor, such as public hospitals and subsidized public transit, are also largely found in cities, although the number of public hospitals has declined significantly over the past two decades.[26]

The local nonprofit infrastructure provides cities with a great resource for building partnerships to address the problems of low-income neighborhoods. Yet, in most cities this infrastructure has developed largely haphazardly and struggles to meet the growing needs created by the recession. Nonprofits found it difficult to stay solvent in this tightly restricted fiscal climate. A 2010 study by the Urban Institute revealed that 42 percent of nonprofits ran a deficit in 2009 as funds dried up or payments from state governments fell behind. Smaller nonprofits, which typically have little cushion, were hardest hit. A 2011 survey of human service nonprofits in Los Angeles County found that half were stable and half struggling.[27] The survey revealed that organizations providing basic services for the poor—including shelters and affordable housing—failed at twice the rate of other services. It also showed that organizations in neighborhoods with a high percentage of African American residents were far more likely to disband than were organizations in other neighborhoods.[28] Some local governments have made decisions that are likely to harm their nonprofit infrastructures. The city of Lynchburg, Virginia, for example, made headlines in 2010 when it decided to withhold CDBG funds from nonprofits and instead use them exclusively for city projects.[29]

While fiscal stress may result in a stronger organizational base by promoting mergers and efficiencies, this outcome is most likely when an umbrella organization can oversee a planned process of change. It is unlikely to occur spontaneously from below. However, few metropolitan areas contain organizations with the capacity or authority to promote wholesale reorganization. The survey of Los Angeles nonprofits, for instance, noted only "a few examples of innovative collaborations, partnerships, mergers, or social enterprise initiatives."[30] In some regions, associations of nonprofits sought to cope with the pressure by encouraging nonprofit organizations to merge or share functions. Yet, resistance to such strategies meant that some groups folded during the recession.[31]

The recession also sparked new partnerships among city governments, counties, and nonprofits that represent steps in the right direction. In many of these cases, local government did not act as the system builder but supported others actors, including nonprofits and counties. Given the housing crisis associated with the recession, many of these collaborations concerned homelessness. For example, Fairfax County, Virginia, in suburban Washington, D.C., assumed the role of system builder in a major anti-homeless campaign that began in 2008. The county took the lead in building an effective partnership between the cities of Fairfax and Falls Church and a wide array of nonprofit organizations, faith groups, and corporate sponsors to launch an anti-homelessness campaign. The campaign, which became a national model, reduced homelessness by 16 percent in Fairfax despite the recession.[32]

Local governments have also supported collaborations initiated by private and nonprofit organizations. In Portland, Oregon, Habitat for Humanity—with the help of a major private donor—bought a number of foreclosed properties and abandoned lots. The city, with its strained finances, played little part in the initiative but plans to build public support around this sizeable private investment in affordable housing.[33] Across the country, the combination of local initiative and additional funds available through ARRA had a significant impact. The National Coalition to End Homelessness reported in 2011 that homelessness did not increase during the recession.[34]

The end of the federal stimulus funds requires that cities use existing funds as effectively as possible. Several cities have embarked on system building in hopes of making the most of diminishing funds. For example, in 2012, the city of Chicago launched a plan that aimed to end homelessness by redeploying existing city funds to provide permanent supportive housing, implementing strategies designed to prevent homelessness, and creating more effective administration through a partnership with Catholic Charities of the Archdiocese of Chicago.[35] The city also introduced new funding to promote a more coordinated system of early childhood education.[36] Similarly, in 2012, New York City redesigned its child care programs to make the system more effective.[37] The new program, EarlyLearn NYC, merged three funding streams (child care, Head Start, and universal prekindergarten), set new requirements on providers, and targeted funds more directly on low-income neighborhoods.

System building at the regional level is much more difficult because it involves the participation of multiple governments. Building regional systems for redistributive issues confronts especially formidable barriers since local governments often prefer to shield themselves from the costs of low-income residents. However, the Chicago region's proposed pilot program, the Chicago Regional Housing Choice Initiative, shows that regional collaboration around redistribution can occur under the right conditions.[38] This pilot program established a consortium among five local housing authorities to make housing choice vouchers more portable across the region. Overseen by the Metropolitan Planning Council, a business-linked civic organization, the initiative represented the work of a cluster of philanthropic and civic organizations, as well as the Chicago Metropolitan Agency for Planning (the region's metropolitan planning organization) and the Metropolitan Mayors Council (a forum that promotes collaboration among the region's mayors).

INNOVATORS Cities can also act as innovators in designing new approaches to strengthen the safety net. Not surprisingly, affluent cities with some fiscal slack are more likely to initiate significant innovations. In the past decade, San Francisco and New York have embarked on pioneering—but very different—strategies for assisting low-income residents. With the support of organized labor and a large contingent of liberal-minded residents, San Francisco launched the health care access program Healthy San Francisco in 2007. Funded by a tax on businesses that do not provide health insurance for their employees, the program offers health services to uninsured residents whose annual income is at or below 300 percent of the national poverty line. In 2003, San Francisco voters approved a citywide minimum wage that was higher than the state minimum and that rises every year to keep pace with inflation.[39] While San Francisco has followed a strategy championed by organized labor and its allies, New York City has pursued a path charted by transnational policy experts.[40] San Francisco's strategy seeks to improve the security of low-income residents, whereas the New York program aims to alter their behavior in hopes of opening new opportunities. In 2006, New York City created a Center for Economic Opportunity (CEO) to incubate bold new ideas about poverty reduction. The CEO has overseen a range of trial initiatives, including developing a new measure for poverty (which showed a higher number of elderly poor than the federal poverty measure). The CEO initiative that has received widespread attention was a pilot program of conditional cash transfers (CCTs), a poverty reduction strategy that had been implemented in the developing world. CCTs provide cash assistance to program participants who meet various behavioral requirements, such as sending children to school, ensuring that family members receive adequate health screening, or undergoing job training. After receiving inconclusive evaluation of the programs' success, however, the city decided not to renew the CCTs after the initial three-year pilot program.[41]

Yet New York continues to experiment with new strategies for social programs. In 2012, the city made headlines when it turned to social-impact bonds to fund a program that aims to reduce recidivism rates among young men.[42] Designed as a strategy to leverage additional funds for social purposes, social-impact bonds elicit investments from private or nonprofit organizations to support social programs. The investors receive a return on their funds only if the program succeeds. The strategy has been used in Britain and Australia, but New York City's program marks the first U.S. use of social-impact bonds. In New York, the private bank Goldman Sachs offered a $9.6 million loan to support the program. Depending on the outcome of the program, it will lose money, make a profit, or come out even. The strategy raises a host of questions about how contracts will be drawn up and how programs will be evaluated. It also provokes a broader set of concerns. How does the prospect of private investment alter public calculations about investment in the safety net? How would increased reliance on private dollars to fulfill public roles affect the way public officials regard local, state, and federal regulation of the firms on which they rely for funds?

Other cities have innovated on a smaller scale, often with nonprofits taking the lead. The city of Seattle worked with the Neighborhood Farmers Market Alliance to enhance the use of food stamps at farmers markets with a program that doubled the value of purchases up to ten dollars a day. Philadelphia has likewise collaborated with a local nonprofit, the Food Trust, to provide supplemental funds for SNAP recipients who shop at farmers markets. These kinds of initiatives can be a win-win for cities since they require little local money or administrative time, and by publicly supporting the programs, city officials draw attention to them, increasing their chances of success.

ADVOCATES Finally, local governments can act as advocates in state and federal arenas to expand safety net programs; draw down additional federal dollars in order to assist low-income residents; or support regulations, such as the federal minimum wage and fair lending, that enhance the economic security of low-income residents.

During the recession, some urban leaders drew on their intergovernmental ties to improve conditions for their low-income residents. Faced with a combination of high unemployment in the construction industry and persistent poverty in many neighborhoods, Los Angeles mayor Antonio Villaraigosa launched a creative campaign to speed up a major rail construction project approved and funded by voters with a half-cent sales tax increase in 2008.[43] Assembling a coalition of state and local officials, the mayor and his allies convinced Congress to include a loan program of federally guaranteed bonds in the 2012 transportation bill. In Los Angeles, the accelerated construction schedule also created an apprenticeship program that set aside half of its slots for veterans of Iraq and Afghanistan and for residents of low-income zip codes.[44] As this case suggests, mayors and other local officials can also attach requirements to various types of federal dollars in ways that will improve conditions for lower-income residents and communities.

Local government support can make the difference in securing competitive federal grants targeted at poor neighborhoods. In order to win funding competitions such as the Obama administration's Choice and Promise Neighborhoods initiatives (directed at building housing and education, respectively), localities must show strong multi-sector community engagement around the plan. Although Promise Neighborhood grants have gone directly to nonprofits, local government engagement is an essential component of successful endeavors.[45] In San Antonio, mayoral leadership and city investment was critical to the collaboration among nonprofits, the San Antonio Independent School District, and the San Antonio Housing Authority that lay behind the successful grant application.

The urban voice is also critical in drawing attention to holes in the safety net. Simply by highlighting existing needs, local officials can draw attention to problems that might otherwise be ignored. Mayors have an incentive to shine a spotlight on national problems that otherwise might be ignored or labeled as urban issues alone. For example, the U.S. Conference of Mayors annual hunger and homelessness survey, released during the holiday season, aims to draw national attention to deficits in basic needs.[46]

Weak Local Governments

Some localities are home to a disproportionate number of low-income residents. Cities have traditionally shouldered this responsibility, although since 1990 the number of poor suburbs has grown. The Great Recession expanded the number of extreme-poverty neighborhoods (those with poverty rates above 40 percent) in the Midwest as well as in a number of Sunbelt cities.[47] Localities with high poverty rates, large clusters of concentrated poverty, and weak fiscal bases confront serious obstacles in strengthening the social safety net.

In places with little inherited infrastructure for addressing poverty, such as poor suburbs, local governments often lack the resources and administrative skills to improve the safety net. Recent research has shown that these areas rarely possess a strong base of nonprofit and philanthropic organizations that can help strengthen the safety net.[48] For example, in a 2010 study, Scott Allard and Benjamin Roth found that the ratio of poor persons to nonprofits was significantly less favorable in high-poverty suburbs than in lower-poverty suburbs.[49] Some poor cities, such as Cleveland, enjoy a strong nonprofit and philanthropic base, but others—especially those in the Sunbelt, such as Fresno, California—lack a tradition of philanthropy and nonprofit activity. The challenge for such places is to assemble a combination of public and nonprofit capabilities that recognize the "interdependent and mutually reinforcing" relationship between these sectors.[50] Yet, given their weak starting point, these localities are unlikely to build such an infrastructure on their own, especially since they are faced with the pressures generated by the recession. Their productive interactions with external governments and agencies are essential for strengthening the safety net. An examination of some strategies these areas have adopted in response to the recession reveals the significant challenges involved in building the safety net in these weak places.

Detroit has taken the extreme step of dissolving several public agencies and transferring responsibilities to nonprofits. In 2012, the city transferred the functions performed by its Department of Human Services to outside social service agencies. A long history of corruption and mismanagement at the department, combined with pressure from the state and federal governments, lay behind the dramatic decision. The city also transferred workforce development activities from the Workforce Development Department to a nonprofit.[51] These moves will have an unknown long-term impact on the local safety net. In the short term, these decisions likely ensure more competent administration and the continued flow of federal funds. But over the longer term they may sideline human services on the city's agenda, leading to disengaged local officials and fewer resources for the local safety net. Likewise, delegating to nonprofits in itself cannot ensure more effective use of resources or guard against corruption. Strong public oversight is essential to effective nonprofit administration.

In other areas, diverse collaborations—involving a mix of governments and nonprofits—have emerged as a strategy for building capacity to address growing need. This strategy has been particularly useful in settings where multiple small poor suburbs face growing poverty. With 273 municipal governments, the Chicago area has long been one of the nation's most politically fragmented metros. Although the city remains home to the majority of the region's low-income residents, suburban poverty grew to represent nearly half of the metropolitan area's poor by 2010. In poor suburbs, such as those in the southern part of the region, decentralization, political fragmentation, and a complex tangle of responsibilities for the safety net has made it difficult to build capacity for funding and delivering human services.[52]

While a degree of coordination has emerged from below, initiative from above is needed to promote broader and more effective collaborations. Philanthropic organizations based in the city of Chicago have worked to build that capacity for over a decade, with generally limited results. The recession and the possibility of accessing new federal funds, however, spurred new collaborations. Supported by the Chicago Community Trust, in 2009, nineteen suburbs in Chicago's hard-hit south suburbs formed a collaborative to apply for federal funds through the Neighborhood Stabilization Program, part of the federal antiforeclosure initiative. The trust supplied the funds for the collaborative to hire a housing director to apply for grants.[53] Although difficult to create, this type of cross-municipality, cross-sector collaboration provides small suburban governments with the administrative capacity necessary to access federal funds.

Looking to nonprofits and establishing collaborations to solve the problems of the local safety net have become widely accepted nostrums. Yet it is clear from the experience of poor suburbs and very poor cities that neither comes easily. Sustained interaction with engaged outside groups and substantial new funds made available through federal stimulus funds accelerated the moves forward in the Chicago region. Yet, many outside groups encounter significant barriers when they attempt to build new capacities in poor places. Distrust and parochialism may scuttle collaborations even with the prospect of additional funds. Without the lure of new funds, it becomes harder to alter existing practices.

In some poor places, the organizational deficit is so severe that experienced city-based or regional agencies cannot gain a foothold. The southern suburbs of Atlanta in Clayton County, where poverty grew rapidly after 2000, had little organizational base for addressing the new needs, a deficit that has made it difficult for more experienced Atlanta-based organizations to step in. As a staff member at one Atlanta nonprofit described the problem, there are "just not enough energy and resources in Clayton to meet both the philanthropists and service providers in that middle ground."[54] Similarly, a Brookings–Federal Reserve study on concentrated poverty showed that such areas often had weak nonprofit sectors and little capacity to attract—and perhaps to use effectively—philanthropic dollars. For example, advocates in West Fresno rued their inability to compete effectively with the Bay Area and Los Angeles for philanthropic dollars but, at the same time, some acknowledged that they lack the capacity to use such funds effectively. Two newly established community development financial institutions in the area likewise noted problems in identifying projects ready for investment.[55] In the absence of adequate services, residents of poor suburbs near cities are likely to turn to already burdened city services, especially if they are recent transplants to the suburbs. But this option is not available to many low-income people. In poor cities, such as Fresno or Youngstown, Ohio, the poor have nowhere to go.

The difficulty of bringing philanthropic investment to poor suburban communities is highlighted in figures 2 and 3. These maps present data about the distribution of philanthropic human services grants from the largest private

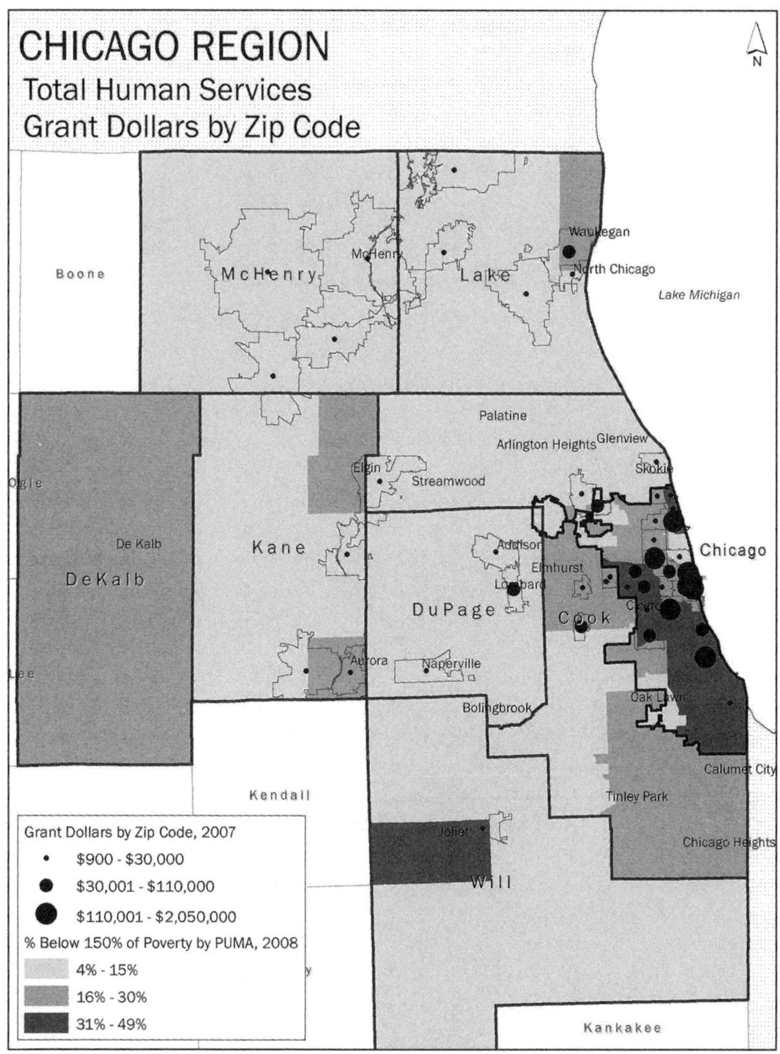

Figure 2. Human Services Philanthropic Grants in Chicago Metro, 2007. Source: Sarah Reckhow and Margaret Weir, "Building a Resilient Social Safety Net," *Urban and Regional Policy and Its Effects*, vol. 4, ed. Margaret Weir, Howard Wial, Harold Wolman, and Nancy Pindus (Washington, D.C.: Brookings Institution Press, 2012), 301. Philanthropic spending includes the largest private foundation in the region as well as all community foundations. For a full description of the methodology, see Reckhow and Weir, 319–20.

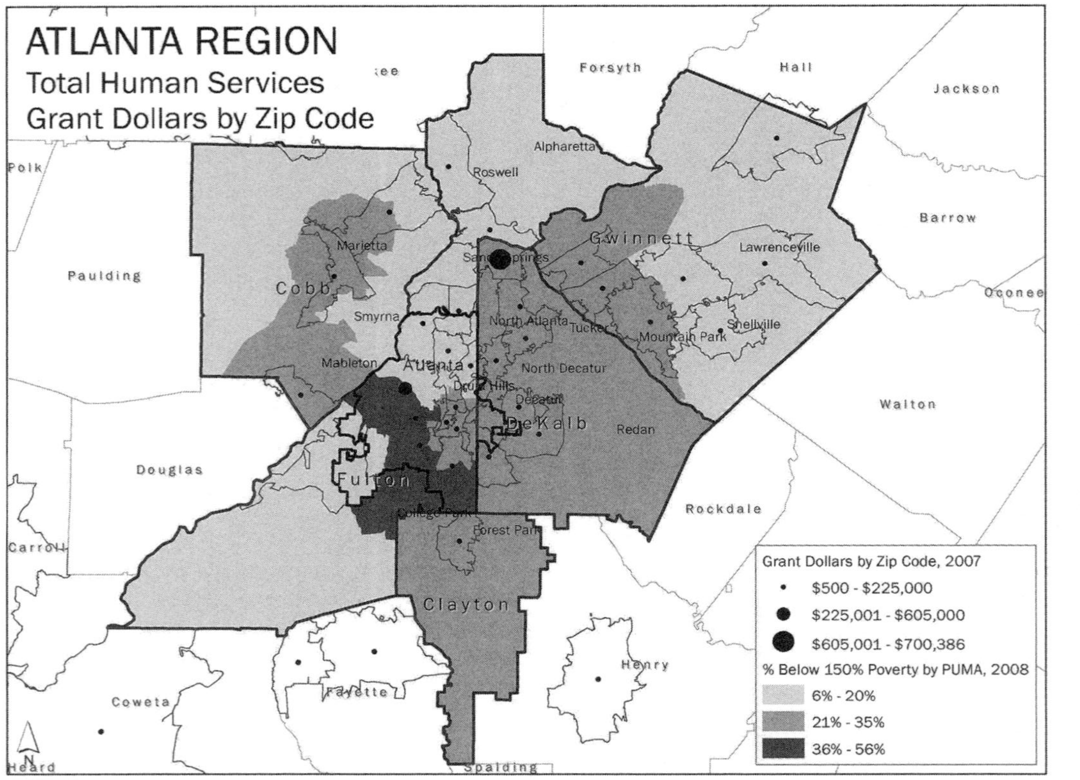

Figure 3. Human Services Philanthropic Grants in Atlanta Metro, 2007. Source: Reckhow and Weir, "Building a Resilient Social Safety Net," 299. Philanthropic spending includes the largest private foundation in the region as well as all community foundations. For a full description of the methodology, see Reckhow and Weir, 319–20.

foundation and community foundations in the Chicago and Atlanta regions for 2007. In both metropolitan areas, philanthropic resources concentrated in cities, to a much lesser extent in affluent and middle-class suburbs, and hardly at all in poor suburban areas.

The importance of sustained engagement and substantial outside funds—both to promote collaboration and to address need directly—suggests that the problems confronting these areas will not be easily solved.

The Avoiders

Perhaps the most common response of local governments is to limit the size of the population that relies on the safety net. The quest to separate residential communities by income is one of the oldest themes in the history of U.S. suburbanization.[56] For a century, the state laws governing municipal incorporation and zoning restricted the supply of affordable housing in most suburbs, preventing low-income people from moving into middle-class and affluent communities. Affluent localities prided themselves on providing a high quality of life for a population that relied on federal programs such as Social Security, Medicare, and the home mortgage deduction but had little need of a local social safety net. Roads, good schools, and perhaps parks were all these residents looked for from local government. These suburban localities have been largely successful in maintaining their status by resisting policies—such as inclusionary zoning and other affordable housing initiatives—that would make their communities more economically diverse.

Even so, demographic and economic changes meant that some traditionally middle-class and affluent localities saw an influx of lower-income residents during the 1990s and 2000s. Some of the shift can be traced to immigration. In an effort to find housing near job centers, growing numbers of low-income immigrants settled in affluent suburban communities, often relying on multiple wage earners in a single household to pay the housing costs.[57] The growing numbers of lower-income residents in affluent suburbs has also grown through what Alan Ehrenhalt has called "demographic inversion"—the relocation of well-off whites to the city and the movement of middle- and lower-income African Americans to the suburbs.[58] Finally, the recession has also boosted the number of needy residents in many suburban communities. Exurban localities, in particular, have experienced high foreclosure rates.

Middle-class localities have responded to the growth of low-income populations in several ways. Many have sought to reduce the number of low-income immigrants with measures including anti-immigrant ordinances;

enforcement of housing codes in order to limit the number of residents in a single dwelling; and police agreements with the federal government through the 287(g) program and the Secure Communities program.[59] Although anti-immigrant initiatives reflect fear and resentment of immigrants, they are often explicitly linked to concerns about disproportionate use of city services by low-income immigrants.

Local governments can also make it difficult for agencies that serve the poor—immigrant oriented or not—to locate in their area. They can enable and reinforce NIMBYism by failing to assist nonprofit organizations seeking to create new services. Services associated with the very poor—such as homeless shelters—often have a difficult time locating in affluent suburban communities.[60] Some middle-income or affluent suburbs that decline to support a safety net regard such activities as beyond the scope of government responsibility and therefore best left to religious organizations and volunteers. Nor has the quest of the affluent to separate from the poor abated. Fulton and DeKalb Counties in Georgia, for example, saw a spate of municipal incorporations after 2005 as the lower-income populations in these counties grew and county governments sought tax and service increases to address new needs.[61] Since they have historically had little need for safety net services, affluent and middle-class localities have weak nonprofit infrastructures.[62]

Yet affluent suburbs have the advantage of financial and institutional resources when advocates do try to build a local safety net. Especially when county governments offer support, efforts to create a stronger nonprofit capacity to address new needs have achieved some success even when local governments remain on the sidelines. For example, in the affluent suburban DuPage County in the Chicago metropolitan area, the DuPage Federation on Human Service Reform relied on the county, local philanthropy, and a local university for financial and administrative support as it built an infrastructure of support for the small but growing low-income population.

Even though some counties and nonprofits are collaborating to build a safety net infrastructure in affluent suburbs, these initiatives require stronger support from other levels of government. Efforts to build the safety net in the suburbs encounter specific difficulties. The dispersed character of poverty in the suburbs means that need is likely to be less visible than in cities. Simply providing information about the growth of poverty is an important undertaking for suburban nonprofits. The dispersion of the poor and the lower density of suburban life mean that ensuring effective transportation to services is a critical element of the safety net. Moreover, because suburbs lack the inherited base of services available in cities, they may decide to forego some services or find them too hard to create anew. For example, access to specialist health care has been particularly difficult for low-income residents in the suburbs. In the absence of adequate services in the suburbs, those in need may rely on already overburdened city services, a phenomenon some researchers have referred to as "suburban free riding."[63]

STRATEGIES FOR THE FUTURE

As local governments confront strained finances and high levels of need that have lingered well after the recession officially ended, what strategies should they consider for the future? The agenda of possible policy strategies calls on local governments to engage actively as connectors, system builders, innovators, and advocates. But the strategies for enhancing the social safety net and the quality of life in cities are not just tasks for local government; they require activating other sectors and levels of government and building new kinds of regional collaborations. The following are among the critical areas for action and policies where local initiative is needed:

Eliminate local barriers to the take-up of federal benefits and create outreach campaigns. Local governments can identify and eliminate barriers to take-up of federal benefits, including unresponsive bureaucracies, poorly located agencies, and unnecessary red tape. Local governments are ideally situated to launch outreach campaigns that can reach program beneficiaries who otherwise would not know they are eligible or may be reluctant to accept benefits. The low take-up rates of SNAP benefits among immigrants suggests that targeted outreach to immigrants is a critical area for the connector strategy.

Look for opportunities—and avoid problems—that will emerge with the full implementation of the Affordable Care Act. The full implementation of the ACA will provide opportunities for linking health care systems with human service systems. As states implement the act, big-city governments, in particular, should have a seat at the table to ensure that the systems they have already created are not adversely impacted by implementation of the ACA. Likewise, engagement with ACA implementation will allow city governments to take advantage of opportunities to link human services to health care.[64] Local governments also need to be attentive to the ways that the ACA may present new challenges for safety net hospitals on which low-income residents rely.

Build coherent regional systems for delivering services. Over the past four decades, the federal government with great fanfare devolved responsibilities to state and local governments and encouraged contracting out of government services. Yet, in promoting devolution and privatization, Washington took little note of the need for coherent delivery systems. The current process for creating and locating nonprofit service providers is too bottom-up to achieve goals of efficiency and effectiveness in service delivery.

While national and regional nonprofit intermediary organizations have sought to build more coherent systems and local governments have, on occasion, tried as well, states can adopt a stronger role in ensuring adequate capacity in places where need exists. Connecticut has taken a step in this direction by creating a cabinet level position that liaises with the nonprofit world.[65]

Because there is no regional government, states or Metropolitan Planning Organizations can monitor shifts in the location of need and identify holes in the safety net. Federal policy can help by incentivizing the formation of regional coalitions. Regional coalitions not only promote learning across the system, they also provide critical support for advocates seeking to create services in localities where local officials offer little support or stand in the way of developing services for low-income residents.

Address the special problems of highly distressed suburbs and cities. Poor suburbs and highly distressed cities have little capacity—either administrative or financial—to address the needs of their low-income residents. State governments can take the lead in organizing consortia of these areas and create new models of multiservice nonprofit development. States can also reform systems of funding services in small low-income communities, especially when these systems are overly decentralized.

The federal government can revamp its grant system to enable consortia of low-income suburbs to apply for federal grant programs. Reflecting their focus on big cities, current grant rules assume considerable knowledge and coherence among applicants. To allow poor suburbs to compete for grants, the federal government may need to offer funds for creating and sustaining a consortium of local governments.[66]

The weakness of the public sector in poor suburbs and highly distressed cities means that the federal government may need to offer special assistance so these areas can receive the kind of support they need. The model offered by the HUD Strong Cities, Strong Communities pilot program could be deployed more widely. The program brings federal employees from various agencies in close collaboration with local officials, helping them develop revitalization strategies and connecting them with the federal resources that will help them achieve their goals.[67]

Open housing opportunities for low-income residents in job-rich affluent and middle-class suburbs. Since 1987, the housing voucher program has been linked to the goal of poverty deconcentration with provisions that allow voucher holders to "port" their vouchers to locations outside of the issuing jurisdictions. Yet, in most jurisdictions, only a handful of housing voucher recipients take advantage of this provision. The Chicago region's pilot program, the Chicago Regional Housing Choice Initiative, has taken steps toward pooling housing choice vouchers between the city and four suburban housing authorities. Federal support for pooling housing vouchers and making them truly portable will allow low-income families to locate in areas closer to jobs, and often with better schools.

Reengage local governments as advocates for low-income residents in state and federal arenas. Local governments cannot be expected to spend substantial sums on redistribution. But they can play an important role in advocating for federal and state policies that strengthen the safety net.

The recession made it clear that the safety net is poorly equipped to respond to sharp growth in need. Although the fully federal program SNAP expanded rapidly to meet growing need after 2008, the TANF block grant program has proven far less responsive to the growth in poverty.[68] The work-oriented welfare system performs poorly in a period when jobs are scarce. Moreover, TANF increasingly resembles, in MDRC president Gordon Berlin's words, "a form of revenue-sharing for the states."[69] States have used TANF funds for a wide variety of programs that make it difficult for them to shift back to cash assistance in periods of urgent need.

One of the strategies permitted by the TANF Emergency Fund, authorized as part of ARRA, was to allow states to create subsidized jobs for TANF recipients.[70] However, the program ended in 2010 when the ARRA stimulus funds dried up. Local officials who seek to strengthen the local safety net should mount a lobbying effort to make such a program part of TANF reauthorization in the future.

Notes

The author thanks Mike Pagano, Rachel Gordon, Nik Theodore, Julia Stasch, Terry Mazany, and Bill Barnes for their helpful comments.

1. Elizabeth Kneebone and Emily Garr, *The Suburbanization of Poverty: Trends in Metropolitan America, 2000 to 2008*, Metropolitan Policy Program at Brookings, January 2010.

2. Richard M. Musgrave, *The Theory of Public Finance* (New York: McGraw-Hill, 1959); Paul E. Peterson, *City Limits* (Chicago: University of Chicago Press, 1981).

3. Richard Florida, *The Rise of the Creative Class: And How It's Transforming Work, Leisure, Community and Everyday Life* (New York: Basic Books, 2002).

4. See, for example, John Logan and Todd Swanstrom, eds., *Beyond City Limits: Urban Policy and Restructuring in Comparative Perspective* (Philadelphia, Pa.: Temple University Press, 1991).

5. Edward W. Glaeser and Matthew E. Kahn, "From John Lindsay to Rudy Giuliani: The Decline of the Local Safety Net?," *FRBNY Economic Policy Review*, New York Federal Reserve, September 1999.

6. Florida, *Rise of the Creative Class*, 3.

7. Thomas L. Gais, "Stretched Net: The Retrenchment of State and Local Social Welfare Spending before the Recession," *Publius* 39:3 (2009): 557–79.

8. On ARRA see Arloc Sherman, "Despite Deep Recession and High Unemployment, Government Efforts—Including the Recovery Act—Prevented Poverty from Rising in 2009, New Census Data Show," Center on Budget and Policy Priorities, January 5, 2011, http://www.cbpp.org/cms/index.cfm?fa=view&id=3361, accessed June 6, 2013.

9. For example, Mayor Rudolph Giuliani of New York altered the administration of AFDC in ways that sharply reduced the numbers of recipients. See John Krinsky, "The Urban Politics of Workfare: New York City's Welfare Reforms and the Dimensions of Welfare Policy Making," *Urban Affairs Review* 42:6 (July 2007): 771–98.

10. See Derek S. Hyra, *The New Urban Renewal: The Economic Transformation of Harlem and Bronzeville* (Chicago: University of Chicago Press, 2008).

11. Steven Rathgeb Smith and Michael Lipsky, *Nonprofits for Hire: The Welfare State in the Age of Contracting* (Cambridge, Mass.: Harvard University Press, 1992); Martha R. Burt, Nancy Pindus, and Jeffrey Capizzano, *The Social Safety Net at the Beginning of Federal Welfare Reform: Organization of and Access to Social Services for Low-Income Families*, Assessing the New Federalism Occasional Paper No. 34, Washington, D.C.: Urban Institute, 2000.

12. See Jodi Sandifort, "Nonprofits within Policy Fields," *Journal of Policy Analysis and Management* 29:3 (2010): 637–44; Jack Krauskopf and Bin Chen, "Administering Services and Managing Contract: The Dual Role of Government Human Services Officials," *Journal of Policy Analysis and Management* 29:3 (2010): 625–28; Steve Smith, "Nonprofit Organizations and Government: Implications for Policy and Practice," *Journal of Policy Analysis and Management* 29: 3 (2010): 621–25.

13. Scott W. Allard, *Out of Reach: Place Poverty and the New American Welfare State* (New Haven, Conn.: Yale University Press, 2009), 154.

14. See the discussion of youth services in Linda Harris, *Learning from the Youth Opportunity Experience: Building Delivery Capacity in Distressed Communities* (Washington, D.C.: Center for Law and Social Policy, January 2006).

15. Ester R. Fuchs, *Mayors and Money: Fiscal Policy in New York and Chicago* (Chicago: University of Chicago Press, 1992), 114–17.

16. Peter Eisinger, "City Politics in an Era of Federal Devolution," *Urban Affairs Review* 33:3 (January 1998): 308–25; Margaret Weir, Harold Wolman, and Todd Swanstrom, "The Calculus of Coalitions: Cities, Suburbs and the Metropolitan Agenda," *Urban Affairs Review* 40:6 (July 2005): 730–60.

17. National League of Cities, *Combating Poverty: Emerging Strategies from the Nation's Cities*, www.nlc.org, accessed August 28, 2012.

18. Alice O'Connor, "Swimming against the Tide," in *Urban Problems and Community Development*, 77–137, edited by Ronald F. Ferguson and William T. Dickens (Washington, D.C.: Brookings Institution Press, 1998).

19. Scott W. Allard and Benjamin Roth, *Strained Suburbs: The Social Service Challenges of Rising Suburban Poverty*, Metropolitan Policy Program at Brookings, 2010.

20. U.S. Bureau of the Census, table 2, Poverty Status of People By Family Relationship, Race, and Hispanic Origin, 1959 to 2011, http://www.census.gov/hhes/www/poverty/data/historical/people.html, accessed June 6, 2013.

21. This paragraph draws on Steve Holt, *Ten Years of the EITC Movement: Making Work Pay Then and Now*, Metropolitan Policy Program at Brookings, April 2011.

22. These are county figures—see Food Research and Action Center, "SNAP Access in Urban America: A City-by-City Snapshot," January 2011, 1. California had a fingerprinting requirement, which may also help account for the lower take-up rates in San Diego and Los Angeles (California dropped the requirement in 2012).

23. John Eligon, "Cuomo Pushing City to End Food-Stamp Fingerprinting," *New York Times*, May 18, 2012, A25.

24. Nicole E. Marwell, *Bargaining for Brooklyn: Community Organizations in the Entrepreneurial City* (Chicago: University of Chicago Press, 2007).

25. Based in Elgin, Illinois, and with efforts throughout the state except in Chicago, the Grand Victoria Foundation is an exception to this pattern, although it is still small when compared to large private foundations and city community foundations.

26. Laurie E. Felland, Johanna R, Lauer, and Peter J. Cunningham, *Suburban Poverty and the Health Care Safety Net*, Center for Studying Health System Change Research Brief No. 13, July 2009.

27. Zeke Hasenfeld, Hyeon Jong Kil, Mindy Chen, and Bill Parent, *Stressed and Stretched: The Recession, Poverty, and Human Services Nonprofits in Los Angeles The Annual State of the Sector Report, 2002–2012* (Los Angeles: UCLA Luskin School of Public Affairs, Center for Civil Society, 2011), vi.

28. Ibid., 13 and 14; the figure for African American neighborhoods is 39.9 percent versus 14.3 percent for other neighborhoods.

29. Alicia Petska, "City Cuts CDBG Funding for Nonprofits," *News and Advance*, September 28, 2010. The decision drew considerable criticism because a large portion of the CDBG funds went to pay off a loan for a private mixed-use project.

30. Hasenfeld et al., *Stressed and Stretched*, vii.

31. Jonathan O'Connell, "Nonprofits Struggle to Survive and Maintain Services," *Washington Post*, November 8, 2010, 16; Jonathan Walters, "Nonprofits Seek Relief and Support from States," *Governing Magazine* (May 2011), http://www.governing.com/topics/health-human-services/nonprofits-seek-relief-support-from-states.html, accessed June 6, 2013; Hasenfeld et al., *Stressed and Stretched*.

32. Tom Jackman, "Fairfax Reduces Its Homeless Population, Even in Recession," *Washington Post*, June 16, 2011.

33. Kirk Johnson, "Habitat for Humanity Tries Big-Scale Approach to Housing in Oregon," *New York Times*, May 11, 2012.

34. National Alliance to End Homelessness, www.endhomelessness.org/library/entry/no-increase-in-homelessness-despite-recession, accessed September 13, 2012.

35. Meribah Knight, "New Attention Paid to Homeless Youth and Families," *New York Times*, November 3, 2011.

36. Noreen S. Ahmed-Ullah, "Emanuel to Pour $10 Million into Early Childhood," *Chicago Tribune*, August 4, 2012.

37. Brooke Rosenberg, "Mixture of Hope and Concern for City's New Daycare Program," *City Limits*, July 27, 2012.

38. See "Chicago Regional Choice Housing Voucher Proposal" for a description of the program and the additional support requested from HUD, Metropolitan Planning Organization, http://www.metroplanning.org/uploads/cms/documents/FINAL_CRHCI_Proposal_to_HUD.pdf, accessed November 15, 2012.

39. Santa Fe also enacted a local minimum wage in 2003; in 2012, voters in Albuquerque, N.M., and San Jose and Long Beach, Calif., also enacted city minimum wages.

40. Jamie Peck and Nik Theodore, "Recombinant Workfare, across the Americas: Transnationalizing 'Fast' Social Policy," *GeoForum* 41: 2 (March 2010).

41. Neil deMause, "Bloomberg Cash Rewards Program Gets Mixed Reviews," *City Limits*, April 29, 2010.

42. David W. Chen, "Goldman to Invest in City Jail Program, Profiting if Recidivism Falls Sharply," *New York Times*, August 2, 2012, A14.

43. Harold Meyerson, "Los Angeles Gets Innovative on Jobs," *Washington Post*, August 2, 2012.

44. The implementation of the program is in some doubt, because a local measure designed to support the program received just shy of the two-thirds majority to win approval.

45. Tim Mudd, "Federal Promise Neighborhoods Grants Awarded to 20 Communities," National League of Cities, January 9, 2012, www.nlc.org/media-center/news-search/federal-promise-neighborhoods-grants-awarded-to-20-communities, accessed September 15, 2012.

46. United States Conference of Mayors, *Hunger and Homelessness Survey: A Status Report on Hunger and Homelessness in America's Cities: A 25-City Survey*, December 2012, http://usmayors.org/pressreleases/uploads/2012/1219-report-HH.pdf, accessed June 6, 2013.

47. Elizabeth Kneebone, Carey Nadeau, and Alan Berube, *The Reemergence of Concentrated Poverty: Metropolitan Trends in the 2000s*, Metropolitan Policy Program at Brookings, November 2011.

48. Pascale Joassart-Marcelli and Jennifer R. Wolch, "The Intrametropolitan Geography of Poverty and the Nonprofit Sector in Southern California," *Nonprofit and Voluntary Sector Quarterly*, 32:1 (March 2003): 70–96; Sarah Reckhow and Margaret Weir, "Building a Resilient Social Safety Net," in *Urban and Regional Policy and Its*

Effects, 275–323, Building Resilient Regions, vol. 4, edited by Margaret Weir, Nancy Pindus, Howard Wial, and Harold Wolman (Washington, D.C.: Brookings Institution Press, 2012).

49. Scott W. Allard and Benjamin Roth, "Strained Suburbs: The Social Service Challenges of Rising Suburban Poverty," Metropolitan Policy Program at Brookings, 2010.

50. Kristen Grønbjerg and Steven Rathgeb Smith, "Nonprofit Organizations and Public Policies in the Delivery of Human Services," in *Philanthropy and the Nonprofit Sector in a Changing America*, 139–171, edited by Charles T. Clotfelter and Thomas Ehrlich (Bloomington: Indiana University Press, 1999).

51. It also considered transferring the responsibilities of the city health department to a nonprofit.

52. Rebecca Hendrick and Karen Mossberger, *Uneven Capacity and the Delivery of Human Services in the Chicago Suburbs: The Role of Townships and Municipalities*, Report for the Chicago Community Trust (Chicago: University of Illinois at Chicago, 2009). Townships have responsibility for general assistance, and other services are optional; for municipalities, all assistance is optional.

53. *Evidence Matters*, Policy Development and Research, HUD (winter 2012): 18.

54. Sarah Reckhow and Margaret Weir, "Building a Resilient Social Safety Net."

55. David Erickson, Carolina Reid, Lisa Nelson, Ann, O'Shaughnessy, and Alan Berube, eds., *The Enduring Challenge of Concentrated Poverty in America: Case Studies from Communities Across the U.S.*, Board of Governors of the Federal Reserve System, 2008, 31.

56. Jon C. Teaford, *The Political Fragmentation of Metropolitan America, 1850–1970* (Baltimore, Md.: Johns Hopkins University Press, 1979); Gary Miller, *Cities by Contract: The Politics of Municipal Incorporation* (Cambridge, Mass.: MIT Press, 1981).

57. Robert Suro, Jill H. Wilson, and Audrey Singer, *Immigration and Poverty in America's Suburbs*, Metropolitan Policy Program at Brookings, August 2011.

58. Alan Ehrenhalt, *The Great Inversion and the Future of the American City* (New York: Knopf, 2012).

59. For an overview see Monica Varsany, ed., *Taking Local Control: Immigration Policy Activism in U.S. Cities and States* (Stanford, Calif.: Stanford University Press, 2010).

60. See, for example, Dianna M. Aáñez, "Ambitious United Way Program Targets Homelessness," *Republic*, August 22, 2012.

61. April Hunt, "Local Control: More Cities May Need New Metro Landscape," *Atlanta Journal-Constitution*, September 19, 2011.

62. Joassart-Marcelli and Wolch, "Intrametropolitan Geography of Poverty and the Nonprofit Sector in Southern California."

63. Els De Graauw, Shannon Gleeson, and Irene Bloemraad, "Funding Immigrant Organizations: Suburban Free-Riding and Local Civil Presence," paper presented at the APSA 2012 meeting, http://papers.ssrn.com/sol3/papers.cfm?abstract_id=2107385, accessed November 13, 2012.

64. Cari DeSantis, APHSA National Workgroup on Integration, *Bridging the Divide: Leveraging New Opportunities to Integrate Health and Human Services* (Washington, D.C.: American Public Human Services Association, 2011).

65. Walters, "Nonprofits Seek Relief and Support from States."

66. See Elizabeth Kneebone and Alan Berube, *Confronting Suburban Poverty in America* (Washington D.C.: Brookings Institution Press, 2013).

67. See *Evidence Matters*.

68. LaDonna Pavetti and Liz Schott, "TANF's Inadequate Response to Recession Highlights Weakness of Block Grant Structure," Center for Budget and Policy Priorities, July 14, 2011.

69. Gordon Berlin, "Rethinking Welfare in the Great Recession: Issues in the Reauthorization of Temporary Assistance for Needy Families," Testimony of Gordon L. Berlin, President, MDRC, Before the Senate Finance Committee, September 21, 2010, 4, http://www.npc.umich.edu/news/events/safetynet/rethinking-the-safety-net-readings.pdf, accessed November 3, 2012.

70. Clifford M. Johnson, Amy Rynell, and Melissa Young, "Publicly Funded Jobs," *Reducing Poverty and Economic Distress after ARRA*, Urban Institute, July 2010.

Low-Wage Work and the Fraying of the Social Safety Net

DISCUSSANT: NIK THEODORE,
UNIVERSITY OF ILLINOIS AT CHICAGO

Redistributive programs for the poor have never ranked highly on the policy agendas of U.S. cities, where variants of public choice theory have long held sway. Inspired (knowingly or not) by a selective reading of Charles Tiebout's "pure theory of local expenditures," which argues that residents, as voter-consumers, will relocate to jurisdictions that provide them with their preferred bundle of public goods, local politicians have been reluctant to increase the share of municipal budgets devoted to pro-poor programming.[1] While Tiebout's argument was initially conceived to theorize the provision of public goods in general, it has since been applied with particular force to redistributive programs. Paul Peterson's influential "city limits" thesis extends the application of public choice theory to urban politics, arguing that upper-income residents will shun the tax burdens associated with social spending, expressing their discontent with pro-poor redistribution by "voting with their feet" and relocating to jurisdictions with lower rates of taxation. According to Peterson, "the pursuit of a city's economic interests . . . makes no allowance for the needy and unfortunate members of the society. Indeed, the competition among local communities all but precludes a concern for redistribution."[2] Instead, municipalities should pursue developmental objectives, such as those that attract jobs and investment to an area. In a political environment in which urban policies must pass certain "market tests," redistributive programs that favor lower-income residents typically fail such tests.[3]

Margaret Weir makes a convincing case that although local governments play a relatively small role in directly funding social programs, they have a critical role to play in ensuring that a strong safety net exists for residents in need. She characterizes these roles as connector (maintaining a sound bureaucracy to assist needy residents in accessing federal benefits), system builder (managing decentralized systems of service delivery), program innovator (developing new program models and approaches), and advocate (bringing political pressure to bear on higher levels of government to support pro-poor spending). These roles take on new urgency, she argues, in the wake of the Great Recession and the mounting fiscal stresses facing municipalities across the country.

And it is not just city coffers that are suffering. With rates of poverty and unemployment remaining persistently high well into what has been an extraordinarily anemic economic recovery, many city leaders are dedicating local resources to ensure both that low-income residents receive the social benefits for which they are eligible, and that entities in the public, private, and nonprofit sectors that are responsible for program development, funding, and delivery meet their responsibilities. The Great Recession has starkly revealed a set of problems that may appear to be cyclical—increasing economic hardship and growing demands on the social safety net—but that actually is part and parcel of a secular trend toward growing inequality and economic insecurity in U.S. cities. Well before the calamitous events that led to the 2007–8 recession, warning signs were evident that the foundation of middle-class living standards—stable jobs that provide fringe benefits and opportunities for upward mobility—was being eroded. Captured in the phrase "working poor" was the troublesome increase in jobs that pay below a "living wage," the growth in involuntary part-time work and temporary employment, and the loss of middle-income union jobs, especially in manufacturing and construction sectors. Policy has played a part in this, as well, in particular the erosion of the minimum wage, whose value has fallen fairly consistently in real terms (adjusting for inflation) since its historic high in 1968. The working poor, then, have come to symbolize those at the bottom of the wage structure, those who have "played by the rules" and retained an active attachment to the job market, but who nevertheless find themselves struggling near or below the poverty line.

Historically, economic expansions have been accompanied by falling poverty rates and reductions in social spending. But, state expenditures on many programs that help working families make ends meet have increased, despite the overall tightening of benefit eligibility rules that has occurred over the past two decades. When jobs pay too little to support a household, families often turn to various social safety net programs—such as child care subsidies, food stamps, and the Earned Income Tax Credit—to supplement their low earnings. When jobs don't come with health insurance, or when the cost of buying into an employer's plan is too high, families either make do with emergency room visits or they enroll in public programs such as Medicaid. In short, when work does not pay enough to support a family, the public sector steps in to fill the gap between family income and family needs. In Illinois alone, hundreds of thousands of working families turn to public benefits programs to help them make ends meet. This support to workers and their families represent the hidden public costs of low-wage work.

Using publicly available administrative and survey data, Theodore and Doussard estimated the share of social safety net spending going to working families in Illinois, and identified the leading industries that employ low-wage workers.[4] As the Illinois economy slowly rebounded from the early-2000s recession, each year approximately 475,000 families with a worker who was employed year-round were receiving benefits from one of the state's social safety net programs. Low wages were the principal reason working families received benefits: two-thirds of the year-round workers in families receiving public benefits earned ten dollars an hour or less. Surprisingly, perhaps, this was not driven by part-time and temporary employment: 79 percent of those families were supported by a full-time worker employed at least thirty-five hours a week, and more than 92 percent of the dual-worker households receiving public assistance were supported by more than seventy hours of weekly employment.

The health services, retail trade, and arts-and entertainment services sectors are the largest employers of year-round workers with families receiving public assistance. Together, they accounted for 36 percent of all working Illinois families enrolled in public programs, and for 39 percent of program benefits to working families. Notably, one-third of the year-round workers with families receiving public assistance were employed at firms with a thousand or more workers.

The safety net programs supporting the neediest families are indispensable, and they contribute in no small measure to the high quality of life enjoyed by most Illinoisans. But when profitable industries fail to pay family-supporting wages, workers have great difficulty being productive at work under such conditions, and the state has to step in to help them make ends meet. But many employers have essentially pushed their costs onto social-assistance programs, and in turn onto the state and its taxpayers. A case, therefore, can be made that the social benefits received by workers who are employed year-round (and typically working a full-time job) are an implicit subsidy to their employers who have paved a path to profitability by radically cutting labor costs. And employers benefit from this social spending, since it fills the gap between what they pay and what workers need in order to be stable and productive employees.

As the statistics from Illinois suggest, the need for low-income families to access safety net programs is great, and the local government roles of connector, system builder, program innovator, and advocate identified by Weir remain as important as ever. But can localities do more? Because they are hidden, the costs of maintaining the social safety net are rarely included in debates over local economic development. Economic development expenditures are an investment in a municipality's future. But when public programs support low-wage employers, taxpayers pay twice: first, through the many state and local programs designed to attract and retain businesses; and, second, through the billions of dollars spent every year to support families that rely on low-wage jobs in highly profitable industries.

It takes more than new jobs to build a healthy economy. In Illinois, as in many other states, too many of the jobs created since about 1990 are poorly paying and offer no fringe benefits. As a result, Illinois is confronted by what at first seems to be a paradox: economic expansion and employment growth have been accompanied by rising state expenditures on public benefits programs to help working families make ends meet. These are crucial programs. They help pay for health care, child care, food, and other daily needs, and they ensure a basic standard of living for everyone in the state. But their worthy public purposes are subverted when employers pursue low-road business strategies based on holding down wages and avoiding benefits obligations, in the process shifting greater costs and responsibilities onto public benefits programs.

Notes

1. Charles E. Tiebout, "A Pure Theory of Local Expenditures," *Journal of Political Economy* 64:5 (1956): 416–24.

2. Paul E. Peterson, *City Limits* (Chicago: University of Chicago Press, 1981), 37–38.

3. Jamie Peck, "Neoliberal Suburbanism: Frontier Space," *Urban Geography* 32:6 (2011): 884–991.

4. Nik Theodore and Marc Doussard, *The Hidden Public Costs of Low-Wage Work in Illinois* (Chicago: University of Illinois at Chicago Center for Urban Economic Development, 2006).

Social Safety Nets

Subsidies and Place

DISCUSSANT: RACHEL A. GORDON,
UNIVERSITY OF ILLINOIS AT CHICAGO

As a social scientist, I think about the interlocking contexts that surround families and children. The safety net is one of these contexts. We know a good deal about the extent to which that net truly supports families—as well as where it sags or breaks. In reading Margaret Weir's contribution, however, I realized that the sociology and developmental literatures don't discuss how living in a particular municipality matters for children and families' well-being. One longstanding interest of mine is how children and families' well-being depends on the fraction of people in their community who are like them. In some ways, similarity can be a disadvantage: A poor child who lives in an area of concentrated poverty is often exposed to high crime and under-resourced schools, for example. In other ways, dissimilarity can be a *dis*advantage: If a child is poor, she may be less likely to get social assistance when there are "too few" other poor people in the area for local programs, information, and infrastructure to have grown up to support them. The latter possibility intersects well with Weir's typologies of municipalities, and seems ripe for cross-disciplinary conversation and research. It is also a topic of considerable policy interest, for example, as low-income families are displaced from inner-city high-rise public housing to suburban subsidized housing and as immigrant families move to places where historically there were few others like them.

My colleagues and I offer a recent example of the potential of wedding Weir's typologies to other social science research.[1] We looked at national data about a USDA food subsidy program for child care providers that is similar in many ways to the School Lunch Program. Most of the rules for this program are at the federal level, rather than at the state or local level. Even so, we found that the chances of a preschooler receiving the food subsidy depended largely on whether her neighbors were also poor. If she lived among others who were better off, she was less likely to receive this assistance. The differences were significant, especially among children cared for in for-profit centers where fully two-thirds of poor two-year-olds received the program when they lived in the highest poverty zip codes, versus less than one-third of those living in lower poverty areas. Because the subsidy flows through the child care provider, rather than going directly to children and families, we anticipated that this differential occurs because it is not worth it for the child care center to go through the administrative hurdles of signing up for the program if few children qualify. This decision leaves the child without the nutrition benefits that the program is meant to offer.

The 2012 Chicago Area Study that I directed supports these interpretations and further illuminates the relevance of Weir's typologies.[2] We surveyed child care center directors in thirty-three zip codes on the North and West Sides of the Chicago metropolitan area. We interviewed 70 percent of all directors in these areas, 229 in all. We asked providers if they participated in several federal and state programs, including the food subsidy program, and if they didn't, why not. We found that just over half of all directors of centers not participating in the food subsidy program said they hadn't signed up because not enough families qualified. Within the subset of directors who said that they had enough qualifying families, another 20–25 percent reported that the amount of paperwork prevented them from signing up. These barriers were reported even within the poorest zip codes, where nearly one-quarter of providers said the lack of qualifying families was a barrier to participation and 20 percent reported that paperwork was an obstacle. Again, this situation may make sense in the director's calculus, but it is problematic from the perspective of low-income children, since they can benefit from the food subsidy program only if their provider participates. In fact, among centers located in low-income zip codes that did not enroll in the food subsidy program, fully 70 percent participated in other programs aimed at low-income children, such as subsidies to pay their basic tuition. Even within higher-income zip codes, over one-third of centers not offering food subsidies reported participation in other programs for low-income children. These findings suggest that the food subsidy program may be unique in terms of provider knowledge or administrative burdens.

Municipalities can help address such situations, so that the quality of the safety net depends less on where a child or family lives (and thus less on whether enough residents are similar enough to support programs). The roles Weir defines of connector and system builder are relevant for the food subsidy program that we studied, especially in areas that are relatively better-off, with limited or emerging pockets of poverty. Although many child care providers—especially centers and licensed family day care providers—will be aware of the food subsidy program, some may not be, especially when the families they typically serve are not poor. Thus, municipalities can perform the connector role by helping providers learn about the program. Even though providers are the recipients of the subsidy—so they can serve more nutritious food in their programs—municipalities can do outreach to parents in order to document demand for the program. In making such connections, municipalities may be most successful if they use another of Weir's strategies—system building—to complement existing outreach efforts by the state agencies and local child care resource and referral agencies that typically oversee the program.

There may also be municipal roles for program innovation and advocacy around the food subsidy program. Municipalities could develop creative strategies to reduce the administrative burdens of participation, especially for the smallest centers and family day care providers who likely have the least in-house capacity. This might, for example, involve designating a floating staff person to travel among centers to help them sign up for the food subsidy program and fulfill any ongoing programmatic requirements. Municipalities might also advocate for changes to the program to make it easier for providers to participate, again especially in localities where fewer children qualify. Small family day care providers that are exempt from licensing do not qualify for food subsidies in all states, even though these providers care for approximately 20 percent of toddlers and preschoolers nationally. Therefore, this would be an area particularly ripe for advocacy, especially in municipalities where these license-exempt providers are common.

I am aware of no existing data sets documenting such municipal action, at least none covering large geographical areas. Thus another activity ripe for municipal action and collaborative research is better developing such data sets. The city of Chicago's Early Learning portal, for example, allows parents to learn interactively about child care options in their area.[3] The U.S. Department of Education has been encouraging states to development Longitudinal

Data Systems to provide better information on teachers and schools.[4] Such databases can serve multiple purposes. Municipalities can use them to learn what others are doing. Families can use them to search for needed services (and potentially use them in residential decisions). Scholars can use them to study how the multiple contextual layers surrounding children and families help or hinder their well-being. Each of these purposes requires data structured somewhat differently, and innovations in information gathering and dissemination have led to a myriad of user interfaces. From the social scientist lens, efforts to capture and centralize data in structures conducive to research (back-end comprehensive spreadsheets) will best support a next generation of collaborative research about the ways in which the local safety net matters for the life course of children and families.

Notes

1. Rachel A. Gordon, Robert Kaestner, Sanders Korenman, and Kristin Abner, "The Child and Adult Care Food Program: Who Is Served and Why?," *Social Service Review* 85 (2011): 359–400.

2. Rachel A. Gordon, Maria Krysan, and Anna Colaner, *2012 Chicago Area Study*, 2012, http://igpa.uillinois.edu/cas/2012-chicago-area-study, accessed June 10, 2013.

3. City of Chicago: Early Learning Portal, http://www.ecechicago.org/, accessed June 10, 2013.

4. Donald Hernandez, *PreK–3rd: Next Steps for State Longitudinal Data Systems* (New York: Foundation for Child Development, 2012).

Resilient Economic Development

Challenges and Opportunities

RAPHAEL W. BOSTIC

UNIVERSITY OF SOUTHERN CALIFORNIA

The question of what makes and keeps local and regional economies and societies resilient is an important one. In an increasingly global and competitive world, the market and other forces that influence a local and regional economy can change quickly, altering the competitive balance in ways that can significantly disrupt local economic dynamics. Many have noted the important role that public policy can play in shaping how a city or region responds to these changes, both in the short and long run.[1]

Events since the turn of the millennium have only increased interest in this issue. Hurricane Katrina and the 9/11 terrorist attacks made clear that resilience is relevant and important for natural and noneconomic political forces in addition to economic competitive forces. The longer-term, ongoing struggles of rust-belt cities such as Detroit (Mich.) and Cleveland (Ohio), as well as struggles in Memphis (Tenn.), Chester (Penna.), Fresno (Calif.), and elsewhere—and the different strategies each has pursued—sharpen the issue even further.

This chapter explores whether resilience requires specific ingredients to ensure that economic development proceeds effectively and continuously. It provides a blueprint for how regions and communities might achieve resilience in the face of fluctuating economic and public fiscal capacity. How do economic and fiscal contractions influence the set of initiatives and policies that localities employ, and how can localities minimize the adverse effects of these contractions on their economic development efforts?

The Great Recession of 2007–9 brings this question into sharp relief, as states and cities across the country face significant fiscal challenges in its wake. If the depth and intensity of this economic downturn represents a "new normal" of greater economic volatility after forty years of increasing stability in macroeconomic measures, then this question may be increasing in importance.[2] While this is not a consensus view, the past twenty-five years have been marked by three significant recessions (1988–91, 2001–2, 2007–9) and one period of historic growth (the late 1990s). It appears that having coherent and effective local strategies for implementing policies that promote economic growth and development that remain impactful in varying economic circumstances will likely be critical for sustained robust economic development.

THE CONTEXT: ECONOMIC DEVELOPMENT AND RESILIENCE

Economic development is the result of the interaction of policy with the prevailing economic forces. In turn, policy's efficacy is a function of how successfully and effectively the governmental and other institutional organizations interact and collaborate. This section reviews the nature of these relationships, which provides a framework to help us consider how policy might change in the face of changing fiscal capacity. In addition, I highlight the important issue of geographic scope—economic development can happen at various levels, and each level features unique dynamics.

Economic Development: The Economics of Growth

Economic development must first and foremost leverage the forces and dimensions that generate and sustain economic growth and prosperity. Urban places are created as a result of the agglomeration forces driving density and production.[3] And, the agglomeration is in turn driven by a number of economic factors. The most basic of these are the needs of production and consumption. In general, people must come together in order to produce and exchange most goods. Innovations in technology have reduced such needs in some cases. For example, a great deal of retail activity takes place remotely through eBay and other e-commerce vehicles. Similarly, email, telework, and teleconferencing have reduced the need for employees to be near one another to conduct business. However, these innovations have not yet created transformations that suggest that production and consumption agglomeration forces are waning and likely to disappear. In fact, the demand for retail space, while reduced in some sectors, has remained robust despite the increased prevalence of technological alternatives. Similarly, the demand for office space has evolved rather than disappeared, and we now see new arrangements, such as Silicon Beach and other models, that leverage resource sharing in new ways.[4]

In addition to these agglomerative forces, urbanized places develop and thrive because they offer opportunities to realize increasing returns to scale and positive production externalities.[5] Increasing returns arise when an increase in output reduces average total costs per unit of production, a situation that occurs for many industries, including those for computers and music. Other agglomeration externalities focus on positive spillovers associated with the exchange of information. These spillovers can occur either within industries or across industries, creating beneficial situations for urban places that boast either a more specialized industry mix (for within-industry spillovers) or a diverse industry mix (for across-industry spillovers).[6] More specialized urban places also can deliver services more efficiently, as infrastructure can evolve in ways that streamline access to productive inputs and the ability to move final products to market.

In order to understand and shape the nature and extent of economic growth, however, we must also consider the negative aspects of agglomerative forces. For example, if it is not managed effectively, agglomeration can increase density and development to a degree that creates adverse congestion. This congestion increases the cost of transporting goods and commuting to work, and it can reduce the relative competitiveness of a locale. If adverse factors such as these are not addressed, efforts to promote economic development and growth and, by extension, to establish resilience, are likely to be less successful than they otherwise could be.

Economic Development: The Policies

Governments at all levels have at their disposal a number of strategies to promote economic development. These can be grouped into several broad strategies: direct subsidies, tax expenditures, zoning and land use changes, infrastructure investment, and order-and-disorder approaches targeted at providing signals for commerce and investment. Each one can promote economic development and increased prosperity. This section briefly reviews these various approaches and considers some of the evidence that evaluates the effectiveness of these strategies. The literature shows that policies in each category can be effective, although success is generally not guaranteed. Although the discussion of policy examples skews toward affordable housing policies, programs using each strategic category exist in all the major economic development policy areas, including workforce training, small business development, and neighborhood revitalization.

DIRECT SUBSIDIES. Direct subsidies are associated with grants and low-cost funds, usually from public sources and often through place-based formulas and competitive grants. Federal programs in this category include the Community Development Block Grant (CDBG) program, the HOME Investment Partnerships Program, the Jobs Corps, the Workforce Investment Act Adult Program, and the Economic Development Administration Grant Program. Also in this category are proceeds generated by the issuance of municipal bonds, which typically have lower interest rates than can be obtained in the broader market, and local policies that offer subsidies such as down-payment assistance. The effectiveness of these programs varies widely. Programs targeting the labor force have received considerable attention from researchers and have yielded useful findings that have shaped program design. In contrast, despite their strong support among policy makers, there has been virtually no research assessing the impact of the CDBG and HOME programs.

TAX EXPENDITURES. Tax expenditure policies, which do not require explicit appropriations but which impact budgets nonetheless, operate through federal or state budgets (e.g., the low-income housing tax credit, the Earned Income Tax Credit, redevelopment areas, enterprise zones, and free-trade zones) as well as at lower levels of government, sometimes as a supplement to existing federal programs (e.g., state enterprise zones) and at other times as a stand-alone program (e.g., tax increment schemes associated with redevelopment). Evidence about these types of programs suggests that they can be effective economic development strategies in some circumstances. But, as with direct subsidies, the overall evidence on the program effectiveness of tax expenditures is mixed, both in terms of depth and effectiveness. For enterprise zones, for example, Bostic and Prohofsky, Papke, and others show positive impacts, while Kolko and Neumark and others report limited effects at best.[7] The similar mixed record of results for evaluations of other strategies suggests an important, unfilled role for local context in determining ultimate program effectiveness.

ZONING AND LAND USE. Zoning and land use policies typically are targeted to specific local areas and, since land use is generally determined by specific jurisdictions, tend to be enacted locally. However, some land use policies, such as urban growth boundaries, are implemented at higher geographic levels, which makes this class of policies applicable at multiple geographic levels. The empirical evidence is that zoning and land use policies impact the value of assets and thereby impact the potential for economic development.[8]

Most of the research emphasizes the negative aspects of the restrictions this zoning generally introduces, but these negative findings reveal the important role that zoning and land use can play for economic development. Moreover, anecdotal evidence suggests that efforts in this category can catalyze economic development and private investment.[9]

INFRASTRUCTURE INVESTMENT. Industry efficiency increases with higher-quality infrastructure, as better infrastructure lowers the cost of moving goods and people to and from places of work and commerce. Regions with better infrastructure are better positioned to leverage future economic developments, grow robustly, and weather tougher economic winds. Investments in this area include establishment or expansion of public transit, widening of streets to accommodate more modern transport and production technologies, and bolstering of the power grid to increase its ability to carry load. Ample evidence shows that investment in public infrastructure enhances economic performance at various geographic levels, though the magnitude of effects appears to vary with time, industry, and geography.[10]

"ORDER-AND-DISORDER" POLICIES. Since about 1980 we have seen increasing emphasis on using policies designed to improve neighborhood conditions in ways that appeal to private investors, who in turn can make investments that spark economic development. Such policies have the goal of improving the perceived appeal of locations as investment targets and new private investment activities. These include major policy initiatives, such as those seeking to reduce crime rates, as well as smaller-scale efforts targeting sources of disorder, such as those with objectives to eliminate graffiti, fix broken windows in buildings, and convert significant sources of blight. Regulatory and enforcement actions like code enforcement represent another potential component of an "order-and-disorder" strategy, as building and health codes can be used to shutter nuisance properties and allow for their conversion to community assets.[11] The empirical evidence is clear that aggressive policies can reduce crime, though there is debate about the effectiveness of enforcing laws that target minor infractions, such as broken windows.[12] Given the widely recognized negative relationship between crime incidence and private investment, these policies have a clear positive link to economic development.

Economic Development: The Vital Role of Institutions

While economic development typically focuses on the economic environment and policy levers that prevail either regionally or at more local geographic levels, the institutional context is a critical factor in determining the success or failure of an economic development program. Every policy must be implemented, and implementation occurs through specific institutional vehicles.

Prevailing wisdom had long held that public-sector institutions would be the primary implementer of policies, and those policies will then impact the private and nonprofit sectors. Increasingly, however, we have observed nonprofit and private sector actors to be key in policy execution. Affordable-housing production is an exemplary model of this. At the outset of federal housing policy in the 1930s and 1940s, the federal government was positioned as the developer of housing units to be occupied by those needing housing assistance. However, in the wake of the failure of high-profile public-housing projects, this model was thrown out in the early 1970s. In the replacement policy, the public sector provides subsidy financing to private and nonprofit housing developers that build housing meeting governmental guidelines, which include requirements for lower, more affordable rents. Today, virtually all new affordable-housing units are produced by private or nonprofit developers.[13] This intersectoral model of institutional support or direct partnership now prevails in many policy arenas, including homelessness, community development, small-business development, environmental preservation and protection, and infrastructure production.[14]

Academics have long understood the importance of effective implementation of policy. For example, scholars at the time of the Great Society were deeply concerned with the challenges of implementation and the implications for policy efficacy. Within the resulting body of work—Rittel and Weber's seminal writing on "wicked problems" is of this era—are key pieces emphasizing the multidimensional challenges that implementation offers.[15] Sabatier and Mazmanian create a more formal conceptual framework of policy implementation that highlights the importance of institutional capacity, embodied in staff skill and resource availability, the prevailing rules for decision making and institutional relationships.[16] For the latter, a key evaluative criterion is whether or not the various organizations share incentives and are ideologically aligned. Such alignment is not preordained. For example, there is a long-documented adversarial relationship between cities and suburbs and among suburbs.[17] These frictions can limit the efficacy of policy and the extent to which economic development is realized.

Since the 1970s, the profile of implementation concerns in scholarly contexts has waned somewhat, and the application of scholarly insights regarding implementation to real-world contexts has lagged.[18] As a consequence, challenges of implementation remain significant for many. Current federal policies acknowledge this. The Obama administration's Strong Cities, Strong Communities (SC2) initiative and HUD's OneCPD (Office of Community Planning and Development) technical assistance modernization are but two policy initiatives that seek to make implementation less of a hurdle. SC2 seeks to "assist communities that have faced long-term challenges in developing and implementing their economic strategies."[19] It features on-the-ground assessments of local capacity, the embedding of skilled federal experts within local government agencies to supplement capacity and enhance program implementation, the provision of resources to enable coordinated interagency local and regional planning, and a technical assistance network to provide ongoing support to policy implementers as needed. The OneCPD initiative represents a new way of providing technical assistance to local governments. It explicitly recognizes that local capacity challenges are not program specific but rather tend to be common across programs, which demands that they be addressed in a holistic, comprehensive manner. Technical assistance is delivered with this philosophy in mind.[20] Both efforts represent an explicit acknowledgment that implementation problems threaten the effectiveness of policies seeking to transform communities.

Economic Development: Defining Geography

The appropriate geographic scope must be considered in any economic development strategy. Each level of geography—region, city, neighborhood—requires an emphasis on different considerations. A natural geography to consider is the region, as economic activity is typically organized at a regional scale. Economic models show that economic and agglomerative forces shape the built environment without consideration of jurisdictional boundaries, with the forces that drive supply and demand also determining the location, scale, and trajectory of land uses, whether they be for production, residential, or retail. Indeed, a significant body of evidence confirms that central city and suburban economies are closely tied together and that weaknesses in one adversely impact growth in the other and in the aggregate.[21] Clearly, regional policies that improve coordination and strengthen the region or its component jurisdictions can potentially effect positive change.

Despite the important role that regions play in economic development and performance, regional policy is relatively rare, as most regions are governed in a disaggregated fashion by a large number of independent towns, cities, and counties. This reality makes the city a natural unit of geography to consider as the site to originate economic development policy. Most economic development policies are implemented by cities, and the public-sector resources flowing to a region often are directed to cities rather than to regions. Moreover, cities, particularly centrally located cities, are often the drivers of major infrastructure investments that can strengthen the relative position of a region. For example, local officials, including Los Angeles mayor Tom Bradley, played vital roles in driving the investment in and growth of the Los Angeles–Long Beach port and Los Angeles International Airport, which catalyzed their positions as the dominant transport hubs in the western United States.[22] We see many similar city-based efforts taking place elsewhere.

A third geography to consider is the neighborhood. Within a city, economic activity and welfare are not evenly distributed; neighborhoods and communities lag behind others. Lagging neighborhoods often are isolated from the broader city or regional economic engine and suffer from social problems that draw resources from other productive uses. Much government effort—at the local, state, and federal levels—seeks to transform the trajectory of these struggling places and help them better contribute to and benefit from the city and regional economic engines. Neighborhoods can also be the focus of targeted economic development efforts that leverage place-specific opportunities, such as those embodied by enterprise zones.

The geographical area of interest will determine the activities and considerations that should receive the most attention regarding government policy. Regional assessments and strategies should focus on establishing which economic and agglomerative forces dominate and how they play out in terms of industry mix, labor force needs and skills, and capital and infrastructure requirements. By contrast, local neighborhoods and, in most cases, individual city policies must consider the roles each plays in contributing to the regional economy and then further identify areas of weakness, strength, and opportunity. Importantly, these policies must have a connective element, as the residents and resources will necessarily relate and interact with residents and resources in other proximate communities to create the regional economy. Approaches that are more isolated in their orientation are unlikely to yield successful and sustained economic development and improvement.

Volatility in Economic Performance and Public Finance

The existence of business cycles—and their effect on public-sector finance—has long been recognized. Since the 1800s, the United States has experienced more than twenty-five economic cycles of growth, each followed by a contractionary period of varying intensity and length.[23] Business cycles are not unique to national economies, but rather occur at nearly every level of economic organization. Thus, we observe significant fluctuations at the state, regional, city, and neighborhood levels. California in recent years has suffered from a major spike in unemployment and from volatile output. At the regional level, a number of regions have experienced cyclical boom-bust periods over both short and longer terms. This is perhaps most clearly seen in regional economies driven by oil, gas, and other natural resources, as with the boom-bust oil-based economies of Denver and Houston and the more recent major expansions in parts of North Dakota and western Pennsylvania due to oil shale extraction innovations. But regional cyclicality has also been observed throughout history as broader economic trends have caused industry sectors to ebb and flow. For example, the declines of New Bedford and Lowell, Massachusetts, and of other textile markets of New England have been well-documented, and the rapid decline of historical rural population and economic centers of the Great Plains, which began in the early 1900s, continues.[24]

While economies often operate on a regional scale, economic declines and cyclical performance need not be geographically regional. Indeed, some central cities have seen lengthy recessionary periods, which at times could be considered chronic declines, while the region at large can be deemed growing healthier or, at a minimum, demonstrating cyclicality. For example, Hill et al. show that, over the past thirty years, the Detroit metropolitan area experienced periods of growth even while the city Detroit continuously declined.[25] Neighborhoods show similar cyclical dynamics.

The ebb and flow of economies suggests an ebb and flow of public-sector finances, as the amount at a public institution's disposal depends on the level of economic activity and the value that activity creates. The degree of volatility in public finance is closely tied to the nature of the economic fluctuations (i.e., which sectors of the economy are growing or shrinking), the tax structure, and the relative importance of revenues across various sources. Thus, although business cycles drive the direction of public budgetary volatility, the magnitude of their importance for tax revenue and, by extension, the provision of services and programs, vary.

The recent Great Recession highlights the extent to which the nature of the economic fluctuation affects public-finance volatility. In the run-up to this recession, public budgets swelled due to ever-increasing tax revenues from higher incomes, sales, and property values. In 2007–8, data from the U.S. Census of Governments indicate that aggregate state and local public budgets were at record highs. The 2007–8 budget levels were more than twice as high as receipts in 1995, 50 percent higher than levels in 2002–3, and had grown by 22 percent in the previous three years. These higher budgets supported, among other things, increases in the provision of educational, public works, and other services; more public-sector employment; and increased investment in neighborhoods.

The Great Recession precipitated a sea change for public budgets. The loss of jobs and full-time employment in the general economy resulted in a major decline in public-sector revenues arising from income and sales. Income tax revenues fell by 14.6 percent to $260.3 billion between 2008 and 2010. Declines in retail sales caused sales tax revenues to fall by 4.2 percent between 2007 and 2009. This distress was exacerbated by subsequent troubles in major industries, perhaps most clearly represented by the auto industry. In 2009, as part of the Troubled Asset Relief Program (TARP), General Motors and Chrysler together reduced their dealership network by about two thousand dealers, which represented about 25 percent of their aggregated total.[26] Such a hit to a powerful economic engine that drives sales revenue and jobs additionally hurt states and localities, particularly those more dependent on the industry as an employment base and on such sales as a major producer of tax revenue.

The housing crisis added to these woes. While the loss of sales tax revenue was significant, the crisis had two additional effects. First, it reduced investments in housing-related activities that require permitting—in particular, new construction measured by permits fell by 73 percent, and home improvement activities as measured by loan amounts fell significantly, as well. As a consequence, revenues from the permits required for these activities tumbled. Second, declining values mean that property tax revenue stagnates or even declines. Instead of being revenue generating, as it had historically been, the rebenchmarking of tax basis that occurs in many states after a sale more frequently worked to the detriment of a jurisdiction's fiscal interests. For example, data on repeat sales show significant declines in many metropolitan areas between 2006 and 2009, meaning that the sale price of a given house was lower than the most recent prior sale of that house. Lower sale prices are likely to result in a fiscal loss for the jurisdiction in the many states that permit property owners to petition for a reassessment of a property's value, an option usually pursued only when selling prices have recently dropped. And indeed we have witnessed a significant uptick in the frequency of requests for reassessments of property. In Washington, D.C., for example, reassessment requests in 2012 resulted in new assessments that reduced property values by an estimated $2.6 billion, which then "cost" the District $48 million in lost tax revenue.[27] In the aggregate, the billions in reductions in revenue resulted in difficult decisions for jurisdictions faced with balancing their budgets. Unlike the federal government, which can run deficits over years, local and state governments generally are legally required to balance their budgets over the course of a fiscal year.

RESPONDING TO NEED WHEN BUDGETS SHRINK

The volatility of public resources conflicts directly with the often intractable stability of need for goods and services. Independent of the business cycle, the citizens of a jurisdiction will still demand education, trash collection, police, fire, and other services. Thus, strains are placed on the budget when economic contraction occurs. Similarly, local governments are continually seeking to improve the status of their jurisdictions and to stabilize economic trajectories. There are many communities of need that lack public safety, good education, job opportunities, and other basic amenities viewed as fundamental to American values of liberty, freedom, and choice. In these places, need is often not cyclical—instead, the demands are consistent and long-standing.

Thus there is ongoing demand for programs from the suite of economic development policy options, even during times of acute fiscal constraint. However, some of the classes of economic development strategies discussed above are more difficult to maintain during times that require public-sector belt-tightening.

Because direct-subsidy programs often represent direct budgetary line items, they are generally weighed against all other public obligations in discussions of priorities. Economic development often fares poorly when policy makers weigh it against core governmental functions such as policing and education, resulting in its receiving lower priority. Decisions at the federal level, which are influenced by a similar dynamic, can exacerbate these effects. As part of the federal budget reductions in 2011, for example, HUD opted to cut expenditures for its block grant programs (such as CDBG) rather than reduce the resources committed to rental assistance.

Tax expenditures are generally believed to be associated with less political risk than direct-subsidy programs because they are triggered automatically and typically do not require annual deliberations. As a consequence, one might expect that this class of strategies would be less susceptible to fluctuations as fiscal conditions shift. While that is generally true, this class of policies is not immune from being reduced. For example, in 2011 California eliminated a powerful tax expenditure program—the redevelopment agency—in a quest to shore up the state's shaky finances.[28] Redevelopment agencies in California functioned based on a tax increment structure, whereby the extra taxes gained through the increased value generated from the agency's investments were added to local budgets in order to finance a set of diverse community and economic development activities. The loss of redevelopment has cost local governments $5 to $6 billion in available funds, with fully 20 percent of that reserved for affordable housing. This represents a significant blow to California's local economic development efforts.

Unlike subsidies and tax expenditures, zoning and land use policies are rarely eliminated when budget challenges arise. Because these policies generally represent an evolution of collective decision making and politics, they are generally able to withstand budgetary challenges. However, their effectiveness relies on vigorous engagement from private, nonprofit, and philanthropic sector partners, and the first two types of organizations (though not the philanthropic ones) are likely to experience troubles comparable to what the public sector encounters during times of stress.

The challenge for maintaining infrastructure investments is that the bulk of the benefits for these investments are realized well into the future, while the bulk of the resource demands are felt contemporaneously. Both of these situations pose problems. In difficult budget environments, large line items with limited immediate payoffs become easy targets. The elimination of high-speed rail programs in Florida, Ohio, and Wisconsin all are examples of this.[29] Moreover, because the benefits accrue mainly in the future, it is more difficult to construct sizable vocal and active coalitions capable of winning a political battle regarding such investments. So this strategy is also at risk.

Order and disorder can also be adversely affected. These policies are often labor-intensive, which can make them relatively expensive to operate. For example, effective implementation of a rigorous property inspection program could require significant increases to a jurisdiction's inspector corps in order to meet increased expectations and workloads such a program creates. Thus, acute pressures to reduce public-sector staff can be a threat to the effective operation and positive impacts of these types of programs. So although they can often survive the "chopping block," the efficacy of order-and-disorder programs can be significantly reduced.

On balance, reliance on purely public approaches for economic and community development is likely to leave communities and regions vulnerable to public funding cycles. As discussed in the next section, resilience then is threatened if support and energy are tapped only from public sources. A broader approach is needed to involve players from across all sectors and to draw from the diverse skill set in a community or region.

RESILIENT ECONOMIC DEVELOPMENT

Successful economic development, whether at the regional or more local level, requires sustained collaboration and coordination. Economic development efforts rarely run their course over six months, a year, or even five or ten years. Rather, economic development typically occurs incrementally over long periods of time, as the investments in new and latent opportunities that are made require time to take hold, evolve into mature enterprises, and become engines of growth. There is inherent risk in this process. The enterprises that result from the economic development strategy will necessarily be start-ups, and we know that start-ups have a high failure rate.[30] If these foundational organizations are left to their own devices, then, economic development will occur at a far slower pace, since a number of essential cogs will inevitably fail and need to be replaced.

To minimize lost time in the midst of this dynamism, regions and communities pursuing coordinated economic development will benefit from having a party or parties that own the effort from its beginning and sustain ownership and leadership over time. This "ownership entity" will monitor the progress of the overall initiative, identify significant trouble spots or threats, and bring interests together to galvanize direct responses as needed to help ensure that the initiative doesn't fail outright. The public sector can play this "ownership entity" role, but, as already noted, the public sector's engagement can wax and wane as broader economic and political environments evolve.

Thus, a preferred structure is one in which this ownership entity extends beyond the public sector to include members representing the broader civic network, as has seen success in New Orleans, Cleveland, and Chicago. These collaboratives allow for both an influx of resources that are somewhat independent of public fiscal realities, and a diverse set of ideas informed from experiences beyond the public sector.

Given this overall structure, three important elements can jump-start and sustain resilient economic development efforts:

- self-awareness, both of weaknesses and opportunities;
- coherent institutional structure, such that a cogent collaborative can be constructed; and
- creative strategies that establish new partnerships that introduce new energy and access to resources that can help spark the needed private-sector activities.

Emerging from this discussion is a set of recommendations for regions, cities, and communities considering pursuing resilient economic development.

Self-Awareness

Step 1 of Alcoholics Anonymous, the quintessential self-help program, reads as follows: "We admitted we were powerless over our addiction—that our lives had become unmanageable."[31] Indeed, a basic tenet of all self-help programs is that, before healing, recovery, and restoration can occur, one must first recognize that there is a problem that warrants attention and help. One can view economic development initiatives as a form of self-help, in which the region or neighborhood is seeking to improve its position and to evolve into a stronger and more enduring entity. If one accepts this view, then an essential element of economic development is self-awareness.

Self-awareness among municipal leaders has prompted difficult and necessary conversations. For example, in a sober assessment of Detroit's fiscal condition, after taking office in 2009 Mayor Dave Bing declared that the city could no longer provide all services to all neighborhoods, especially those that had lost considerable population.[32] Similarly, executive director of recovery management for the city of New Orleans Ed Blakely argued in 2007 that New Orleans's social, infrastructure, and economic challenges made it difficult for wholesale economic development to take root there in the wake of Hurricane Katrina.[33]

In addition to facilitating problem recognition, self-awareness can afford economic development coalitions with a perspective that facilitates preparation and prompt response to changing economic conditions and realities. It allows for identifying opportunities and risks facing neighborhoods, cities, and regions through ongoing analysis of trends, and it allows quick, real-time—or even proactive—responses. Even if needs are not extreme or acute, gazing through an analytical lens can allow regions to zero in on problems or potential threats or opportunities and then to face them directly.

A key to being resilient is being cognizant of local and regional strengths and weaknesses. Self-awareness is a hallmark for success in many aspects of personal life, but it is less often emphasized in developing strategies for success in collective contexts. However, it is no less important. At the regional level, this can be seen in targeted investments spearheaded by local and regional leaders. Los Angeles has been investing heavily over the past decades in infrastructure to improve the efficiency and lower the cost of goods movement. Mayor Bradley and other civic leaders in the 1970s understood that commerce, trade, and goods movement were an important part of the L.A. economy and could become even more so with the appropriate investments. Hence they championed deepening the port to accommodate the larger ships that were becoming the standard in shipping, expanding of the Alameda Corridor connection between the port and key rail yards that bring goods to interior markets, and redeveloping the airport to capture a burgeoning freight and people transport demand.[34]

The approach here is the same as that espoused by Michael Porter and put into action via his Initiative for a Competitive Inner City. ICIC's mission is to "drive economic prosperity in America's inner cities through private sector investment to create jobs, income and wealth for local residents."[35] Its approach is to identify local comparative advantages—that is, build awareness of local opportunities—and support the community strategies and organizations that leverage them.

The power of self-awareness holds regardless of the broader fiscal condition in which a jurisdiction or region finds itself. However, if the public sector is the sole resource being deployed, public fiscal conditions will impact—and limit—the set of responses that can be embarked upon. Indeed, in some circumstances, fiscal weakness can take certain types of interventions off the table completely, thereby limiting the set of tools with which to effect change, and reducing the probability of short- and long-run success. This suggests that long-term economic success will depend on supplemental support, which is the focus of the next two necessary characteristics.

Coherent Organizational Structure

Given the seeming inevitability of the cyclicality of public-sector support for economic development activities, one must turn to other sectors and organizations in order to have a more diversified support base. The task then becomes one of identifying essential partners for a broad-based coalition and determining which of those are strong enough to make meaningful contributions. Partners must represent the broad range of sectors that need to be involved. Experts and leaders along at least five dimensions must be present: finance and banking, community-based organizations, business, political representatives, and conveners and translators. Ultimately, the set of players derives from the prevailing theory of change in the region or community—all who can contribute to driving the growth and change as envisioned in the overarching strategy should be sought for inclusion in the coalition.

The conveners and translators, consisting of academics, foundations, and others, are important, as they often have independent relationships with many sectors and can serve as a bridge between them. Translation is an especially important role, as those in the various categories use different language to describe the same situation, which can result in the factions talking past each other rather than to each other. These translators can act as the bridge builders and connective tissue to ensure that there are open lines of communication and that all parties understand each other's perspectives and views.

In addition to representing a diverse set of interests in economic development plans and efforts, these interests must have adequate skills to develop good strategies and to execute them. Implementation is an essential element of any policy and, as I noted earlier, implementation problems can be a major impediment. Communities must make sure they don't hamstring themselves by placing in key positions people or organizations who are unprepared or unable to embrace those roles fully and effectively. This is clearly a concern for economic development at more local levels (i.e., cities and neighborhoods), where public agencies and even leading community-based organizations may lack the skills—perhaps due to a lack of training—or the scale to advance plans effectively. As a general matter, capacity must be assessed and steps taken to expand it for those with key roles who fall short. This is one motivation behind the SC2 and OneCPD programs now in place. Both are predicated on the reality that public-sector agencies often have too few people with the requisite skills to execute sometimes sophisticated strategies.

All regions and communities already have pieces in place that can be springboards for establishing an organizational structure that in turn can be the basis for a sustained economic development strategy. Chambers of commerce, community-based consortia, and public commissions can bring together interests that contribute to the broader effort. These groups should be approached, common interests identified, and ways to work together agreed upon. Existing relationships and partnerships can be particularly important, as they can validate the economic development concept and be vehicles to advance bold vision. But initial efforts may instead be modest. If these groups do not have a history of working together, trust must be developed first. Once established and nurtured, this trust can then be leveraged for more ambitious objectives.

Ultimately, a coherent organizational structure has vital internal and external value. Internally, it allows for a focusing of resources and a potentially efficient pursuit of strategy, while also establishing an infrastructure that can endure over time and provide stability that can weather fluctuations in public-sector resource capacity. Externally, it can serve as a signal to potential allies outside the region or community, and help spark the deployment of private capital by external investors who might see the more formal structures as reducing the risks associated with such investment. An infusion of private capital is critical. Economic development, even in the short run, cannot thrive without it.

Supplementing this institutional structure must be personal leadership and a capacity to build enduring public consensus. The experiences following the flashes of self-awareness in Detroit and New Orleans (and elsewhere) demonstrate that self-awareness on the part of the leadership is a necessary but not completely sufficient condition. Significant proportions of the electorate must concur and be willing to incur costs, if they arise. In Detroit, Mayor Bing's proposals faced considerable challenges from many fronts.[36] And in New Orleans, Blakely resigned after a tumultuous tenure during which few of his proposed plans moved forward, a failure that has been attributed both to his sometimes abrasive style and to a lack of implementation capacity in his organizational leadership.[37] In both cases, parties that would incur sometimes significant costs balked at the suggestions, and no solutions were found to assuage their concerns. In both cases, progress slowed as resource deployment was either delayed (New Orleans) or not possible (Detroit, since resources were not freed up).

Creative Strategies

High-quality information and functional institutions are indisputable prerequisites for successful resilient economic development. However, these might not be sufficient, especially in times of weak public fiscal capacity. Indeed, public-sector weakness might undermine key strategies being pursued, particularly if the strategies rely on traditional relationships and governmental programs. As resources for such programs dwindle, the viability of these strategies may be called into question, putting at risk the entire initiative. In the face of such a reality, one approach to increase resilience is to diversify the program's support base by incorporating nontraditional partners. In nearly every context, there are potential partners with similar goals and objectives but who are not present in the institutional coalitions, whether for historical, programmatic, or other reasons.

Consider housing, which has long been the domain of affordable-housing developers, advocates for lower-income families and the homeless, and the fair-housing and civil-rights communities. A growing body of evidence shows that housing success contributes to improved physical and mental health outcomes, better attendance and performance in schools, reduced interaction with the justice system, more sustained job attachment, and neighborhood stability, among other positive associations. This suggests that health care, education, criminal justice, labor and employment, and community development professionals should be natural allies in supporting the provision of high-quality affordable housing. As allies, they may be able to contribute funds to support its development or devise new ways to support its production. In building a comprehensive sustained affordable housing policy, then, it might be advantageous to incorporate these potential partnerships as strategic opportunity areas that can diversify the base and reduce volatility as conditions change.

There are movements in this direction at the federal level. The Obama administration's Neighborhood Revitalization Initiative is a collaboration of agencies with a limited history of significant agency-level cooperation. Similarly, new collaborations between HUD and the Department of Health and Human Services as well as among the Department of Transportation, HUD, and the Environmental Protection Agency demonstrate a new commitment to this approach. One must hope that federal efforts—and the resources such efforts bring to the table—serve as a model that is replicated at the state, regional, and local levels, so that myriad new partnerships can thrive, supporting sustained economic development. Grantees associated with all of these programs represent a first wave that may well establish a new development model.

This sort of creativity need not be applied only in the context of public agencies. The net for collaboration and coordination should be cast widely beyond institutional relationships. Actors from nonprofit, for-profit, and philanthropic sectors are increasingly playing a leading role in providing services and driving policy. Perhaps these entities can be molded into stable and sustained organizational forces that can drive economic development efforts independent of abundant public resources. Such partnerships already exist in Baltimore, Cleveland, and Detroit, for example, where foundations have joined with local community-based organizations to pursue innovative economic development programs. Similarly, local entrepreneurs should be recognized as potential key contributors to economic development initiatives, and means for more fully incorporating them should be explored.

Finally, it is important to understand that the opportunity for broadening such coalitions is perhaps greatest in times of fiscal stress. In such times, because fiscal stress will not generally be localized to a single sector but rather stretches across sectors, the partners that the economic development strategist will be seeking are likely also looking for new partners. Win-win solutions will be in great demand and more possible.

RECOMMENDATIONS AND CONCLUDING THOUGHTS

Economic development is hard. Regions and communities must overcome many difficult hurdles in order to show successful economic development. Economic development is much harder when public sources for funding are reduced or in flux. Because of the long gestation period, economic development efforts require sustained and continuous engagement, which is threatened when public-fund availability is cyclical. Effective resilient economic development requires, at a minimum, self-awareness, institutional coherence, and a broad base of allies and partners who have been creatively convened. A bit of good fortune will help, as well.

This reality suggests some recommendations for those seeking to embark on the path of resilient economic development:

- *Identify and devote resources to develop a sober assessment of the prevailing landscape, with a focus on weaknesses and opportunities.* There may be value in commissioning an outsider to produce this assessment, as an outsider is more likely to candidly identify the sensitive issues that insiders might have difficulty articulating.
- *Establish a small committee of leaders tasked with identifying organizations with adequate capacity to take a leadership role in executing the ongoing economic development strategy.* This committee should be diverse and include members who have strong personal relationships, since an important function of this committee will be to honestly highlight weaknesses among organizations and individuals. These conversations will not be productive if relationships are nascent and if trust has not been established. This committee might also become a convener to bring the target organizations to the table.
- *Encourage regular bilateral and multilateral meetings between "unnatural" bedfellows.* These meetings should include public-sector agencies as well as nonprofit, private-sector, and philanthropic organizations active in the relevant geography, and focus on points of commonality and intersection. The focus of the first few meetings will necessarily be to build familiarity, with later meetings delving deeper into possible ways to collaborate and coordinate.

Enacting these three recommendations can help set communities on a path that creates the infrastructure necessary for resilient economic development.

The recommendations also prompt a fundamental question: who? This discussion has focused on high-level principles and processes without trying to answer this question, although clearly it is of paramount importance. The people who take on these roles must have credibility both within the community and external to it, as well as demonstrate talents that match the tasks. A lack of consensus about who should be on this roster can introduce significant barriers to success. Moreover, there is the question of who (which individual or entity) decides the ultimate course to be followed. There are many examples of a strategy having excluded the views and considerations of important, often underserved, populations who might be the target recipients of the assistance. Such "people" issues must be resolved satisfactorily. If not, the goal of resilient economic development could prove elusive.

One can only hope that generalizable models of sustained and resilient economic development emerge out of the Great Recession—a crisis is a terrible thing to waste—and from the many federal and local efforts to cope. If so, there is hope that many regions and communities that have fallen behind will find a pathway to increased prosperity and well-being.

Notes

1. R. Andersson, J. M. Quigley, and M. Wilhelmsson, "Urbanization, Productivity, and Innovation: Evidence from Investment in Higher Education," *Journal of Urban Economics* 66 (2009): 2–15.

2. M. Sensier and D. van Dijk, "Testing for Volatility Changes in U.S. Macroeconomic Time Series," *Review of Economics and Statistics* 86:3 (2004): 833–39.

3. J. Quigley, "Urban Diversity and Economic Growth," *Journal of Economic Perspectives* 12:2 (1998): 127–38.

4. J. Graham, "Silicon Beach Emerges as a Tech Hotbed," *USA Today*, July 16, 2012, http://usatoday30.usatoday.com/tech/news/story/2012-07015/silicon-beach/56241864/1, accessed June 10, 2013.

5. See, e.g., Alfred Marshall, *Principles of Economics* (London: Macmillan, 1890); P. Krugman, *Geography and Trade* (Cambridge, Mass.: MIT Press, 1991); M. Porter, *The Competitive Advantage of Nations* (London: Macmillan, 1990); A. Potter and H. D. Watts, "Evolutionary Agglomeration Theory: Increasing Returns, Diminishing Returns, and the Industry Life Cycle," *Journal of Economic Geography* 11 (2011): 417–55.

6. J. Jacobs, *The Economy of Cities* (New York: Random House, 1969).

7. R. W. Bostic and A. C. Prohofsky, "Enterprise Zones and Individual Welfare: A Case Study of California," *Journal of Regional Science* 46:2 (2006): 175–203; L. E. Papke, "Tax Policy and Urban Development: Evidence from the Indiana Enterprise Zone Program," *Journal of Public Economics* 54 (1993): 37–49; J. Kolko and D. Neumark, "Do Some Enterprise Zones Create Jobs?," *Journal of Policy Analysis and Management* 29:1 (2010): 5–38.

8. See, e.g., J. K. Brueckner, "Urban Growth Boundaries: An Effective Second-best Remedy for Unpriced Traffic Congestion?" *Journal of Housing Economics* 16:3–4 (2007): 263–73; G. Knaap, "The Price Effects of Urban Growth Boundaries in Metropolitan Portland, Oregon," *Land Economics* 64:1 (1985): 26–35; E. L. Glaeser, J. Gyourko, and R. Saks, "Why Is Manhattan So Expensive? Regulation and the Rise in Housing Prices," *Journal of Law and Economics* 48:2 (2005): 331–69.

9. USC Professor Alex Saunders noted that the city of Los Angeles's amending of the mixed-use ordinance for downtown was followed by significant private commercial investment in housing and retail space.

10. See, e.g., D. Aschauer, "Is Public Infrastructure Productive?," *Journal of Monetary Economics* 23 (1989): 177–200; A. Munnell, "How Does Public Infrastructure Affect Regional Economic Performance?," *New England Economic Review* (September/October 1990): 11–32; C. Morrison and A. Schwartz, "Public Infrastructure, Private Input Demand, and Economic Performance in New England Manufacturing," *Journal of Business and Economic Statistics* 14:1 (1996): 91–101.

11. J. Kromer, *Fixing Broken Cities: The Implementation of Urban Development Strategies* (New York: Routledge, 2010).

12. B. E. Harcourt and J. Ludwig, "Broken Windows: New Evidence from New York City and a Five-City Social Experiment," *University of Chicago Law Review* 73:1 (2006): 271–320; H. Corman and N. Mocan, "Carrots, Sticks, and Broken Windows," *Journal of Law and Economics* 48:1 (2005): 235–66.

13. E. Graddy and R. W. Bostic, "The Role of Private Agents in Affordable Housing Policy," *Journal of Public Administration Research and Theory* 20 (2010): 81–99.

14. D. Suarez, "Creating Public Value through Collaboration: The Restoration and Preservation of Crissy Field," USC Price School working paper, 2012; Y. Wang and E. Graddy, "Risk Management and Innovation in the Delivery of Public Infrastructure," USC Price School working paper, 2012.

15. H. Rittel and M. Webber, "Dilemmas in a General Theory of Planning," *Policy Sciences* 4 (1973): 155–69.

16. P. A. Sabatier and D. Mazmanian, "A Conceptual Framework of the Implementation Process," in *Public Policy: The Essential Reading(s)*, 153–73, edited by S. Theodoulou and M. Cahn (Englewood Cliffs, N.J.: Prentice-Hall, 1995).

17. H. Maier, "Conflict in Metropolitan Areas," *Annals of the American Academy of Political and Social Science* 416:1 (1974): 148–57.

18. See, e.g., D. Gastwirth, *Policy Implementation: Prospects for Research and Programmatic Development*, USC Bedrosian Center report, 2012; H. Saetren, "Facts and Myths about Research on Public Policy Implementation: Out-of-Fashion, Allegedly Dead, But Still Very Much Alive and Relevant," *Policy Studies Journal* 33:4 (2005): 559–82; L. O'Toole, "The Theory-Practice Issue in Policy Implementation Research," *Public Administration* 82:2 (2004): 309–29.

19. White House, "Obama Administration Establishes White House Council on Strong Cities, Strong Communities," press release, March 15, 2012, http://www.whitehouse.gov/the-press-office/2012/03/15/obama-administration-establishes-white-house-council-strong-cities-stron, accessed June 10, 2013.

20. OneCPD Resource Exchange (2012), "What Is OneCPD?," https://www.onecpd.info/about-onecpd/, accessed June 10, 2013.

21. See, e.g., R. Voith, "Changing Capitalization of CBD-oriented Transportation Systems: Evidence from Philadelphia: 1970–88," *Journal of Urban Economics* 33 (1993):

361–76; R. Voith, "Do Suburbs Need Cities?," *Journal of Regional Science* 38 (1998): 445–64; A. Haughwaut, R. Inman, and J. V. Henderson, "Should Suburbs Help Their Central City?," *Brookings-Wharton Papers on Urban Affairs*, 2002, 45–94.

22. S. Erie, *Globalizing L.A.: Trade, Infrastructure, and Regional Development* (Stanford, Calif.: Stanford University Press, 2004).

23. National Bureau of Economic Research, *US Business Cycle Expansions and Contractions*, 2012, http://www.nber.org/cycles.html, accessed June 10, 2013.

24. H. Yen, "Rural US Disappearing? Population Share Hits Low," *Bloomberg Businessweek*, July 27, 2011, http://www.businessweek.com/ap/financialnews/D9OODOEG0.htm, accessed June 10, 2013. On New England decline, see S. L. Wolfbein, *The Decline of a Cotton Textile City: A Study of New Bedford* (1948; reprint AMS Press: New York, 1968); L. F. Gross, *The Course of Industrial Decline: The Boott Cotton Mills of Lowell, Massachusetts, 1835–1955* (Baltimore, Md.: Johns Hopkins University Press, 1993).

25. E. Hill, T. St. Clair, H. Wial, H. Wolman, P. Atkins, P. Blumenthal, S. Ficenec, and A. Friedhoff, "Economic Shocks and Regional Economic Resilience," in *Urban and Regional Policy and Its Effects*, 193–274, Building Resilient Regions, vol. 4, edited by Margaret Weir, Howard Wial, Harold Wolman, and Nancy Pindus (Washington, D.C.: Brookings Institution Press, 2012).

26. Office of the Special Inspector General for the Troubled Asset Relief Program, *Factors Affecting the Decision of General Motors and Chrysler to Reduce Their Dealership Networks*, SIGTARP-10-008, Washington, D.C., July 19, 2010.

27. D. Cenziper, N. Stewart, and T. Mellnik, "Surge in D.C. Tax Office Settlements Reduces Commercial Property Owners' Bills," *Washington Post*, August 7, 2012, http://www.washingtonpost.com/investigations/surge-in-dc-tax-office-settlements-reduces-commercial-property-owners-bills/2012/08/07/5af75372-d1c4-11e1-8bea-6dc0b4879aab_story.html?hpid=z1, accessed June 7, 2013; M. Neibauer and D. J. Sernovitz, "D.C. Property Owners, Attorneys React Cooly to Washington Post Assessment Story," *Washington Business Journal*, August 8, 2012, http://www.bizjournals.com/washington/news/2012/08/08/dc-property-owners-attorneys-react.html?page=all, accessed June 7, 2013.

28. D. Walters, "California Redevelopment Is Dead; Long Live Redevelopment," *Sacramento Bee*, September 7, 2012, http://www.sacbee.com/2012/09/07/4796017/dan-walters-california-redevelopment.html, accessed June 10, 2013.

29. M. Grunwald, "High-speed Rail Goes Off the Tracks in Wisconsin," *Time*, October 29, 2010, http://www.time.com/time/nation/article/0,8599,2028182,00.html, accessed June 19, 2013.

30. D. Gage, "The Venture Capital Secret: 3 Out of 4 Start-Ups Fail," *Wall Street Journal*, September 19, 2012, http://online.wsj.com/article/SB10000872396390443720204578004980476429190.html, accessed June 19, 2013; Small Business Administration Office of Advocacy, *Frequently Asked Questions*, September 2012, http://www.sba.gov/sites/default/files/FAQ_Sept_2012.pdf, accessed June 19, 2013.

31. Alcoholics Anonymous, "How It Works," chapter 5 in *Alcoholics Anonymous*, 4th ed., Alcoholics Anonymous World Services, June 2001, http://www.aa.org/big bookonline/en_bigbook_chapt5.pdf, accessed June 10, 2013.

32. C. Angel, "In Detroit's Distressed Areas, the Neighbors Left, and Now Services Disappear," *Detroit Free Press*, May 20, 2012, http://www.freep.com/article/20120520/NEWS01/205200478/In-Detroit-s-distressed-areas-the-neighbors-left-and-now-services-disappear, accessed June 10, 2013.

33. A. Nossiter, "Steering New Orleans's Recovery with a Clinical Eye," *New York Times*, April 10, 2007, http://query.nytimes.com/gst/fullpage.html?res=9507EEDD15 3FF933A25757C0A9619C8B63&sec=&spon=&pagewanted=1, accessed June 10, 2013.

34. Erie, *Globalizing*, 18.

35. Initiative for a Competitive Inner City, *Who We Are*, http://www.icic.org/about, accessed February 12, 2013.

36. M. Helms, "Bing Frustrated by Slow Progress in Fixing Detroit's Money Troubles," *Detroit Free Press*, October 10, 2012, http://www.freep.com/article/20121010/NEWS01/121010045/dave-bing-interview-with-free-prese-board, accessed June 10, 2013.

37. S. Grace, "Blakely and Nagin Are Two of a Kind," *New Orleans Times-Picayune*, May 11, 2009, http://blog.nola.com/stephaniegrace/2009/05/stephanie_grace _blakely_and_na.html, accessed June 10, 2013.

Economic and Policy Cycles and the Great Recession

DISCUSSANT: RACHEL WEBER,
UNIVERSITY OF ILLINOIS AT CHICAGO

The problems facing cities in the wake of the Great Recession of 2008—punishing public and private debt, constrained budgets, record unemployment, rising health care and pension costs, and deteriorated infrastructure—are numerous and overwhelming. Such problems are the result of bad economic development decisions and fiscal mismanagement, but also of changes outside of the purview of administrators. In 2001, median household incomes in the United States had dropped to approximately $50,000, their lowest level since 1996 (adjusted for inflation).[1] Middle-income jobs have rapidly disappeared, only to be replaced by low-wage temporary and part-time work.[2] More than half of the college graduates who received their degrees since 2006 cannot find a full-time job.[3] What should city governments do now?

THE RELATIONSHIP BETWEEN ECONOMIC AND POLICY CYCLES

Before pundits jump to conclusions and propose quick fixes, they first need to think through the evolution of policy solutions in a way that is reasonable and historically valid. Decision makers anxiously await a recovery that will resemble the upturn of 2001–8 and will allow them to return to business as usual. In contrast, analysts suggest that urban economies and fiscal conditions have moved into such unfamiliar territory that they will require radically new policy tools. Should business conditions and economic development policies be considered cyclical, or have we entered a "new normal" that will endure for the long term?

Raphael Bostic identifies a comfortable middle ground in these debates about the temporal progression of economy and policy. Regional business cycles, he tells us, have coexisted alongside path-defining, structural trends. Some community needs ebb and flow based on labor and housing markets, while others are chronic. Economic development approaches change with differing economic contexts, but certain approaches allow cities to be resilient not just in coping with the current contraction but in facing a future of more rapidly fluctuating conditions.

The notion that the policy strategies of a local government move in tandem with its economic base makes sense. However, the directionality of those strategies—that is, their relationship to business and building cycles—is not clear a priori. In theory, for example, the economic development functions of local government should be countercyclical. The public sector is supposed to be the funder of last resort, providing gap financing when the private sector is hibernating and rationing credit. The reverse should also be true: when business cycles peak, developers, landlords, and corporations have access to large amounts of capital, and city governments should be off the hook. They can step back to do a little planning, regulating, and service provision because during such periods "the market" will basically take care of itself.

Instead, we witness just the opposite. During the economic and subsequent building boom that spanned the millennium, major cities like New York, Las Vegas, and Chicago, and smaller suburbs like Stockton (Calif.) and Allen Park (Mich.), played what has been called an "activist" and "entrepreneurial" role.[4] They underwrote major redevelopment projects, subsidizing business and selectively reducing tax and regulatory burdens. They built tech parks and infrastructure when their economies still seemed to be growing. They partnered with private investors, did deals, and "devoted themselves to reinforcing (the) expansionary tendencies" of the private developers and firms.[5]

Bostic wisely suggests that municipal governments engage in this kind of paradoxical behavior because public finances (tax revenues as well as capital improvement and program budgets) depend on economic activity. As such, cities have the capacity to be most active when they are least needed.[6] Conversely, they are most hamstrung when their services could be of most use to residents and businesses.

Moreover, I would add that cities, private firms, and developers respond to similar kinds of financial incentives—namely the cost of borrowing—and that the public sector has easier access to bond markets during the upcycle. Access to the bond market allows cities to pay for ambitious economic development projects. In the first decade of the century, states and municipalities across the country borrowed heavily, much of which was for investment in economic development expenditures. Between 2000 and 2010, the total outstanding state and municipal bond debt more than doubled, growing from $1.2 trillion to $3 trillion when adjusted for inflation.[7] Borrowing does not always prove helpful to the economic base. During the last boom, a self-reinforcing cycle ensued: cheap debt validated the city's desire to undertake development schemes, and development caused property values to appreciate, which fueled a confidence to undertake additional public investment schemes with more debt. Many a municipality "bit off more than it could chew" and then used heavy debt service payments as justification for not making redistributive types of investments.

Not all municipalities borrowed so heavily. Wealthier places often assumed an antigrowth posture that allowed them to convert their wealth into freedom from financial-market dependence. In other cases, some cash-strapped municipalities were ignored by financial markets altogether, while others had to "pay to play," becoming encumbered by high-interest debt on usurious terms because of their lower ratings.[8] Bond ratings are partly a function of a strong economic base and growth prospects but also depend on the management decisions of city government, which are often independent of the local economy.

Such variation leads us to look more closely at the role played by political ideology and power. As scholars of urban regimes have pointed out, some mayors and city council members may see their role during booms as accommodating business and development, while others seek to parlay their leverage into more inclusive and redistributive policies—for example, linking new commercial development with an affordable-housing trust fund (more common with so-called caretaker regimes). As such, public-sector responses to booms and busts and the strategies they choose to employ may be different depending on the particular administration. Some cities are allocating scarce resources to retrain laid-off workers or making what Bostic calls "order-and-disorder" investments that reduce crime in low-income neighborhoods, while others are adopting harsh austerity measures in every area but business services.

In other words, needs and resources alone do not determine spending priorities; ideas matter, too, as a local government's theory of job creation and economic growth will influence how and where funds are raised and spent. When one is thinking through the temporal relationship between government activity and economic base, such mediating factors must be taken into account.

THE PATH OF LEAST RESISTANCE

Even during good times, but especially during economic contractions, local governments tend to gravitate toward a limited menu of quick-fix policies that are highly visible instead of dealing with the longer-term challenges of creating more good jobs. For example, they focus on real-estate projects, conflating economic development with property development. It makes sense for cities to choose this easy out as real estate leverages private investment, produces noticeable physical improvements, and can be influenced by commonplace municipal tools, such as zoning. Cities also gravitate toward financial incentives, both the direct subsidies and the tax expenditures that Bostic describes. Like real estate, incentives such as sales tax rebates and tax increment financing (TIF) give the impression that cities are doing something tangible to strengthen local economies.

Unfortunately, incentive-subsidized property development merely gives the illusion of economic development. Inflated property values are not the same as prosperity, new office construction does not mean there are new jobs, and more supermarkets and big-box stores do not signal either population or income growth. This is because real estate has a tendency to detach from underlying economic fundamentals, responding more to what is taking place in global capital markets than to occupant needs within localities.[9] Moreover, academic evaluations of incentives show that they are not particularly effective at job or wealth creation (for a summary of such studies, see Kenyon, Langley, and Paquin 2012).[10] Copycat behavior dilutes the power of incentives, taxes constitute too small a share of operating and development costs to influence location behavior, and incentives are not passed onto employees but instead improve return rates for management and shareholders. Even their staunchest advocates admit that incentives are procyclical—they rarely work in poor places or in recessionary periods. And certainly on national and regional levels, we would be better off without them (one seasoned economic developer was quoted in the *New York Times* as saying "there ought to be a law against what I'm doing").[11]

The time is ripe to reduce municipal reliance on building solutions and incentives, which cost state and local governments an estimated $70 billion annually.[12] Democratically controlled California has taken advantage of steep deficits to get rid of its TIF program, and business attraction or redevelopment there is unlikely to come to screeching halt. However, I do not suggest drastic action without putting alternatives on the table. Republican governor Rick Snyder eliminated the Michigan Economic Growth Authority (MEGA) tax credit while also lowering corporate income taxes.

Several alternatives could aid both business and workers and more directly confront the issue of job creation. For example, cities can use the money they would have spent on firm-specific subsidies and one-off projects to fund robust capital improvements plans. Investing in area-wide infrastructure more systematically will make commercial districts more attractive to business, connecting them with employees, suppliers, and customers. It also allows the city more control over job creation. Public works programs eliminate the challenge of overseeing whether a subsidized private business actually created employment while helping employees accrue the work experience, soft skills, and networks that prepare them for unsubsidized work in the future.[13] Moreover, at the end of the day, cities have a modernized public realm that endures long after any individual business leaves.

Cities can also restructure existing community college and vocational high school curricula so that they are responsive to sector-specific needs. Done well and targeted to particular kinds of employer, investments in occupational preparation can help businesses grow while also extending the prosperity enjoyed by the city's professional classes into lower-income households and neighborhoods.

In short, we need to return to a more job-centered definition of economic development. But cities will need help getting there because the temptation to resort to short-term nonsolutions like incentives and property development is so strong. Moreover, cities keep playing the incentive game because they are caught in a prisoner's dilemma that requires everyone or no one to play it. Since Bostic draws an analogy with Alcoholics Anonymous, I will extend the metaphor to say that cities will need sponsors—namely states and the federal government, along with local community organizations—to help them quit their expensive addiction. In addition to passing higher minimum-wage laws, higher levels of government can rein in city spending on white-elephant projects and encourage a return to more proven growth strategies. Moreover, to weather changes, Bostic rightly urges municipal governments to create responsive, flexible structures that build on a realistic appraisal of their comparative advantages. They need to pursue "sustained collaboration and coordination" with nontraditional stakeholders, such as social service providers and local foundations. In other words, institutional knowledge and the organizational infrastructures to mobilize it will be critical to riding out current and future storms.

Notes

1. Jeff Madrick, "Our Crisis of Bad Jobs," *New York Review of Books*, October 2, 2012; National Employment Law Project, *The Low-Wage Recovery and Growing Inequality*, New York, August 2012.

2. National Employment Law Project, "Filling the Gaps in the Unemployment Safety Net," http://www.nelp.org/content/content_issues/category/Filling_the_Gaps_in_the_Unemployment_Safety_Net/, accessed February 11, 2013.

3. Carl Van Horn, Cliff Zukin, Mark Szeltner, and Charley Stone, *Left Out. Forgotten? Recent High School Graduates and the Great Recession*, Work Trends, John J. Heldrich Center for Workforce Development, Rutgers University, June 2012.

4. David Harvey, "From Managerialism to Entrepreneurialism: The Transformation of Urban Governance in Late Capitalism," *Geographiska Annaler* 71B (1989): 3–17; Bob Jessop, "The Narrative of Enterprise and the Enterprise of Narrative: Place Marketing and the Entrepreneurial City," in *The Entrepreneurial City: Geographies of Politics, Regime, and Representation*, 77–99, edited by Tim Hall and Phil Hubbard (West Sussex: Wiley 1998).

5. Susan Fainstein, *The City Builders: Property Development in New York and London, 1980–2000*, 2nd ed., rev. (Lawrence: University of Kansas Press, 2001).

6. Unfortunately, empirically testing such a proposition would prove challenging. Measuring changes in economic development policy longitudinally is complicated by "innovations" in policy making, by the lack of a standard measure of policy usage, and by the need to control for administrative and political changes.

7. Federal Reserve, table D3, "Credit Market Debt Outstanding by Sector," in *Flow of Funds Accounts of the United States: Flows and Outstandings, Fourth Quarter 2012*, December 6, 2012, http://www.federalreserve.gov/releases/z1/current/z1.pdf, accessed December 20, 2012.

8. Rachel Weber, "Selling City Futures: The Financialization of Urban Redevelopment Policy," *Economic Geography* 86:3 (2010).

9. Rachel Weber, *Why We Overbuild*, forthcoming.

10. For a summary of such studies, see Daphne Kenyon, Adam Langley, and Bethany Paquin, *Rethinking Property Tax Incentives for Business* (Cambridge, Mass.: Lincoln Institute of Land Policy, 2012).

11. Louise Storey, "As Companies Seek Tax Deals, Governments Pay High Price," *New York Times*, December 1, 2012.

12. Kenneth Thomas, *Investment Incentives and the Global Competition for Capital* (Basingstoke: Palgrave MacMillan, 2010).

13. Thanks to Laura Wolf-Powers for her raising this point, and for her more general insights into New York City's workforce development system.

An Interrelated International Urban Economy

DISCUSSANT: GEOFFREY J. D. HEWINGS,
UNIVERSITY OF ILLINOIS AT URBANA–CHAMPAIGN

The practice of urban economic development in metropolitan economies has undergone a series of transformations. The "smokestack chasing" of the 1970s and 1980s morphed into more sophisticated incentive-based approaches that persist today.[1] In the interim, an era of growth center formation was followed by one of cluster-based approaches, some consideration of optimal portfolio theory (wherein the urban region's mix of industries was treated rather like a stock portfolio, with attention to the risk and return trade-off), then attraction of the creative class until today, when the orientation seems directed toward sustainability and resilience. Many of these approaches have similar roots, but their implementation and the expected outcomes were often very different; furthermore, measurement of the impacts of the policies proved to be even more difficult, leading some cynics to suggest that their promotion was often nothing more than "faith-based" economic development. Bostic provides an impressive overview of some of the major issues and challenges facing metropolitan regions as the second decade of the century unfolds. My remarks offer a complementary perspective: understanding urban resilience requires understanding how urban economies interact with the rest of the world (external interdependencies through trade) and how they work internally (internal interdependencies). Remarkably, very little attention is paid to these dimensions, yet they hold the key to understanding how an economy works, its responsiveness to changes, and its capacity to absorb both positive and negative shocks.

Since about 1980, in the United States we have witnessed how decreases in the real costs of transportation have propelled a dramatic increase in interstate trade, much of it centered on flows between metropolitan regions. This interstate trade growth is exceeding the growth of gross metropolitan products. Illinois is now part of a five-state region whose interstate trade would rank it sixth or seventh in the world. Sadly, our political leadership in the Midwest has failed to comprehend and exploit the advantages of this remarkable economy over which they preside. Instead, they have engaged in negative advertising that has extended the wasteful, counterproductive strategies of attempting to steal economic activity from neighboring states.[2] Individual metropolitan communities and their home states fail to appreciate the complex interdependencies that exist between their economies; the net benefits (after financial incentives are factored in) from relocation are often very small and in some cases could even be negative.

Gains from trade are well-documented, but urban systems have been profoundly changed by the hollowing out of economies due to the fragmentation of production chains. The degree of interdependence—the sharing of the purchases and sales between establishments that occurs within a local economy—has declined while the concomitant share of dependence on sources of inputs sourced from outside the local economy and the percentage of sales to customers outside have increased. In addition, firms have dramatically reorganized their production systems to take advantage of these lower transportation costs and to exploit scale economies by producing a larger percentage of their products in a smaller number of locations. As a result, the multiplier or ripple effects of economic change within any metropolitan region have declined, while the interregional or spillover effects have increased. In the recent recession, approximately 20 percent of the indirect effects from jobs losses in any one Midwest state were concentrated in the other Midwest states, demonstrating that interstate or intermetropolitan linkages have strengthened dramatically.

Metropolitan economies are now both more competitive and more complementary with other urban and regional economies—challenging the efficacy of cluster-based development strategies and posing significant challenges for a resilience-focused development strategy. Supply chains in one state provide only the tip of the iceberg of a complex web of interactions that may extend over multiple jurisdictions. Metropolitan economies need to see themselves as part of broader, more spatially extensive regional economies—a phenomenon that the recent Organization for Economic Cooperation and Development (OECD) report on the tri-state Chicago region attempted to establish.

Hence, to understand the resiliency of a single urban economy, we must understand its connections with the national and international urban system, how these are changing, and what opportunities and challenges are likely to enhance or unravel past economic successes. Myopically focusing only on what happens inside our metropolitan regions will miss comprehending the essential new economic geography of development. While we need to know how our internal economies function and operate, it is the connection with the external world that provides the key to future success. Urban resilience now involves placing a specific urban economy in a much more complex web of interconnections. Failure to do this will undermine any policy initiatives to enhance economic resilience or to promote sustainability that are promulgated without this understanding. The opportunity cost of directing scarce development resources into inappropriate initiatives has never been higher.

Notes

1. See G. LeRoy, Kasia Tarczynska, Leigh McIlvaine, Thomas Cafcas, and Philip Mattera, *The Job Creation Shell Game* (New York: Good Jobs First, 2013), for an evaluation of the ways in which economic development agencies have provided subsidies to attract and retain business.

2. Since 2011, the Indiana Economic Development Corporation maintains advertising with the theme "Illinoyed? Consider a location in Indiana."

How Cities Collaborate While Competing in the New Economy

RICHARD C. FEIOCK
FLORIDA STATE UNIVERSITY

Five years after the onset of the "Great Recession," its aftereffects continued to limit the economic opportunities of cities. Yet the Great Recession also unleashed forces to reshape the way that metropolitan regions are governed. By accelerating both competition and collaboration, this restructuring creates the potential for metropolitan regions to be more resilient.

Competition and collaboration are often assumed to reflect conflicting values. Thus, in conventional urban theories, these two offer alternative paths for organizing metropolitan areas: one based on competitive markets for public goods with tax and policy competition for residents and tax base; and the other based on collaboration through centralized planning and authority to integrate the metropolitan area as a system. I argue instead that competition and collaboration operate in complementary and reinforcing ways. Visionary local leaders are pursuing this stance by addressing local and regional issues in ways that take advantage of the innovative energy produced by aligning competitive and collaborative goals.

The study of urban politics has been slow to catch up with this reality. Debates over the desirability of centralized versus decentralized systems have dominated discussions of the structure of government and public service provision in metropolitan areas for almost half a century.[1] Following Tiebout, advocates of intergovernmental competition in the delivery of public goods treat decentralization and competition as synonymous. This treatment leads much of that work to be blind to mechanisms other than competition that can coordinate and integrate decisions among local governments in jurisdictionally fragmented areas.[2]

Since about 1990 a new regionalist perspective has emerged that recognizes that collaborative regional governance solutions are possible in jurisdictionally fragmented settings. This work seeks to replace competition with collective governance mechanisms by creating associations, partnerships, districts, or regional councils through which the collective interests of a region can be pursued. This research has made important contributions, but scholarship in the new regionalism tradition suffers from three limitations that prevent it from advancing a more general explanation of urban governance that can inform both theory and practice. The limitations are an implicit or explicit assumption that collaborative mechanisms are substitutes for, rather than complements to intergovernmental competition; neglect of the transaction costs and collective action problems inherent in forming and maintaining the regional governance institutions they prescribe; and the scholarship's disregard for bilateral mechanisms based on networks, contracting, and bargaining, which impose lower costs, have greater political feasibility, and in at least some instances provide a more effective solution to regional problems.

This chapter address these issues by offering a framework based on institutional collective action theory that charts potentially promising paths for both the study and practice of local governance in U.S. metropolitan areas. After review of the public-goods market and new regionalism perspectives, I describe a recently developed taxonomy of collaborative regional governance mechanisms. I then link these instruments to contemporary urban problems to describe both the advantages and the limitations of self-organizing mechanisms. This approach is illustrated by examining how self-organizing network governance can mediate competition and collaboration for local economic development. Finally, I discuss the implications and limitations of multiplexity and self-organization for metropolitan theory and practice.

INTERLOCAL COMPETITION, COLLABORATION, AND EFFICIENCY

Scholars of public administration and metropolitan political economy agree on the importance of regional governance for solving collective problems but disagree on the form that governance should take.[3] Much of the debate on how best to organize local government hinges on the interpretation of key normative values and on how those normative values are measured in empirical analysis. In particular, the value of efficiency is a central theme, but because efficiency can be defined in different ways, each side has tended to talk past the other.

In policy discussions, two types of efficiency are recognized: technical (or productive) efficiency and allocative efficiency. Technical efficiency is the relationship between inputs and outputs. The higher the output of some productive process relative to the input, the more technically efficient that process is. Thus, at any given level of input, citizens are better off the more technically efficient the production. Allocative efficiency is a relationship between demand and supply. The closer the match between the type and level of service that citizens want and what they receive, the greater the allocative efficiency. Comparisons of consolidated versus fragmented government have tended to focus on either technical efficiency or allocative efficiency in isolation.[4]

A multiplicity of rival service providers might enhance both allocative and productive efficiency—the former by enabling heterogeneity of services, the latter through competitive processes that drive down costs and mitigate the excesses of public-monopoly-induced rent seeking. The earliest modeler of such competition was Tiebout, who suggested that fragmented governments in large metropolitan areas compete by inducing households to locate in those jurisdictions that provide them with the optimal tax-service packages. Allocative and productive efficiency would occur if the signals provided by such geographical mobility were strong enough to induce policy change.[5]

Major policy change through mobility alone is unlikely because it is costly to move and because voice (i.e., politics) constrains exit effects. The recession and collapse of the housing market since 2008 reinforces this constraint, with many households "stuck" and unable to move despite their desires to do so. Competition also works for businesses through tax incentives and subsidies.[6] Incentive competition leads to lower business taxes and thus advantages business over households, as jurisdictions find themselves in a prisoner's dilemma situation.

In terms of technical efficiency, intergovernmental competition is rationalized by the logic that competition-induced spending reductions make government more efficient. One problem is that, in practice, efficiency is measured based on costs without considering output variations. Technical efficiency requires that the same level of service is provided at lower cost. Thus, spending cuts do not necessarily result in efficiency gains. Competition can mean a race to the bottom if politician's governments feel that reelection is influenced more by tax rates rather than service quality. Although some work reports that interjurisdictional competition promoted service efficiency, others report little or no impact.[7]

This approach treats cooperation and competition as incompatible because cooperation between units is assumed to reduce the efficiency of competitive processes.[8] But collaboration might enhance both productive and allocative efficiency if it corrects market failures. For services with economies of scale in production, lack of coordination leads to inefficiencies and higher service costs. In many policy arenas, conflicting policies produce spillover effects as decisions in one community impose costs on surrounding communities.

Interlocal competition can enhance technical and allocational efficiency through innovation and incentives, but it can also be destructive if it produces negative spillovers that undercut regional gains, as illustrated by economic development incentive competition. The traditional alternative to intergovernmental competition is to centralize authority through multipurpose districts, regional authorities, city-county consolidation, or state authority. The focus on centralization reflects this convention that intergovernmental fragmentation makes voluntary self-organizing solutions to metropolitan problems infeasible. This conventional wisdom has never been true universally, and the pressures of economic decline have produced alternative governance arrangements that illustrate the potential for resilient self-organizing governance to reconcile competition and collaboration.

COLLABORATION IS THE NEW COMPETITION

Since about 2000, the conversation has changed. Local public officials are looking outward to understand the metropolitan role in the broader national and global economy. At Bill Clinton's Chicago Summit in 2012, Colorado governor John Hickenlooper boldly asserted that "collaboration is the new competition." This assertion is valid both in the sense that collaboration has become the trend and buzzword in discussions of urban governance and that collaboration has proven to be a viable, efficient, and successful strategy for coping with the current fiscal environment.

Collaboration is replacing competition on important issues not only because of economic and service pressures within the community, but also because metropolitan regions now have to collaborate to compete in the global economy.[9] Recent work explores collective actions of local governments to create and maintain collaborative alternatives to centralized governmental provision of services. Institutional collective action (ICA) dilemmas arise directly from the fragmentation of service responsibilities among local governments and authorities because fragmentation creates diseconomies of scale, positive and negative externalities, and common property resource problems. Independent service provision decisions made by jurisdictions acting alone may hinder the ability of government officials to take advantage of opportunities to improve outcomes or reduce the average cost of public services to their residents.

Cooperation results from bargaining and negotiation among the officials of affected jurisdictions. Leaders in each community weigh the utility they expect to receive cooperatively against the utility they gain when acting *non*-cooperatively, since cooperative exchanges are not without transaction costs. The joint gains produced by collaborative arrangements may be insufficient to stimulate the collective action necessary for local actors to create these mechanisms.

In fact, collaboration might be more effective in a competitive environment, and thus be a complement to competition. If competition provides information about citizen preferences and the goals and strategies of other actors, it makes information less of a barrier to collaboration than it is in more competitive settings. This means potential collaborators may be able to take information for granted and instead focus on addressing the problems of securing credible commitment.

Intergovernmental exchange relationships are embedded in larger social, political, and economic systems. Thus, economic and social-network theories provide a basis for identifying benefits and transaction costs of collaboration.[10] If we assume that institutional actors act self-interestedly by selecting the available strategy that most enhances their short-term interests, then the outcomes of individual choices will lead to collectively inefficient decisions. Production efficiencies are lost if local authorities are too small to efficiently produce on their own a service that each government wishes to provide. In addition, production of the service by small, fragmented units produces externalities that spill across jurisdiction boundaries.

The study of urban politics has traditionally focused on regional or central authorities as the mechanism for solving collective action problems. Consolidation of governmental authority mitigates the collective dilemma by eliminating independent authorities, but it does so at a high cost. Centralization creates uncertainties about the balance of authority between levels of government, disrupting ongoing governance activities. Instead, I argue that there are an array of mechanisms for integration that vary in the extent to which self-organization is evident in their creation and use. The next section describes regional governance institutions and classifies them by whether their scope is narrow or encompassing, and by the degree of autonomy retained locally.

INSTITUTIONS FOR RESOLVING INSTITUTIONAL COLLECTIVE ACTION DILEMMAS

Feiock and Scholz discuss the range of institutions that have emerged to mitigate ICA and array them according to the autonomy they provide local actors.[11] Feiock elaborates this dimension by defining three types or zones of enforcement authority: centralized authority, mutually binding contracts or agreements, and network embeddedness. These are the general mechanism types to integrate decision making across local government units in a metropolitan area.[12] Under centralized authority, a new governmental unit is created or a higher level government intervenes to consolidate authority and internalize ICAs. Under contracting, individual governments legally bind themselves to mutual action. Under embedded relations, agreements among local units are coordinated and enforced through a network of social, economic, and political relationships rather than through formal authority.[13] These mechanisms are not mutually exclusive and can complement each other.[14] The nature of these mechanisms makes them more or less costly for individual governments to exit the collaboration. Exit is most difficult with collaborative arrangements mandated through governmental authority and easiest with cooperation based on voluntary relationships and social constraints.

Feiock defines a second dimension based on the scope of relationships the institution addresses.[15] At one end of the range is narrow collaboration focused on individual relationships, such as exchanges of information, resources, and commitments related to a single-service function or policy among a limited set of actors. At the other end of the range is extensive collaboration, in which relationships are multiplex and collective, thereby addressing multiple functions and services and applied collectively to all affected actors. Narrowly targeted exchanges include informal networks of dyadic relationships, service contracts, and even mandated agreements. Encompassing collaboration arrangements include informal relations, but most often they involve collective governance achieved through decision bodies representing all of the affected government units. The public administration and new regionalism literature looks to these types of authoritative governance bodies to mitigate ICA dilemmas.[16]

Table 1 depicts nine general categories of ICA mitigation mechanisms classified according to how narrow or encompassing the scope of negotiation is, and to whether or not the coordination mechanism allows individual units to enter or exit relationships autonomously—ranging from agreements enforced through social embeddedness to those enforced by centralized authority. The top row of the vertical dimension reflects institutions that enjoy highly complex relationships involving multiple services or functions that

Table 1. Regional Integration Mechanisms for Institutional Collective Action Problems

	Embeddedness	Contracts	Centralized Authority
Encompassing	7	8	9
complex / collective	multiplex self-organizing systems	councils of governments / metropolitan planning organizations	centralized regional authorities
Intermediate	4	5	6
	working groups	partnerships / multilateral interlocal agreements	constructed networks / multipurpose districts
Narrow	1	2	3
single issue / bilateral	informal networks	service contracts	mandated agreements / special districts

are coordinated collectively. The last row reflects more narrowly defined institutional relationships that are directed to a single function or policy and often involve dyadic relationships through networks and agreements. The center row encompasses mechanisms that are broader in scope and can address related functions and multilateral relationships.

Entities on the right side of table 1 rely on exogenous resources and authority, usually higher-level governments. To the middle along this dimension, local units delegate some level of authority by voluntarily entering into associations or contractual arrangements that bind themselves to some degree but that rely on mutual consent. To the left, relationships are informal and coordination is enforced by embedded social interactions. Institutions in cell 1 rely exclusively on self-organization and social embeddedness to coordinate decisions in a single domain, while preserving the autonomy of the involved policy actors. Although given less attention in the regionalism literature, evidence from education, natural resource, and economic development policy arenas suggests that policy networks play important roles in coordinating actions among decentralized actors.[17]

FOUR TYPES OF ICA PROBLEMS

The preference of local actors for specific institutions to mediate ICA will depend on the nature of the problem and existing institutions in place, as well as on the transaction costs facing local governments.[18] Based on the general proposition that *incentives will favor the type of mechanism that provides the greatest gain for the least cost*, institutions that ensure autonomy, such as those found in cell 1, emerge where the risk of defection by any of the participants is low. Mechanisms that broadly restrict autonomy, such as those in cell 9, are favored as defection risks become very high.[19] The trade-off between autonomy for local actors and effectiveness in dealing with complex ICAs defines the diagonal in table 1 corresponding to cells 1, 5, and 9. Risk in the underlying ICA reflects the cost of collaboration when others defect, which has both a relative component (the relative gains to collaboration over the loss from defection, and the impact of this difference on the likelihood that others will collaborate) and an absolute component (the total size of commitments and gains in terms of both dollars and the number of participants). The credibility of commitments required to mitigate dilemmas with higher levels of risk is achieved by imposing greater restrictions on autonomy. As the level of risk imposed by a dilemma increase, transaction costs required to achieve optimal effectiveness for a given mechanism will also increase and the level of achievable effectiveness will decline.

The type of problem or service and the relative size or interests of cities are likely to be critical factors in whether or not cities collaborate with each other as well as what governance structure is necessary to achieve it. For the nine governance mechanisms classified in table 1, their emergence and effectiveness in addressing regional problems will depend on which of the four types of collective action problems cities are trying to solve: coordination gains from matching service delivery activities across jurisdictions; capturing economies of scale in the production of infrastructure; minimizing a common-property resource problem; or internalizing externalities imposed by other local governments. With each problem, local governments confront a different set of incentives, which then influences the likelihood they will cooperate.[20]

The achievement of coordination gains and scale economies in service production has become more urgent with the financial cutbacks local governments have experienced since about 2009. Cost savings or economic efficiencies are sometimes possible for governments simply by coordinating ongoing activities with other jurisdictions. The informal mechanisms to the left on table 1 in cells 1, 4, and 7 have the potential to solve such coordination problems while retaining each jurisdiction's autonomy. Coordination to achieve scale economies is more complex for urban services involving large-scale, capital-intensive investments. Here coordination produces lower average costs for all the affected governments because they will not duplicate the expensive infrastructure within their smaller geographic areas, creating compatible incentives. However, a large investment in a specific fixed asset puts at risk the government that commits to its provision. Other governments' contributions are needed to help pay for the service, in order to cover what would otherwise be unused capacity. The largest government in the area may take the lead and provide the service, but it will likely only commit to the larger scale if the smaller governments will guarantee they will pay their share. The high risk associated with building excess capacity may require mechanisms (see right side of table 1) that rely on contractual enforcement or governmental authority, such as a special district or long-term service contracts with all the participating governments. Since each government service achieves economies of scale at different levels and only a handful experience extreme scale effects, these issues will be handled as single issues with a narrow scope (see the bottom row of table 1).

Common property resource (CPR) problems have partially compatible incentives for most units. Cooperation will lead to greater preservation of the underlying resources; however, while there is an incentive to preserve the good, there is also an incentive to extract as much of the resource as possible at the same time that other incentives continue to constrain their use. Tensions between cooperation and competition need to be managed in the governance mechanism deployed. The risk in a CPR problem is typically smaller than for scale problems, but it continues across time, so each participating government repeatedly decides if it will honor the lower demand placed on the CPR. Where future benefits from continued cooperation remain high, embeddedness and contractual authority may be adequate to sustain the effectiveness of the governance mechanism. Embeddedness in networks or working groups mildly reinforces continued working relationships and greater information about the participants. As the individual benefit increases when a city defects from the agreement, stronger structures are needed. This could take the form of more formal arrangements, such as movement to legal contracts or partnerships, or an increase in connectivity or scope of relationships, so that the cost from defecting in the CPR arena may jeopardize benefits gained in another policy arena.

Externality problems are most difficult for local governance because incentives of local governments are directly opposed. The city that imposes a negative externality on its neighbors has no incentive to alter its behavior. Each jurisdiction directly benefits from oversupplying the negative externalities or undersupplying the positive ones. Both establishing an initial agreement and maintaining it over time are problematic. If the costs of the continuing externality situation are extremely high, the resolution is likely to require a single authority with the capacity to integrate the impacts across a larger geographic area. (See mechanisms, right-hand side of table 1.)

Across all four collective action problems, the size of the cities involved is likely to matter.[21] Size will affect which cities can address the problem on their own and then look for partners (an informal arrangement or contractual arrangement). Size also is likely to affect a city's objectives and therefore which other communities are potential partners for cooperation. In economic development, for example, the government of the city of Chicago may not believe that any suburban jurisdiction can provide enough resources to make a partnership valuable. Across suburban communities, similar places such as Naperville and Downers Grove may cooperate with each other but not with Dolton or Calumet City, and vice versa.

THE RESILIENCE OF SELF-ORGANIZING GOVERNANCE

Regional institutions based on embeddedness and self-organization (table 1, cells 1, 4, 7) are the most pervasive but least understood mechanisms for local governments and community actors to address ICA dilemmas. By relying on social, economic, and political relationships rather than on formal authority, network embeddedness offers flexibility for rules, procedures, and exchanges to be decided locally while preserving the autonomy of the actors.

The concept of embeddedness—the level of direct and indirect involvement of an actor within a network—has generated attention across the social sciences and has been linked to organizational survival, performance, and outcomes.[22] Regional intergovernmental networks increase the credibility of commitments by transforming short-term relationships into repeated ones, linking participants across policy arenas, and increasing opportunities to punish local governments that engage in opportunistic behavior in their regional interactions. A densely clustered network structure contributes to regional social capital by providing extensive monitoring mechanisms and by facilitating development of mutual reciprocity, trust, and conformance to the rules of the game.[23]

There are numerous advantages to self-organizing mechanisms. Networks reduce uncertainty by defining and regulating participants' behaviors and expectations, and they offer several potential advantages over more formal solutions. By allowing more local autonomy, network embeddedness overcomes individual governments' reluctance to delegate authority to newly established arrangements and avoids the political conflicts of revoking existing authority from local governments. By requiring consent of all members, self-organizing mechanisms enhance the search for the mutually advantageous resolution of collective dilemmas, and such mechanisms reduce the potential conflicts resulting from majorities imposing solutions on unwilling minorities.[24]

Policy network structures that emerge from planned and unplanned interactions among local actors offer flexibility for rules, procedures, and exchanges to be decided locally. This produces greater adaptability to governance structures.[25] Nevertheless, some conflicts cannot be resolved voluntarily and require governmental authority. Yet the scope of ICA dilemmas amenable to collaborative solutions enforced only by embedded social relations may be broader than is acknowledged. To illustrate, we examine local economic development, an area noted for intense intergovernmental competition and arguably the most difficult test for collaboration. We review recent studies conducted in the Orlando, Florida, metropolitan area to demonstrate that development competition and collaboration are complementary, with public officials identifying the same governments as collaborators and competitors. An analysis of the structure of the networks of communication on development issues among local governments finds strong statistical evidence that local actors reduce risk by embedding relationships in transitive network relationships. Results from a national study are then reported to provide evidence that local governments' development policy networks positively influence the attraction of firms and jobs.

THE ECONOMIC DEVELOPMENT EXAMPLE

Metropolitan regions are increasingly recognized as the engines of economic activity and economic development in a globalized world.[26] Even areas outside metropolitan regions benefit from robust metropolitan areas due to the geography of economic and energy supply chains. Regionalism as a development approach is distinctive. It encompasses the role of industry-specific regional clusters and the provision of regional public goods and infrastructure necessary for development.[27] Industries tend to cluster in metropolitan areas, where they can draw on regional transportation infrastructure, research and technology, skilled workers, particular tax and regulatory climates, and buyer-supplier networks.[28] In other words, metropolitan areas constitute coherent and at least partially integrated areas that are large enough to achieve economies of scale. Yet metropolitan regions are also small enough to allow organizations to establish working relationships and to develop trust among partners, which would be difficult to achieve on a global, national, or state level where less face-to-face interaction occurs. Taken together, this means that individual jurisdictions benefit tremendously by pursuing economic development together rather than individually.

Conventional economic development strategies focus on offering financial and other incentives to businesses. Competition among local governments to attract new investment and development operates the same way an economic market does. However, this quasi-market is subject to market failures, and strategies are driven by political, not just economic, considerations.[29] To be successful, local officials need to identify the regional institutions and the physical, human, and social capital that will enhance their economic position.

The economic development arena is characterized by competition that is often "zero-sum." Competition not only can limit the capacity of local units to solve common problems, but it also makes collaboration risky. Because the revenue benefits of attracting development are jurisdiction specific, one government can use shared information opportunistically to gain competitive advantage over its partners, setting up a classic prisoner's dilemma situation.[30] This makes economic development an ideal policy arena for examining competitive and collaborative relationships together.[31]

COMPETITORS AS COLLABORATIVE PARTNERS

Regional governance strategies can be successful only if they are reconciled with the competitive environment in which they are applied. Collaborative efforts may be hampered by distrust among local jurisdictions, conflicting interests among potential participants, or imbalances in powers and resource endowments.[32] Nevertheless, even among competitors there is pressure not to be isolated from various types of potential collaborative activities that might bestow advantage.[33] Diverse values and perceptions about other jurisdictions shape behaviors and the configuration of regional governance systems.

Leaders' predispositions and orientation toward cooperation or competition with other jurisdictions play critical roles in regional collaboration. However, extant research pays little attention to how perceptions of competitive or collaborative environments relate to interlocal policy network relationships. This section examines at a microlevel how perceptions of cooperation and competition as well as institutional and environmental factors influence regional collaboration. I use the Orlando metropolitan area as a laboratory to investigate how competitive and cooperative development environments influence the structure of informal policy networks.

Local jurisdictions have strategic incentives to keep track of competitors' activities. Goetz and Kayser found that 85 percent of municipalities surveyed in the Twin Cities perceived high levels of development competition, but they split evenly with regard to whether this competition was beneficial.[34] However, interlocal competition can foster a willingness to learn from each other.[35] Differences may be lessened out of mutual understanding, which in turn mitigates inevitable problems of collective action such as distrust and conflicting interests among potential partners.

Where local officials are politically risk-averse, the cost of being left behind offsets the potential loss from sharing information with their competitors. Being isolated from ongoing activities of neighboring jurisdictions places local officials in a politically risky position, especially when citizens expect them to produce tangible outcomes.[36] Local officials benefit from collecting information, benchmarking, and participating in joint activities that are visible to citizens. The information needed to successfully compete is useful in collaboration, again making collaboration with competitors more feasible.

Competition increases the risk of defection, but it also allows the partners to focus exclusively on this problem. Collaboration with competitors means local governments already know the resources, problems, goals, and strategies of potential partners, which allows them to design collaborative mechanisms that address the problems of securing credible commitment, rather than focusing on information and coordination issues.

Repeated interactions are manifestations of networked relationships that help control uncertainties and overcome defection risk.[37] Since information about actors and their previous behaviors is relatively open to network participants, certain policy network structures might reduce the possibility of breaking the trust established among participants. They might also provide monitoring mechanisms that facilitate mutual trust and conformance to the rules of the game.[38] Consideration of reputation, communication, trust, and social norms impose constraints on defection and opportunism to increase the stability of a regional governance structure.[39]

Network relationships generally make local governments willing to forge relationships not only with their cooperative partners, but also with existing competitors. Lee, Feiock, and Lee test this statistically by asking each local government development official his or her perceptions of each of the city and county governments in the region. Respondents were asked the extent to which they viewed each jurisdiction as a development competitor and the extent they viewed them as a collaborator. Network regression using quadratic assignment process estimation techniques reveals that competition and collaboration were not inversely related. In fact, there was a significant positive correlation between perceptions of competitiveness and collaboration.[40]

EMBEDDEDNESS AS CONSTRAINT ON DEFECTION

The same forces that link competition and collaboration constrain local governments from opportunistic behaviors. The dilemma for local actors working on economic development is that cooperation with other jurisdictions provides potential benefit if it results in new development, but it poses greater risks in other areas. Cooperative projects are like a prisoner's dilemma game because if one government shares valuable information or commits investments in a project, its partners face the temptation to minimize their own investment or to defect. Joint efforts to attract new development to the region involve opportunities where partners might engage in shirking, deception, less than full disclosure of information, or efforts to direct investments primarily to their own jurisdiction. Joint projects will then be unattractive unless credible commitments can be made by each party.

In practice, local governments work with partners to solve the collective action problems of regional development within both formal and informal networks that link communities in a region. Existing agreements among the parties increase the likelihood of future cooperative action by reducing information- and enforcement-related transaction costs. Moreover, networks add information beyond that found in the simple dyadic (one-to-one) relationship between contracting local government units. If each organization also participates in related agreements with other local governments, the ensuing series of dyadic relationships evolve into a regional network.

Over time, these embedded relationships capture each participant's reputation for reliability and competency. Cities choose partners on the basis of their prior experience with each other as well as knowledge through common third parties.[41] The common partner in effect vouches for the government units that have not had direct interaction. As the network grows more extensive, information about all participants increases, because members will acquire at least indirect information about others' competency and past performances. Networks increase the credibility of any commitments made by transforming short-term relationships into repeated ones and by linking participants across multiple policy domains. If a city engages in opportunistic behavior in any of these relationships, it is observed and sanctioned by others. A highly clustered, dense network builds social capital by facilitating reciprocity, trust, and conformance to the rules of the game.[42]

Table 1 also offers several institutional mechanisms available for advancing regional governance, ranging from voluntary networks of bilateral and multilateral networks and contracting among jurisdictions and other actors, to regional partnership organizations. But in each case, local actors must overcome collective action difficulties as they try to initiate, nurture, and sustain them.

SELF-ORGANIZING AND INSTITUTIONAL COLLECTIVE ACTION

Can voluntary self-organizing relationships mitigate the risks of cooperating on competitive issues like development? In practice, the answer is clearly affirmative. Defying the prisoner's dilemma prediction, individual jurisdictions often engage in voluntary relationships as they seek advice, share information, and work together to promote economic growth in their communities.[43] Case studies describe how collaborative networks solve problems by discovering or creating solutions within a given set of constraints, including knowledge, time, resources, and even competition.[44]

The network analysis literature argues that embedded relationships, especially reciprocity and transitive bonding, build trust, facilitate monitoring, and provide social enforcement through reputations. Mutual exchanges create the shadow of the future in which defection by one actor can be punished by future defection, thus providing a mutual deterrence on which credible commitments can develop.[45]

Lee, Feiock, and Lee investigated these questions through network interviews with the top economic development administrators in the four-county (Lake, Orange, Osceola, and Seminole) Orlando, Florida, metropolitan region.[46] Information was collected both from elected officials (mayor or council members) and from appointed administrative officials (city manager or executive officials) about which other local governments they had shared advice or information with on economic development issues in the last year. This dyadic information was translated into adjacency matrices. A stochastic network analysis examined whether or not the predicted patterns of embedded relationships had influenced partner selection, controlling for actor and community characteristics and alternative network structures. Figure 1 maps the network of development relationships among cities and counties in the Orlando metropolitan area.

The results of our stochastic network analysis strongly support the hypothesis that transitive bonding structures support cooperation and exert a significant positive influence on the formation of network ties. Local

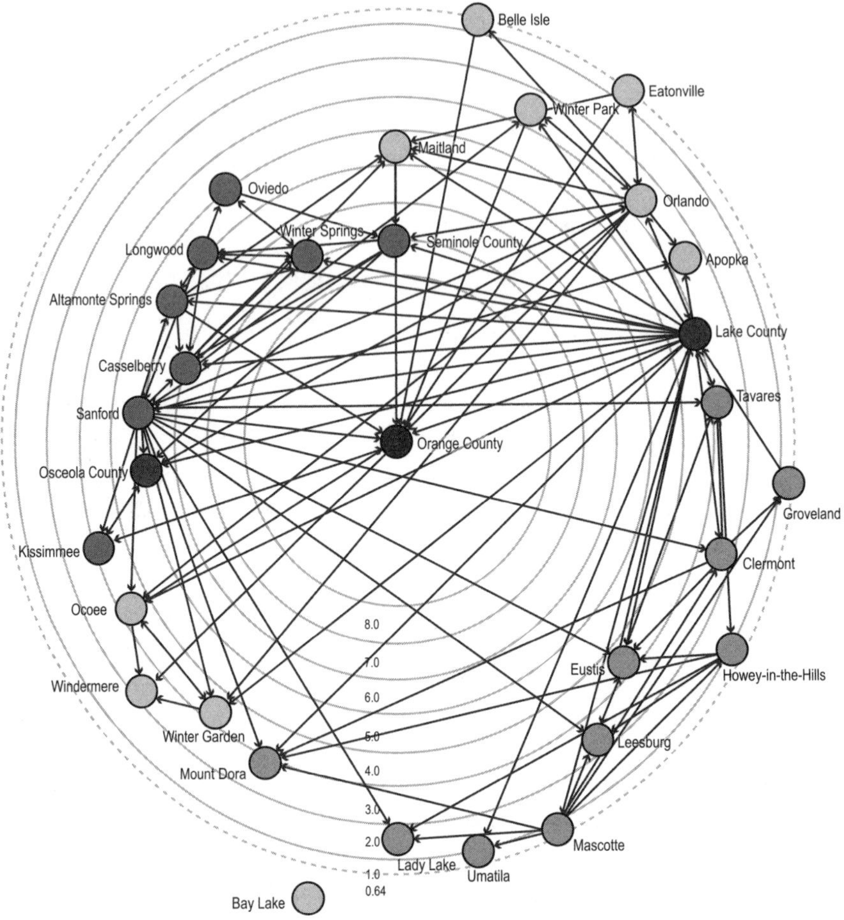

Figure 1. Network of Economic Development Relations among Orlando Local Governments

governments are more likely to share information when they are embedded in a triadic structure. This effect holds for all types of officials and holds even when we consider the actor attributes. "Reciprocity" based on mutual benefits also has a positive coefficient.

The results confirm that when the risks of collaboration are greater, in order to resolve institutional collective action problems, self-organizing actors create mechanisms that enhance trustworthiness. A tightly clustered network bonding structure is advantageous in reducing the transaction costs of enforcing and monitoring the relational obligations, since any actions taken or not taken by a locality are made public. Recent work also demonstrates that local governments endogenously address interdependent problems in service provision through voluntary cooperation.[47] Networks of contractual arrangements thus constitute macrolevel regional governance structures that comprise a set of actors in a social network.[48]

Of course, even if local governments share information and work collaboratively, an agreement is sustainable only if collaboration enhances economic development outcomes for the region as well as for the individual cooperating governments. To bring evidence to bear on this question, Kim and Feiock used data from a 2004 national survey of local economic development officials.[49] The survey asked respondents to identify the local actors with whom they shared information and advice on development issues. In addition to other cities and counties in the metropolitan region, it included regional planning commissions, councils of government, public-private development organizations, and state and federal development agencies. They then estimated the effect of network degree on change in the number of business firms and number of employees from 2002 to 2007.

The statistical results indicate that informal network relationships have a strong and significant influence on economic development. The positive effects on jobs and firms are robust to inclusion of the social and economic characteristics of communities as well as city development programs and incentives.

EXTENDING SELF-ORGANIZING GOVERNANCE TO MULTIPLE FUNCTIONS

We have linked the concept of embeddedness to institutional emergence, sustainability, and performance outcomes, but so far, existing work is limited by its focus on one policy network at a time. A more realistic approach views organizations as embedded in multiple relationships. The combination of all these relationships is expressed by the concept of multiplexity, that is, the degree to which two actors are connected through more than one relationship.[50] Self-organizing regionalism starts with the recognition that network ties are interdependent in complex ways. Through bargaining and logrolling, agreements can be linked in order to address multiple ICA problems. This allows local governments to look beyond dyadic relations to create larger networks to minimize risks and protect against defection across multiple services.

Economic development, land use and energy, and energy-sustainability provide examples of closely interconnected policy arenas that encompass complementary relationships with positive spillovers and as well as conflict and negative spillovers. Unequal resource endowments and needs, inequities in negotiating and bargaining position, uncertainty, and other types of transactions make institutional collective action difficult.

Embeddedness is central to cross-policy coordination. Agreements that are difficult to negotiate individually may be more feasible when they are embedded in a set of relationships for a related policy. Multiple relationships between a pair of actors create more trust and, therefore, greater chances for future exchanges. Likewise, cross-policy reciprocal relationships provide both parties greater assurance for much more stable exchange than if the relationships are one way. Seeking a specific network structure in a multiplex environment can be thought of as engaging in simultaneous multiple games with an overlapping set of actors in multiple policy arenas.[51] The payoffs in each individual game affect the payoff in other games such that the formation of dyadic ties between governments on one service is conditional on relationships on other services. Lubell et al. illustrate this by documenting the efforts to informally coordinate water management, urban planning, and development in California.[52]

Andrew and Kendra examined the evolution of service ties across different sets of activities among sixty-six law enforcement agencies in the Orlando-Kissimmee metropolitan statistical area.[53] They identified a strong tendency for local actors to develop interorganizational ties across different sets of activities. Over time they observe increased multiplexity in the law enforcement activities of sixty-six agencies across the metropolitan area. In addition, they found that services with highly specific assets were coordinated through links with central actors.

LIMITATIONS TO SELF-ORGANIZING GOVERNANCE

We can answer the question of who governs only if we understand how governance operates in contemporary fragmented metropolitan areas. However, we must acknowledge the limitations of self-organizing governance. First, as discussed earlier, in situations where the risk of defection is great, such as with infrastructure coordination or financial cooperation, voluntary solutions may be inadequate, necessitating more centralized and authoritative mechanisms. A second concern relating to equity and accountability has not been given much attention. Because self-organizing networks reflect decisions to cooperate with some actors rather than others, there is a potential for exclusion and for cross-policy reciprocity that in turn may exacerbate regional inequalities. Externalities among related policies and programs might push costs or problems from one policy arena to another. For example, land use development and regulation decisions will have consequences for natural resources, transportation, economic development, and other specialized policy arenas across the region. One advantage of centralized solutions, such as multipurpose regional government, is their potential to authoritatively integrate policies as well as places. If resources and fiscal capacity make some governments a more desirable partner in one area and others less desirable, this advantage may be compounded through multiplexity. Advocacy of self-organizing networks might need to be restrained, and in fact it demonstrably produces collusive relationships in which disadvantage cumulates across policy areas.

Collaboration across multiple service areas exacerbates persistent patterns of advantage and disadvantage in metropolitan areas if communities that have more diverse populations or that are economically stressed are less desirable service partners. Thus, a better understanding of multiplex relations can improve our understanding of coordination and efficiency and more generally provide insights into who governs in contemporary fragmented metropolitan areas.

CONCLUSION

The tasks of governing urban areas in the twenty-first century have become more complex than Robert Dahl could have envisioned when he wrote *Who Governs* in 1961.[54] The problems of fragmentation occur not just among agencies and governments—they exist among services and policies, since policies overlap and are linked in many ways. Scholars of local government must directly confront these issues in order to provide realistic advice and insights for managers and policymakers. Much work remains ahead.

I suggest here that self-organizing relationships can and increasingly do inform local action in ways that improve both the technical and economic efficiency of local governments. While much of the discussion to date has been academic, practical lessons can be drawn that are especially relevant in the aftermath of the Great Recession as collaborative arrangements are considered as alternatives to reduce service costs and promote technical and economic efficiency gains. First, local government officials must be sensitive not just to economies of scale, but also to possible positive and negative spillovers across governments and functional areas that may first appear to be unrelated to each other.

Second, the choices for addressing regional governance issues go beyond conventional comparisons of political markets and regional institutions. I introduce an array of mechanisms that vary in scope and enforcement and that can be deployed to address collective policy problems, describing how these mechanisms can be matched to specific ICA dilemmas. Third, our discussion of the advantages of embedding relationships provides strong grounds for the prescription that local actors design collaborative mechanisms to reduce collaboration risks and make commitments more credible and binding. One way to do this is through multiplex agreements that link more than one service or policy. Logrolling across policies can be a solution to institutional collective action dilemmas.

Fourth, local policy makers and administrators must create new venues and take advantage of existing venues that provide opportunities for face-to-face interactions with both competitors and collaborators in order to build knowledge and social capital that can advance their collective interest. Fifth, decision makers must be aware that the efficiency advantages of self-organizing mechanisms may result in increased service inequality across jurisdictions. A small set of actors cooperating across multiple services produces collusion. Because not every intergovernmental problem can be effectively addressed in a self-organized manner, the ultimate challenge is to design collaborative mechanisms that not only enhance individual and collective efficiency, but that are adaptable to the diverse problems, values, and preferences that define local policy and regional governance.

Notes

1. Joseph F. Zimmerman, "The Metropolitan Area Problem," *Annals of the American Academy of Political and Social Science* 416 (1974): 133–47.

2. Charles M. Tiebout, Vincent Ostrom, and Robert Warren, "The Organization of Government in Metropolitan Areas: A Theoretical Inquiry," *American Political Science Review* 55 (1961): 831–42.

3. Among the public-administration scholars are Luther Gulick, "Metropolitan Organization," *Annals of the American Academy of Political and Social Science* 314 (1957): 57–65; W. E. Lyons, David Lowery, and Ruth Hoogland DeHoog, *The Politics of Dissatisfaction: Citizens, Services and Urban Institutions* (Armonk, N.Y.: M. E. Sharpe, 1992); David B. Walker, "Snow White and the 17 Dwarfs: From Metro Cooperation to Governance," *National Civic Review* 76 (1987): 14–28. Among the metropolitan political economy scholars are Michael Craw, "Taming the Local

Leviathan: Institutional and Economic Constraints of Municipal Budgets," *Urban Affairs Review* 43 (2008): 663–90; Tiebout et al., "Organization," 2; Mark Schneider, *The Competitive City: The Political Economy of Suburbia* (Pittsburgh, Pa.: University of Pittsburgh Press, 1989).

4. Jered Carr and Richard C. Feiock, *City-County Consolidation and Its Alternatives: Reshaping the Local Government Landscape* (New York: M. E. Sharpe, 2004).

5. Charles M. Tiebout, "A Pure Theory of Local Expenditures," *Journal of Political Economy* 64 (1956): 416–24.

6. Ibid., 5; Paul E. Peterson, *City Limits* (Chicago, Ill.: University of Chicago Press, 1981).

7. Studies showing improved efficiency: Craw, "Taming," 4; Schneider, *Competitive*, 4; Jeffrey S. Zax, "The Effects of Jurisdiction Types and Numbers on Local Public Finance," in *Fiscal Federalism: Quantitative Studies*, 79–103, edited by H. S. Rosen (Chicago, Ill.: Chicago University Press, 1988). Studies reporting little or no impact: R. J. Campbell, "Leviathan and Fiscal Illusion in Local Government Overlapping Jurisdictions," *Public Choice* 120 (2004): 301–29; T. J. DiLorenzo, "Economic Competition and Political Competition: An Empirical Note," *Public Choice* 40 (1983): 203–9; G. K. Turnbull and S. S. Djoundourian, "Overlapping Jurisdictions: Substitutes or Complements?," *Public Choice* 75 (1993): 231–45.

8. Alexandra Petermann Reifschneider, *Competition in the Provision of Local Public Goods* (Cheltenham: Edward Elgar, 2006).

9. Richard C. Feiock and In Won Lee, "Economic Development Collaboration: Networks among Elected and Appointed Officials," paper presented at the Harvard Networks in Political Science Conference, Cambridge, Mass., June 13–14, 2008.

10. Mark Lubell, Mark Schneider, John Scholz, and Mihriye Mete, "Watershed Partnerships and the Emergence of Collective Action Institutions," *American Journal of Political Science* 46 (2002): 148–63; Richard C. Feiock and John T. Scholz, eds., *Self-Organizing Federalism: Collaborative Mechanisms to Mitigate Institutional Collective Action Dilemmas* (Cambridge: Cambridge University Press, 2010); Mark Schneider, Mark Lubell, John Scholz, Denisa Mindruta, and Matthew Edwardsen, "Building Consensual Institutions: Networks and the National Estuary Program," *American Journal of Political Science* 47 (2003): 143–58.

11. Richard C. Feiock and John T. Scholz, "Self-Organizing Governance of Institutional Collective Action Dilemmas: An Overview," in *Self-Organizing*, 11.

12. Richard C. Feiock, "Politics, Governance, and the Complexity of Local Land Use Regulation," *Urban Studies* 41 (2004): 363–77; Richard C. Feiock, *Metropolitan Governance: Conflict, Competition and Cooperation* (Washington, D.C.: Georgetown University Press, 2004); Richard C. Feiock, "Metropolitan Governance and Collective Action," *Urban Affairs Review* 44 (2009): 356–77.

13. Feiock, *Metropolitan Governance*, 13.

14. Feiock and Scholz, "Self-Organizing," 11.

15. Richard C. Feiock, "The Institutional Collective Action Framework," *Policy Studies Journal* 41 (2013).

16. David Lowery, "A Transactions Costs Model of Metropolitan Governance: Allocation Versus Redistribution in Urban America," *Journal of Public Administration Research and Theory* 10 (2000): 49–78.

17. Robert Agranoff and Michael McGuire, *Collaborative Public Management: New Strategies for Local Governments* (Washington, D.C.: Georgetown University Press, 2003);, Richard C. Feiock, Mark Lubell, and Edgar Ramierez, "Political Institutions and Conservation by Local Governments," *Urban Affairs Review* 40 (2005): 706–29; Lubell et al., "Watershed," 11; Kenneth J. Meier and Lawrence J. O'Toole, "Public Management and Organizational Performance: The Impact of Managerial Quality," *Journal of Policy Analysis and Management* 21 (2002): 629–43; Schneider et al., "Building."

18. Ramiro Berardo and John T. Scholz, "Self-Organizing Policy Networks: Risk, Partner Selection and Cooperation in Estuaries," *American Journal of Political Science* 54 (2010): 632–49; Feiock and Scholz, "Self-Organizing," 11.

19. Feiock, "Institutional," 16.

20. The author appreciates the insight of Annette Steinacker in developing this section of the paper.

21. Ibid.

22. Mark Granovetter, "Economic Action and Social Structure: The Problem of Embeddedness," *American Journal of Sociology* 91 (1985): 481–510; Brian Uzzi, "Social Structure and Competition in Interfirm Networks: The Paradox of Embeddedness," *Administrative Science Quarterly* 42 (1997): 35–67.

23. James S. Coleman, *Foundations of Social Theory* (Cambridge: Cambridge University Press, 1990).

24. Richard Feiock, In Won Lee, Hyung Jun, Park, and Keon Hyung Lee, "Policy Networks among Local Elected Officials: Information, Commitment, and Risk Aversion," *Urban Affairs Review* 46 (2010): 241–62.

25. Feiock and Scholz, "Self-Organizing," 11.

26. Richard C. Feiock, M. Jae Moon, and Hyung Jun Park, "Is the World 'Flat' or 'Spiky? Rethinking the Governance Implications of Globalization for Economic Development," *Public Administration Review* 68 (2008): 24–35.

27. Feiock, "Politics," 13.

28. Michael E. Porter, "Location, Competition, and Economic Development: Local Clusters in a Global Economy," *Economic Development Quarterly* 14 (2000): 15–34.

29. Richard C. Feiock, "A Quasi-Market Framework for Development Competition," *Journal of Urban Affairs* 24 (2002): 123–42.

30. Elinor Ostrom, *Governing the Commons: The Evolution of Institutions for Collective Action* (New York: Cambridge University Press, 1990).

31. Christopher V. Hawkins, "Competition and Cooperation: Local Government Joint Ventures for Economic Development," *Journal of Urban Affairs* 32 (2010): 253–75; In Won Lee, Richard C. Feiock, and Youngmi Lee, "Competitors and Cooperators: A Micro-Level Analysis of Regional Economic Development Collaboration Networks," *Public Administration Review* 72 (2012): 253–62.

32. Jelle Visser, "Why Fewer Workers Join Unions in Europe: A Social Custom Explanation of Membership Trends," *British Journal of Industrial Relations* 40 (2002): 403–30.

33. Lee, Feiock, and Lee, "Competitors and Cooperators."

34. Edward G. Goetz and Terrence Kayser, "Competition and Cooperation in Economic Development: A Study of the Twin Cities Metropolitan Area," *Economic Development Quarterly* 7 (1993): 63–78.

35. Victoria Gordon, "Partners or Competitors? Perceptions of Regional Economic Development Cooperation in Illinois," *Economic Development Quarterly* 21 (2007): 60–78; M. Smith and M. Beazley, "Progressive Regimes, Partnerships and the Involvement of Local Communities," *Public Administration* 78 (2000): 855–78.

36. Feiock and Lee, "Economic," 10.

37. Lubell et al., "Watershed," 11; Granovetter, "Economic"; Ranjay Gulati and Martin Gargiulo, "Where Do Interorganizational Networks Come From?," *American Journal of Sociology* 104 (1999): 1439–93.

38. James S. Coleman, "Social Capital in the Creation of Human Capital," *American Journal of Sociology* 94 (1988): 95–120.

39. Richard C. Feiock, Annette Steinacker, and Hyung-Jun Park, "Institutional Collective Action and Economic Development Joint Ventures," *Public Administration Review* 69 (2009): 257–70.

40. Lee, Feiock, and Lee, "Competitors and Cooperators."

41. Granovetter, "Economic," 483.

42. Coleman, *Foundations*, 24.

43. Lee, Feiock, and Lee, "Competitors and Cooperators."

44. Agranoff and Maguire, *Collaborative*, 18.

45. Robert Axelrod, *The Evolution of Cooperation* (New York: Basic Books, 1984).

46. Lee, Feiock, and Lee, "Competitors and Cooperators ."

47. John T. Scholz, Ramiro Berardo, and Brad Kile. "Do Networks Solve Collective Action Problems? Credibility, Search, and Collaboration," *Journal of Politics* 70 (2008): 1–14; Manoj Shrestha, "Decentralized Governments, Network and Interlocal Cooperation in Public Goods Supply," PhD diss., Florida State University, Tallahassee, 2008; Manoj Shrestha and Richard C. Feiock, "Governing U.S. Metropolitan Areas: Self-Organizing and Multiplex Service Networks," *American Politics Research* 37:5 (2009): 801–23.

48. Feiock and Scholz, "Self-Organizing," 11; Kurt Thurmaier and Curtis Wood, "Interlocal Agreements as Social Networks: Picket-Fence Regionalism in Metropolitan Kansas City," *Public Administration Review* 62 (2002): 585–98.

49. Sangsoo Kim and Richard C. Feiock, "Networks and Performance: Development Policy Networks and Economic Growth," working paper, Florida State University Local Governance Research Laboratory, 2012.

50. Stanley Wasserman and Katherine Faust, *Social Network Analysis: Methods and Applications* (Cambridge: Cambridge University Press, 1994).

51. Mark Lubell, Adam D. Henry, and Mike McCoy, "Collaborative Institutions in an Ecology of Games," *American Journal of Political Science* 54 (2010): 287–300; Fritz Scharpf, *Games Real Actors Play: Actor-Centered Institutionalism in Policy Research* (Boulder, Colo.: Westview Press, 1997);

52. Lubell et al., "Collaborative," 51.

53. Simon A. Andrew and James Kendra, "An Adaptive Governance Approach to Providing Disaster Behavioral Services," *Disasters: The Journal of Disaster Studies, Policy and Management* 36 (2012): 514–32.

54. Robert Alan Dahl, *Who Governs? Democracy and Power in an American City* (New Haven, Conn.: Yale University Press, 1974).

Collaboration and Competition within the Chicago Metropolitan Region

DISCUSSANT: REBECCA HENDRICK,
UNIVERSITY OF ILLINOIS AT CHICAGO

Many scholars agree that the Great Recession has unleashed forces that will alter the financial landscape of local governments permanently. This will be especially true for Illinois if the state government transfers its pension obligations for local government employees to the local governments in order to help resolve the state's fiscal crises. The question posed by our panel in the context of metropolitan resilience is whether this new landscape of increasing costs and limited resources provides enough incentive for local governments in the United States to collaborate in ways that fundamentally alter how services are provided and regional problems are resolved. Recent publications and sponsored research from professional associations such as the National League of Cities, the International City/County Management Association, and the Government Finance Officers Association advocate collaboration between governments as a means of coping with current financial challenges and delivering services more efficiently. This "new regionalist perspective" also promotes the view that collaboration can occur between governments even in competitive and jurisdictionally fragmented settings and that it can advance the collective interests of local governments within a region. In this book and elsewhere, Richard C. Feiock argues that, indeed, the benefits of collaboration can outweigh the costs for individual governments in many settings. In contrast to the new regionalist perspective that "collaboration is the new competition," he identifies important caveats and qualifications about intergovernmental collaboration that should be emphasized if we want to understand the link between collaboration and competition and promote collaboration in a reasonable way. I discuss some of these caveats and qualifications as they apply to Illinois and local governments in the Chicago metropolitan region.

First, collaboration is expensive and risky, and some types of collaboration are more expensive and riskier than others, as demonstrated by Feiock's table 1. This table shows the types of voluntary or self-organized collaborative mechanisms that might exist based on the number of collaborators in the agreement, and their loss of control over future decisions (e.g., inability to exit, transferring authority to central agent). Two-party agreements are less costly and risky to administer than N-party agreements, and informal agreements are less costly but more risky in terms of defection by participants than are agreements that bind or constrain participants to particular actions. Thus, one might expect there to be more two-party than N-party agreements between governments, and more informal agreements than there are formal. Feiock also emphasizes that collaborative mechanisms must be matched to the type of collective action problem in order to develop, endure, and be effective. In conjunction, these hypotheses raise the question of whether or not self-organized arrangements can solve collective action problems that require many participants to give up a great deal of control over future behavior. In most cases, the costs and risks of these arrangements may simply be too high.

Second, competition and collaboration are not opposite ends of the same continuum, with collaboration increasing when competition decreases. As noted by Feiock in his introduction, competition and collaboration are not substitutes but "operate in complementary and reinforcing ways." The trick to using voluntary collaboration to solve collective and regional problems is to find conditions in which the competitive and collaborative goals of individuals are aligned. For instance, collusion between firms to fix prices or limit production is an example of competitors collaborating to increase the likelihood of market outcomes occurring in their favor, thereby achieving benefits they could not receive by acting alone. Collaboration in this case reduces competition between the firms that are part of the agreement and reduces the costs they incur due to uncertainty and risk, but it does not replace the competitive incentives of the market. An annexation boundary agreement between two or more municipalities that share a common area of unincorporated land that is targeted for development is an example of this type of cooperation by local government. In my own research, I found that such agreements were very common in 2003 and 2004 between municipalities at the suburban edge of the Chicago metropolitan region and were used by them to control development and land use in the unincorporated areas.[1] Although these agreements constitute collaboration, they are not really the same as collaborating to provide public goods, manage common resources, or improve economies of scale in service delivery. To develop voluntarily and endure, collaborations that provide public goods and manage common resources require that the interests of participating governments overlap enough to yield positive payoffs for all. However, overlap among interests and the level of payoffs to individual governments are likely to shrink as governments become more numerous and competitive about the target of the agreement. By comparison, collaboration to reduce the costs of competition is likely to focus on a narrow set of benefits with outcomes that may even be detrimental to broader objectives, such as the effects of price collusion on market efficiency.

Although collaboration and competition are not opposite ends of the same continuum, conditions related to competition between local governments are likely to reduce the compatibility of governments' collaborative interests and increase the costs of collaboration. As noted by Feiock, fragmentation of jurisdictions in metropolitan regions is associated with higher competition. Additionally, both competition and fragmentation are associated with the metropolitan populations being sorted and segregated into homogeneous jurisdictions with dissimilar preferences and qualities relative to each other.[2] Competition also is associated with externality problems, which are the hardest to solve collectively because the interests of those affected directly conflict with each other. The more that competitive outcomes are zero-sum between governments, the smaller the area of goal alignment with respect to those outcomes, the more costly it is to find that area, and the less likely it is that collaboration will be initiated. Similarly, the more dispersed, splintered, or fragmented local governments are in a metropolitan region, the more costly it will be to forge and sustain collective agreements among them.

For instance, the Illinois state government distributes sales taxes to counties and municipalities based on the point of sale, and both municipalities and counties may levy sales taxes, although amounts levied by non–home rule governments are restricted. This increases competition between local governments to attract sales tax–generating enterprises in order to reduce reliance on property taxes and export the tax burden to nonresidents who do not vote. According to my recent statistical analyses, local governments in the Chicago region also are highly fragmented. Thus, I would expect collaboration between local governments in this region on matters of economic development or on events that are affected by economic development to be very costly or difficult to create, compared to collaboration between governments in other regions that are not as competitive or fragmented. I would also expect existing collaborative mechanism in the region to be mostly bilateral and informal or contractually decentralized rather than centralized.

These hypotheses fit well with Feiock's argument that the new regionalist perspective neglects the "transaction costs and collective action problems inherent in forming and maintaining the regional governance mechanisms they prescribe," and overemphasizes multilateral governance mechanisms over "bilateral mechanisms based on networks, contracting, and bargaining." But these hypotheses also raise issues for collaboration that are consistent with the new regionalist perspective. One issue is whether bilateral and informal or contractual networks can resolve the difficult collective action problems facing local governments, especially those at the regional level. For instance, it is difficult to conceive of a situation where a government would voluntarily reduce commercial development that lowers sales tax revenue because the development creates more traffic or other negative spillovers for neighboring governments. Rather, as I observed in the Chicago region, governments in such situations are likely to fight it out in court in response to a lawsuit.

Sprawl, by definition a regional problem, is not likely to be resolved bilaterally and also is notoriously difficult to resolve or affect using voluntary or self-organizing methods.[3] A good example of that difficulty is apparent in the regional planning and development efforts undertaken by the Chicago metropolitan region through a variety of nonprofit- and government-sponsored agencies such as Northeastern Illinois Planning Commission (NIPC), Metropolitan Planning Council, the Chicago Area Transportation Study (CATS), and the Center for Neighborhood Technology. These agencies have helped plan and coordinate transportation and development among governments in the region, and they have provided forums for discussion of these issues among stakeholders, but they have not noticeably reduced sprawl or the continued expansion of development in the region. The agencies have no power to implement plans or veto projects, and therefore have little direct influence on these collective problems except through advice and persuasion.[4] The limitations of voluntary collaboration are also seen in the region's eleven councils of government. As collaborative arrangements, the councils are relatively cheap and focus on solving comparatively easy collective action problems, such as the facilitation of coordination and information sharing, lobbying external governments, and the provision of administrative support functions to member governments (e.g., purchasing pools and surplus equipment auctions). Although several councils are leading discussions to improve collaboration and even consolidation of local governments in the region, little progress has been made along this front.

A second issue raised by the new regionalist perspective about collaboration is whether bilateral mechanisms based on networks and contracting can compensate for the inequality between jurisdictions that is likely to exist in regions with sorted populations. Inequality of jurisdictions creates an unleveled competitive playing field, thereby eliminating or discounting some of the advantages of competition for allocative and productive efficiency. Similarly, poorer jurisdictions cannot bring enough resources to the negotiation of collaborative agreements to ensure that their interests are represented in the terms of the agreement and in the final outcomes. This situation reduces the incentive for poor governments to collaborate, and the discrepancy between rich and poor governments increases the costs of collaboration for both parties. Although the Great Recession may increase the payoffs of collaboration for individual governments and the area of mutual benefit between them, it is not clear that this situation will lead to more self-organized collaboration for all types of collective action problems. With respect to particular problems related to externalities and other thorny collective and regional problems, including inequality between governments, we must recognize that collaborative solutions may not occur voluntarily or that the outcomes may not always be desirable or successful. We also will have to acknowledge the potentially positive role of higher authorities in altering incentives for collaborative arrangements and outcomes. Additionally, higher authorities can reduce the costs of collaboration through statutes that facilitate the ability of individual governments to make joint commitments that are binding and enforceable (credible commitments).

Notes

1. Rebecca M. Hendrick, *Managing the Fiscal Metropolis: The Financial Policies, Practices, and Health of Suburban Municipalities* (Washington, D.C.: Georgetown University Press, 2011).

2. See, e.g., Robert M. Stein, "Tiebout's Sorting Hypothesis," *Urban Affairs Quarterly* 23:1 (1987): 140–60; Gregory R. Weiher, *The Fractured Metropolis: Political Fragmentation and Metropolitan Segregation* (Albany: SUNY Press, 1991); Michael Howell-Moroney, "The Tiebout Hypothesis 50 Years Later: Lessons and Lingering Challenges for Metropolitan Governance in the 21st Century," *Public Administration Review* 68:1 (2008): 97–109.

3. Frances Frisken and Donald F. Norris, "Regionalism Reconsidered," *Journal of Urban Affairs* 23:5 (2001): 467–78.

4. This situation may change somewhat with the merging of NIPC and CATS into the Chicago Metropolitan Agency for Planning, which has been authorized by the state government to rank all proposed federally funded transportation projects in the region.

A Nuanced Perspective of Local Governance Possibilities

DISCUSSANT: ANNETTE STEINACKER

Metropolitan resiliency during hard times will depend on cities' ability to provide services to their residents and to raise revenues to pursue their goals. As Richard Feiock points out in his chapter, one way to increase the ability of cities to achieve both goals is through cooperation with each other, which may be achieved through various governance structures. To assess the value of this framework, additional consideration of the conditions under which cooperation will occur and the outcomes that can be achieved is needed. These nuances are developed in this note. Finally, empirical data on the frequency of the nine governance structures and their use in different services areas would be helpful in assessing the likelihood of collaborative efforts across metropolitan areas.

Interlocal cooperation will depend on two issues: the characteristics of the policy issue, and the characteristics of the cities that could work together. Feiock has discussed some of the first characteristics, but few of the second.

The type of policy issue involved is critical because it determines the incentives that potential collaborative partners face. Any cooperative mechanism requires incentive compatibility in order to be created and then to be effective. Feiock lays out four types of policy issues that would affect prospects of cooperation. Three have been developed before (economies of scale, common property resources, and externalities) and one new issue has been added (coordination problems).[1]

Coordination problems involve cases in which all participants want the same outcome but working together is necessary to achieve that goal. There may be conflict among participants because each would prefer the use of their method to achieve the goal, but the importance of goal attainment outweighs the value of which method is used. In game theoretical terms, this is the Battle of the Sexes. In this analogy of coordination problems, the two people in the couple want to spend time together regardless of the activity, but each would also prefer their most-liked alternative. Men may want to go to a sporting event, women may want to go to the movies. Both prefer being together over each doing their first-choice activity, but to achieve that they need to communicate and perhaps make trade-offs over time (one week sports, the next week movies).

One example of a coordination issue in government is the location of bus routes that cross city boundaries. The suburb may prefer that the route passes through its downtown, the central city prefers that the route stops at a parking lot alongside a highway interchange. The suburb wants to draw people downtown to shop; the city wants a quick and easy pick-up point. But both communities need the bus route to transport suburban residents to city jobs more than they need their preferred stop. Communication and trade-offs over time or across issues are usually sufficient to resolve service coordination problems. This is where networks and social embeddedness can be most helpful. Networks generate more opportunities to communicate with other local government representatives and so discover mutually acceptable outcomes. Networks may also help in creating the longer-term relationships or links across issues. Given the generally high level of incentive compatibility in coordination problems, embeddedness is likely to be sufficient to find a solution.

As we move to policy areas with less compatible incentive structures, the necessary type of governance structure becomes more authoritarian. Services that involve economies of scale may be solved with legal contracts. All parties can pay lower average service costs if they cooperate, but they need binding agreements before risking the initial costly investments. For a common property resource (CPR), either a legal contract or a centralized authority may work. For these problems, there is incentive compatibility across participants in the long term but not in the short term. Which governance system is needed will depend on the extent of commitments needed to solve the problem, the time frame each participant is considering, and the ease of monitoring everyone's CPR use.[2] The greater the differences among participants on these issues, the more likely that a centralized authority will be needed. For negative externality issues, incentives of the involved parties are directly opposed in all time periods—the party generating the externality benefits from continuing to do so while other parties bear the costs. The lack of incentive compatibility makes it very likely that a centralized governance authority will be needed to force change to a more optimal outcome for the region as a whole.

The second critical issue affecting possible collaboration among governments is the distribution of potential city partners. Even in policy areas where cooperation is likely to occur, the choice of partner will depend on the other cities' characteristics.

First, geographic proximity will be necessary for some services. An effective water distribution system must connect contiguous communities, whereas library services can be provided to any community in the metropolitan area regardless of their proximity. Second, population size and the socioeconomic composition of city residents will affect the demand for government services and indirectly the city revenue base available to contribute to any shared services with other government units. Third, the type of land uses within a city will have similar effects on service delivery demands and available tax base. Industrial development may require greater fire protection services or larger water and wastewater treatment systems. Residential development could require more parks and recreation or library services. Land uses drive service needs and again indirectly affect the revenue base available to cities to pay for common services. Finally, revenue capacity needs to be considered directly. Capacity depends both on the size and composition of the tax base and on the tax rate that communities are willing to impose on themselves.

For each of the four policy problems discussed above, cities will consider which other local governments could be viable partners. Even for the simpler cases where the policy arena suggests that collaboration should be likely, the array of potential collaborators may not support an agreement being formed.

For coordination problems, everyone has similar incentives, so a follow-the-leader strategy may suffice to solve the problem. Once the largest player commits to a particular strategy, often by dedicating sunk costs to it, the smaller players also conform. The central city could unilaterally decide on bus routes off interstates and reinforce its commitment by construction of shelters in those places. Suburbs find it easier to accept the routes and not have to pay for shelters; the larger city has lower operating costs in return for small initial shelter costs. Resolution of a coordination problem will be most likely when there is one large government player who can take the leadership role and establish a clear service delivery strategy for the other participants. Network relationships and social embeddedness can help identify which city will act as the leader and what strategy will be acceptable for the other cities.

For many economy-of-scale problems, the likelihood of collaboration also increases with one large city that can build the facility or organize the collective action efforts (the privileged provider in Mancur Olson's work).[3] The best distribution of cities for collaboration would be a significant number of other communities that are too small or too poor to provide the service themselves. Given that the average cost for these services would be extremely high if small communities provided them alone, these cities have a strong incentive to collaborate with a larger partner. Communities falling in the middle—of moderate size and with a moderate-to-high revenue base—are the least likely to participate. They have sufficient scale and resources to provide the service themselves. The per-unit cost would still be higher than in a larger consortium, but it would not be necessarily prohibitive. Retaining autonomy may be worth the higher service costs for these cities, decreasing the likelihood of cooperative actions.

For a CPR problem, the distribution of power across city sizes tends to be the opposite of the preceding two cases. City size is often connected to the level of use of the CPR. Large communities use the greatest portion of the CPR and would benefit the most from managed use and a reinvestment plan. They also have a strong incentive to adopt a longer time horizon because the resource is so valuable to them—they cannot risk losing the good in the future. Other communities value the resource, but because of their smaller sizes, their actions have little impact on the overall level of the CPR or on the length of time before the CPR is depleted. Small and poor communities may feel they have no other option but to continue to draw down the CPR because they need the resource and have no ability to invest in order to maintain it. Large communities can take action on their own, but such action will have little impact on the size of the CPR problem. If they unilaterally reduce their use, the small communities are able to increase their demands on the CPR, which simply results in a shift of use from the large to small users, with no net decrease in the level of overuse. Large communities need the cooperation of smaller ones in this case, and that significantly increases the power of the smaller communities. The best distribution of cities in a metropolitan area for cooperation to emerge is one where there are fewer cities and those cities are reasonably equal in size. The impact of each participant's sacrifice is therefore similar and easier to negotiate. In metropolitan areas where there is a smaller number of cities that have similar levels of CPR use, it is more likely that the negotiated collaboration governance structure will be effective. In regions where there are extreme differences in city size and CPR use, or there are a very large number of communities whose cooperation is needed in order to have an impact on the problem, then the centralized authority governance structure may be needed.

Finally, for externality situations, collaboration is simply difficult regardless of the city distribution of characteristics. Each city benefits from continuing to create its negative externality. The only way to encourage collaboration with contractual arrangements requires links to other issues or across time. City politicians may choose not to impose on a neighboring community by building retail development on its border, which would draw sales tax revenue from neighboring residents while imposing more traffic congestion on them, if they anticipated retaliation by the neighbor in the future or on another issue. This balance-of-power relationship suggests that only similar cities would be likely to collaborate to reduce the mutual harms being inflicted on each other over time. Extreme disparities in city size, land use, or residential composition suggest that the community creating the larger negative externality would not benefit sufficiently from reducing its behavior even if other, smaller communities reduced their externalities, as well. Some norms of "good behavior" across neighbors often exist in a metropolitan area—an implicit recognition of the inevitable geographic ties of place that will continue in the future. However, in most cases, if the externality issue is severe (large irreversible costs imposed on other communities), then a centralized authority imposed by the state will be needed to coordinate activities to reduce the level of the externality.

Notes

1. Annette Steinacker, "The Institutional Collective Action Perspective on Self-Organizing Federalism: Market Failures and Transaction Cost Problems," in *Self-Organizing Federalism: Collaborative Mechanisms to Mitigate Institutional Collective Action Dilemmas*, 51–72, edited by Richard C. Feiock and John T. Scholz (Cambridge: Cambridge University Press, 2009).

2. Elinor Ostrom, *Governing the Commons: The Evolution of Institutions For Collective Action* (Cambridge: Cambridge University Press, 1990).

3. Mancur Olson, *The Logic of Collective Action: Public Goods and the Theory of Groups* (Cambridge, Mass.: Harvard University Press, 1971).

The Legacy Costs of Earlier Decisions

RICHARD P. NATHAN

FORMER DIRECTOR, NELSON A. ROCKEFELLER INSTITUTE OF GOVERNMENT, STATE UNIVERSITY OF NEW YORK

By definition, a legacy is something handed down from the past. This chapter focuses on four types of financial strategies in government that involve acting now and paying over time. Because they are so intertwined, the chapter considers the consequences of financial legacy strategies at both the state and local levels. At the end of the chapter the implications drawn and conclusions reached about how to deal with the problems financial legacy strategies can cause are viewed broadly (from national, state, and local perspectives) in terms of the formidable challenge of instilling fiscal discipline, accountability, and transparency in U.S. public finances in these polarized times.

The subtitle for the UIC Urban Forum refers to the present period as "A Time of Economic Turmoil," implying a special urgency to fiscal challenges. The trajectory of budget deficits and debts at every level of government is prominent and scary. The subject of this chapter—how to diagnose and cope with previously made financial commitments that compound when revenue stresses are rising—is not new. It is rare for political leaders not to be faced with inherited budget challenges and prospective deficits and rising debt. Nevertheless, the raging debate in 2012 about the nation's "fiscal cliff" and the severe challenges facing many state and local governments coincident with the UIC Urban Forum mark economic turmoil of particular strength. A central challenge for the country is this question: How can the kinds of legacy budget practices examined here become well-known and understood widely enough to do something about them?

My all-time favorite analysis of how issues get on the agenda for major action is John W. Kingdon's classic treatment, *Agendas, Alternatives, and Public Policies.*[1] Drawing on the rich insights of Charles Lindbolm and Aaron Wildavsky, Kingdon depicts the "highly fluid and loosely coupled" and unpredictable way in which the "three streams"—problems, policies, and politics—come together to put issues on the agenda for major action and change.

Fiscal responsibility would seem to be a difficult candidate for agenda building. Political leaders are better at giving than at taking away, and at incremental as opposed to decremental budgeting. Compounding this, well-financed interest groups that benefit from public programs (as recipients and providers) are better positioned than are budget experts and government analysts to win support in political processes.

Elected officials live in the present. They care about getting elected (or re-elected) now. There are any number of ways they can satisfy desires now and pay later. The same interests and inclinations are often manifest on the part of appointed officials and agency personnel. This is understandable; people who take jobs in government often believe in, care about, and support the goals being sought by the program they are working on. As a government "inner and outer" (an insider as an appointed official and an outsider as a policy researcher) myself, one experience stands out that dramatizes this situation.

I was a staff assistant in the mid-1960s to Governor Nelson A. Rockefeller of New York. He regarded himself as fiscally responsible (most politicians do). When confronted with demands from public-sector unions, he often took the legacy route: "I love you guys. I want to help you. The best way for me to do so is on pensions and benefits." Promise now, pay later.

In writing about the special problem of budgeting, Kingdon observes that there are times when "perceived prohibitive costs" become what he first describes as "a preoccupation," and then reconsidering, substitutes the word "obsession."[2] We seem to be in such a period now where the kinds of budget issues treated in this paper conceivably could rise to the top of political agendas.

A task force organized by Richard Ravitch and Paul Volcker on the "fiscal crisis of the states" has examined exactly this possibility—and need—at the state and local levels in U.S. government.[3] That is, that there would be what Kingdon calls a coming together of the "loosely coupled, various streams" to produce a "window of opportunity" for high-level attention to fiscal practices and the need for honest scoring of the obligations that state and local governments incur.

Kingdon stresses that agenda setting is a rough-and-ready process, often untidy, unnuanced, and turbulent. He is wary of the classical planning paradigm that assumes planners can understand, know well, and weigh all alternatives in order to make rational choices, which Kingdon says is a model that does not "accurately describe reality."

After describing and analyzing four budget-legacy strategies, I consider agenda-setting tactics for U.S. government that could bring heightened attention to fiscal responsibility.

FOUR FINANCIAL LEGACY STRATEGIES

1. PENSIONS AND BENEFITS. Unfunded workers' pensions and benefits stand out on the list of state-local financial problems that can be caused by budgetary legacy strategies. Failing to fully fund future pension and worker-benefit obligations is tempting and unfortunately common. It is a troublesome cause of financial legacy problems.

2. INFRASTRUCTURE. Few events are more gratifying than ribbon-cutting ceremonies. Investments in capital (buildings, highways, parks, and stadiums) win friends and admiration.

There is nothing intrinsically wrong with funding pension systems over time and amortizing revenue-producing capital assets. But however well this may work in theory, it often doesn't work so well in practice when the financial arrangements needed to accumulate pension-system investment income or pay the interest on municipal bonds are not in place and soundly structured.

3. MANDATE AS REQUIREMENTS FOR ACTION. Mandates are especially troublesome for local governments. A tempting strategy for national and state policy makers is to achieve a valued purpose by requiring somebody further down the federalism food chain to do something without covering the costs of doing it. This is especially tempting in fiscally tight times.

4. MANDATES AS ENTITLEMENTS. This form of mandates is important enough to be treated separately. I refer to permanent appropriations to aid individuals and groups and special tax provisions with similar purposes. Although not strictly legacies because the applicable law can be changed, the real politics of doing so are excruciatingly difficult as current conditions demonstrate.

Out-year financial problems are a function of the tenuousness and often unreliable estimates of the costs of permanent appropriations and tax expenditures, or of the sheer unwillingness to deal with the consequences of these commitments. Unless such obligations are properly accounted for, or a way is provided to adjust automatically for changed conditions, again the temptation is to promise something without recognizing and taking into account the anticipated future costs. This legacy category can be especially hard on states' governments, as shown in the following discussion.

HOW LEGACY-TYPE COMMITMENTS CAN AFFECT STATES AND LOCALITIES

I have had the privilege of serving as an appointed official, assistant director of the U.S. Office of Management and Budget for human resource programs. The first years of the Nixon administration, before Watergate, were actually good times for intergovernmental finances. President Nixon put forward a domestic program called the New Federalism, featuring revenue sharing (basically new and additional and unconditional fiscal assistance payments to states and principally local governments) and block grants with "sweeteners" (i.e., consolidated categorical grants provided on a broadened basis with additional funds intended to win congressional support).

Now in the aftermath of the Great Recession, rather than a New Federalism policy, there is a "no federalism" policy in the form of enacted and anticipated reductions in federal grants-in-aid to state and local governments. This is federalism topsy-turvy. The following sections discuss the state-local consequences of financial legacy strategies in this setting.

Pensions and Benefits

In July 2012, the Ravitch-Volcker task force report on the state budget crisis focused on six major threats, prominent among them underfunded retirement promises.[4] Three months later, the task force issued a widely noted special report on Illinois's fiscal problems, which among its main findings said, "Illinois has the worst unfunded liability of any state, estimated at $85 billion."[5] Then in December 2012, when Donald J. Boyd identified the seven worst-condition state-local pension funds in terms of their unfunded accrued liabilities, he found that Illinois accounted for close to 70 percent of the total.[6]

This problem for Illinois is multifaceted. The state is an outlier among states and localities in terms of its pension and benefit obligations, hence limiting its opportunity to build a coalition for national action.[7] Similar to Donald Boyd, Alicia H. Munnell, in her book on state and local government pensions, concluded that, on the whole, the majority of plans face a manageable challenge.[8] Moreover, while the federal government provides pension fund insurance for private employers, there is no direct way to extend the program to state and local governments.

The dilemma in this area, as in Illinois, is legal, in fact often constitutional, binding the jurisdiction to fulfill its defined-benefit pensions and health benefits. This despite the fact that the situation is changing in jurisdictions that are making pension arrangements similar to those in the private sector. Generally, public workers receive guaranteed pension and health benefits, whereas the Ravitch-Volcker task force notes that, in private employment, such defined-benefit arrangements "are disappearing rapidly."[9]

There are more than 3,400 state and local government pension systems in the United States. Most are at the state level and have trustees that are independent of the government that has a fiduciary responsibility to beneficiaries.

A key issue in this area involves assumptions about the returns earned on pension assets. If the anticipated level of earnings is set at too high a rate (8 percent is common), lower market-level returns that occur (often much lower) can cause serious difficulties, sometimes leading pension managers to skip or underfund payments due. Or even worse, shortfalls can cause them to invest in high-risk assets that can backfire and make an already bad situation much worse.

Efforts in the public sector to increase the retirement age and create special tiers of lower benefits for new hires can help this situation, but the fundamental financial problems remain. For local governments in large urban areas where public services tend to be labor-intensive, this situation can be grim: too many promises and not enough seriousness about how to fulfill them. The result can be situations in which governments that are already crisis-stricken become increasingly desperate and in which overlying and similarly hard-pressed state governments are unable (or at least see themselves in this way) to come to their rescue.

For the country as a whole, a report from the Pew Center on the States showed a widening gap of $1.38 trillion for public employees' retirement systems in fiscal 2010 because of governments failing "to have saved enough to pay retirement bills." This is "a nine percent increase from the year previous."[10] These obligations, which in many states also cover local employee pensions (e.g., teachers, police officer, fire fighters), include health and life insurance benefits, which the Pew report notes tend to be in worse shape; according to the Pew analysis, they are funded on average at a level equivalent to 5 percent of the contributions needed.

A dramatic example of pension and health benefit woes that received wide publicity is the bankruptcy of Stockton, California, which with 300,000 residents is to date the biggest U.S. city to file for bankruptcy protection. Its action triggered a fight between the city's bondholders and its obligations to the California Public Employees Retirement Systems (CALPERS), which has constitutional first rights in "the chain of creditors' claims."[11] (CALPERS pensioners are evenly distributed, with one third each from local governments, school districts, and the state.) The issue of whether public-employee unions and CALPERS are protected could land in federal courts.[12]

Infrastructure

Politicians are sometimes chided for having an "edifice complex"—build now, pay later. Economically, it makes sense to amortize capital investments in cases where an anticipated revenue stream is available to support a bond issue that reflects the useful life of an asset. Federal policy encourages this through the tax exemption for interest on municipal bonds.

While "infrastructure is the foundation of economic growth and development," of all the categories of potential legacy problems, this area is the hardest to assess.[13] Although the American Society of Civil Engineers (ASCE) is a party at interest, the most widely cited source of data on unfulfilled infrastructure needs is the ASCE's annual report card on the nation's infrastructure deficit. In 2012 it was reported at $2.2 trillion. ASCE report cards assign grades to various categories of capital expenditures, with the lowest grades in 2012 assigned to roads, waterways, and water and wastewater treatment systems.

There are, however, no government-provided statistical sources that enable analysts to compare jurisdictions on the size and character of their capital needs or on the soundness of their infrastructure expenditures. How, for example, can analysts assess what is an overinvestment in a public facility because of the apparent ease by which it can be deficit financed or cases in which a politically questionable high-visibility project is viewed by government leaders as "too attractive to pass up"? Infrastructure legacy problems like this can only be detected in the interstices of state and local finances by digging into the descriptions of capital expenditures where the definition of "useful life" can be stretched (sometimes beyond recognition) and where borrowing in capital budgets can inappropriately include funding for operating expenditures.

Some kinds of capital spending are by their very nature a hard sell—for example, maintenance expenditures for a new roof, replacement windows, painting, and pointing on even a favored public facility. Michael Pagano emphasizes this problem, observing that the preservation and maintenance of infrastructure is "notoriously underfunded," and recommends corrective action.[14] Other examples of hard-to-sell capital expenditures are for underground assets (e.g., sewers, water pipes, and broadband wiring), and assets that are not particularly loved, such as waste treatment plants and disposal facilities.

In the political arena, seemingly essential or hurry-up needs can cause questionable infrastructure investments for economic development and job creation purposes. Such attitudes can result in fast-tracking pressured decisions on deals that do not (and maybe never could) produce economic benefits. The argument is "build it and they will come." Or, "if you don't build it, your neighbor will." Construct an industrial park; provide road and utility access for a new factory or commercial development; construct development-related new university buildings and dormitories, even a stadium.[15] The not-so-gentle politics of economic development can cause state and local officials to make questionable political deals or even enter into out-and-out unethical deals.

In 2012 the *New York Times* conducted a ten-month study of business tax incentives, constructing an $80.4 billion database of 1,874 state and local incentive programs. The editors' conclusion was decidedly downbeat, calling such competition "fierce" but also "foolhardy and shortsighted."[16]

A dramatic example of local investment decisions gone bad is derivative and swap transactions and related political payoffs involving bankers, lawyers, and public officials in the Jefferson County, Alabama, sewer-bond scandal. A five-page, seventeen-year timeline from 1996 to 2011 published about this $3.1 billion project shows twenty-one people as having been convicted or pleading guilty to "corruption-related charges in connection with the sewer construction and financing, including three onetime [county] commissioners."[17]

Even under what investment markets regard as acceptable methods, fiscally tight times can be an incentive for entering into questionable long-term financial deals, pushing payments way out into the future. A 2012 *New York Times* article described the financing of a school to be constructed in Poway Unified School District in California, where not "a dime of interest or principal [will be paid] for more than two decades," thereby passing current construction costs to the next generation of residents.[18] The district's most recent bond issue was reported to have a total repayment ratio of 9.3 times the principal amount.

An example of the complicated politics of decisions involving public capital stock is the sale of Chicago's parking meters to a private company. This seems to have been done in order to raise revenue by raising parking rates, which according to one analyst was accomplished in a way "the city council was not willing to entertain."[19] While there is a lot to unpack in this example, economically the legacy result was pretty straightforward—more revenue now for the city and less political anxiety for its leaders. Another Chicago example of a widely used infrastructure legacy technique is tax increment financing (i.e., selling bonds based on the anticipated enhanced future revenue streams attributable to public improvements). This is appropriate if soundly structured, but by its very nature is hard to do, hard to assess, and, indeed, often very hard to find out about.[20]

Mandates from Higher Levels of Government

Since the mid-1960s, mandates from "on high" (particularly federal government mandates) have been cited as examples of legacy-producing financial actions, often in the form of requirements under federal grants-in-aid to state and local governments or state grants to localities. Such requirements often are perceived to be (and actually may be) underfunded or even *un*funded requirements. Over the years, grant-in-aid related mandates have become increasingly controversial.

There is often a catch-22 with grant-in-aid money. By accepting the funds, the recipient jurisdiction accepts requirements, not only about their use, but that also broadly affect the conduct of their affairs far into the future in the aided functional area. A National Science Foundation report referred to such grant-in-aid conditions as "orders that induce responsibility, action, procedure or anything else [and as being] imposed by constitutional, executive or judicial action."[21]

This regulatory effect often occurs for state aid to localities, particularly school aid and support for public safety (police and fire) requirements, which can come with strings that cause underfunded or unfunded obligations to be undertaken. Get the money now. Agree to the requirements attached; pay the consequences later. This point applies both to fiscal subventions and generalized directives from state governments to local governments that are not attached to any form of intergovernmental payment. The latter can be the case, for example, for limitations on and requirements pertaining to the levying of local property and sales taxes. One example in Chicago is state laws requiring the Chicago Transit Authority to provide reduced-fare ridership for seniors and the disabled.[22] The rationale may be laudatory—protecting special classes of people (e.g. seniors, veterans, and the disabled) or assuring particular types of activities (e.g., extra night-time police surveillance and safety devices)—but the result is costly nonetheless.

Over the years, scorecards for mandates under federal grants-in-aid have produced hot controversies for particular functional areas of government, notably environmental protection and aid under the Americans with Disabilities Act of 1990 and the 2001 No Child Left Behind Act (providing federal school aid). The crescendo of these controversies came in the mid-1990s with the 1994 Contract with America, the manifesto that enabled Republicans to gain control of the 104th Congress. The Congress passed and President Clinton signed the Unfunded Reform Act of 1995 (UMRA).[23] This law turned out to be a disaster for the Advisory Commission on Intergovernmental Relations (ACIR), of which I was a member. The law required the commission to report to the Congress on the costs of unfunded mandates.

The ACIR had been established under President Eisenhower. It operated for thirty-seven years until September 1996, when it was defunded by the same 104th Congress that passed the UMRA law as part of the Republicans' program to pare down the number of U.S. government agencies. The commission was small (it had a $1 million budget), hence it was an easy target for congressional agency cutters despite the fact that the ACIR's premise and purpose—to enhance the knowledge of U.S. federalism—would seem to be consistent with Republican doctrine. But, Republican doctrine aside, we could not save the ACIR.

In my opinion, the structure of the ACIR was fundamentally flawed. The commission had too many members. The four categories for its twenty-six members were: six members of Congress appointed by the House and Senate leadership; fourteen state and local officials—four governors, three state legislators, four mayors, and three county officials, all appointed by the president from nominations by the respective national organizations of state and local governments; three representatives of the executive branch appointed by the president; and three private citizens, also appointed by the president.

When the ACIR produced its required mandate report on the cost of existing federal mandates, groups representing environmental and disability interests came at us hammer and tongs. Some of the criticisms were from federal agencies that had officials who were members of the commission. Now they joined in denouncing the report.

The commission caved. In an unprecedented action, we voted to rescind our own report. Nevertheless, the ACIR was legislated out of existence in 1996. The story of what happened to the ACIR dramatizes how hard it is to provide sound, respected analyses of state and local and intergovernmental finances. I return to this experience later in this chapter.

Mandates in the Form of Entitlements

This fourth category of financial legacies involves a particular type of federal grant-in-aid. As I already noted, permanent appropriations and tax expenditures that bestow benefits on favored groups warrant treatment distinct from mandates. The Medicaid program was singled out as first among the "major threats to state fiscal sustainability" by the Ravitch Volcker task force.[24] I use this example and pertinent recent events in what follows.

The U.S. Supreme Court decision on the Patient Protection Affordable Care Act (ACA) broke new ground for federalism pertaining to the Medicaid program. Even though Medicaid is not technically a mandate because states can chose not to receive federal grant funds for this program, all fifty states operate the program. Many requirements come along with this federal money. What the Affordable Care Act did was to substantially ramp up these requirements. In the decision on the constitutionality of the ACA, seven justices agreed to uphold most of the provisions of the new law, but they rejected the mandated eligibility expansion of the Medicaid program that required states to extend Medicaid coverage in 2014 to all persons in households earning up to 138 percent of the federal poverty line (FPL).

Officials from a number of states, particularly conservative states that tend to have the lowest income eligibility levels for Medicaid benefits, pounced on what they saw as a nice political opportunity. They asserted that their state would not adopt this now-voluntary Medicaid eligibility extension despite the generous federal matching funds offered for doing so. But the ink was hardly dry on their statements when interest groups on the other side (including hospitals, physicians, and advocacy groups) jumped into the fray.

Providers, particularly hospitals, claimed that in light of the reduction in the ACA of "their" funding (i.e., the federal aid they receive for treating low-income patients), this is just too much: "This is supposed to be *our* money!" That is to say, it is money they would otherwise lose if their state took advantage of the mandate in the Affordable Care Act to reject the Medicaid expansion to 138 percent of the federal poverty line. Hospital officials in particular stressed the argument that under the ACA they are now required to treat all patients who come to their emergency rooms.

The point for this discussion is that this debate has created enormous uncertainty in American federalism as to the way in which, and the extent to which, the federal government can use conditions on grants-in-aid to convey future obligations to the states. (This question continued to be a major unknown after the 2012 elections in conjunction with the implementation of the ACA.)

IMPLICATIONS FOR STATE AND LOCAL BUDGETING AND FINANCE

Although we have now considered the four types of potential state and local problem-producing legacy-type financial arrangements, it isn't possible to present simple and uniform types of budget reforms that would apply in situations like these that could be dealt with by changing state and local budget procedures and financial practices. The financial factors intrinsic to doing this can't be separated out and treated independently from other fiscal accountability challenges. The kinds of changes that would be needed to ameliorate legacy-producing conditions in state and local budgeting involve fiscal accountability problems such as those discussed below that occur on an across-the-board basis in state and local budgeting and finance.

Failure to Face Up to the Costs of Promises Made

Referring to the transparency of legacy commitments, the Ravitch-Volcker report emphasized pensions and workers' benefits as a major threat to fiscal sustainability.

> In both financial reporting and budgeting, future obligations to repay debt are routinely revealed. However, . . . future obligations to workers' pension and other benefits are inadequately and confusingly disclosed. . . . *liabilities* for pensions and retiree benefits are generally understated on financial statements, although considerable amounts of important data are reported in notes and required supplemental information expenses. Furthermore, expenses on the financial statements are often understated, while the numbers disclosed in footnotes are measured in ways that can underestimate liabilities very substantially in comparison to liabilities estimated in accordance with principles of financial economics. Current accounting, actuarial and disclosure rules make it difficult for non-experts to understand the extent of state and

local governments' liabilities for pensions and employee retirement health care and their likely effects on future budgets.[25]

The Lure of Budget Gimmicks

In the budgeting world in which the bottom line is only what most people hear and know about, the lure of budget gimmickry can tempt even the most professional budget and finance official. One can delay making a payment to the next fiscal year, lowball anticipated costs, overstate anticipated revenues, recommend "old chestnut"–type savings (i.e., relying on perennial budget cuts that never happened in the past and couldn't possibly pass muster now). In this way, budget gimmicks are a type of legacy action to hand something off to the future. Another such tactic, although generally of shorter duration, is to delay the issuance of financial reports (in particular Comprehensive Annual Financial Reports—CAFRs) that are crucial to open government or make them difficult if not impossible to decipher.[26]

The Ravitch-Volcker task force, like other groups, emphasized the need for "rainy-day funds," what might be called legacy-protection devices and discusses how they should be established—*and saved*. But this, too, (i.e., their existence) presents a temptation in situations in which these and other supposedly separate budget accounts can be "borrowed" in hard times.

Interpreting Financial Information for Multiple Local Government Entities

Achieving fiscal responsibility is hardest for the local governments at the bottom of the federalism feeding chain. Three words capture why this is so. The first is *diversity*. Local governments vary tremendously in what they do, what their authority is, what they spend, and how they tax. Not only are they diverse, but there is also a high level of jurisdictional *fragmentation* among them. There are lots of local governments—over 87,000, according to the U.S. Bureau of the Census. Moreover, this diverse and fragmented situation is complicated by the way many local units are triple and quadruple *layered* so taxpayers have little or no idea of who they are paying for what services.

Counties have different roles. In some states, they are very powerful; in others there are no counties at all, or they are merely judicial districts. Likewise, cities, towns, villages (other general-purpose units of government) vary widely in their functions and finances. One reason for this is the complicated way (especially in large urban areas) citizens rely on special districts and public authorities that are responsible for particular local functions and services (e.g., mass transit, sanitation, waste disposal and treatment, parks, utilities, libraries, cemeteries). One can argue that governmental consolidation should be the "solution" for local governmental complexity, but that is not easy to accomplish and, in fact, in some places and cases it is not the most desirable thing to do.[27] All three of these intrinsic local government characteristics are reasons why budget and financial officials in local government have a hard time making their mark.

One would hope professional oversight capability existed in all government levels to decipher, explain, and deal with conditions like these, but finance and budget agencies (which in many states and localities became larger, stronger, and more professional in the post–World War II period) seem to be losing ground. Political exigencies and strategies, like the ones I discuss in this chapter, that are advocated by political leaders often limit the power and influence of the agencies.

What about external oversight? Outside of government, there are precedents of watchdog organizations that promote sound, transparent budgeting and call attention to difficulties that arise. But there aren't enough of such organizations, and there are problems with their role and questions about who sponsors them. The ovararching questions about external oversight come down to who will pay for such oversight, and how will it be staffed and kept honest?

Governmental research bureaus at colleges and universities can play this role, though often they are not in a good position to do this. Often they are small and their work is not the most revered of academic functions. Besides, when public colleges and universities play this role (most such agencies tend to be located there), they frequently have their own agendas and needs that require them to stay on the right side of political leaders.

Budget Theory and Techniques

A body of work in political science treats budgeting as incremental, an annual process of adding to the base of existing commitments. One could argue that what is needed today is not incremental budgeting but professional skills and techniques for *decremental* budgeting—ways to make hard choices. Unlike "blue-ribbon" groups that study how to deal with new problems, the need now is for "red-ribbon" budget systems and techniques to contract lower-priority government programs and constrain public spending.

Decremental public budgeting approaches are not unprecedented. At the national level, military base–closing commissions to wind down Cold War military facilities have been created three times since 1998. No politician wants to close a base in his or her state or district, but most agreed that the ending of the Cold War required reductions in the nation's military establishments. The base-closing commissions produced lists of proposed closures and reductions on a "take-it-or-leave it" basis where the president and the Congress had to vote up or down. They could not change the list proposed. As it turned out, the recommendations of all three commissions were adopted.

One can think of this as a designated-driver approach to budgeting. Politicians knew where they wanted to go and also knew they have habits and proclivities that made it hard for them to get there. The base-closing process, while not simon-pure politically, provided an element of political insulation: "Sorry friends, I had no choice. Really. I tried to keep the 'Our-Town' army reserve base, but the process just wouldn't let me."[28]

At the state level, a process like this was used successfully in New York State in 2005–6 to rationalize acute-care and long-term care health facilities. An eighteen-member commission held hearings in six regions of the state (I chaired this process for the northern region) and submitted proposals to the governor and the legislature on a take-it-or-leave-it basis affecting fifty-seven facilities, including nine closures and a larger number of merger and reorganizations that reduced the state's overall hospital system by 4,200 beds, a 7 percent reduction.

Similar approaches have been tried without as much success, to institute sunset provisions and triggers for meeting budget-reduction goals in other functional areas. When the prescription drug benefit was added to Medicare in 2003, the Congress instructed the president that if the Medicare actuary found that the program was "under fiscal duress," he was to present cost-saving proposals to the Congress that required facilitated action. The first two things happened: there was "fiscal duress," and presidential proposals to deal with it that were submitted to the Congress. But, the third thing—facilitated action—did not occur. The Congress quietly adopted a rule that relieved its members of having to consider the president's proposals.[29]

POSSIBLE APPROACHES

The state-local public sector accounts for 18 percent of the gross domestic product and employs one in six workers in the national labor force. The lack of information and understanding of the finances of state and local governments obscures a growing fiscal crisis. There is in my view a crucial need for regular, accessible, user-friendly, trusted, unbiased reports on the conditions and challenges of U.S. state and local finance. Small organizations, particularly those that have an agenda of their own, can't fill this void despite the fact that their work is valuable and serves many important purposes.

Returning to John Kingdon's insightful writing on how public policy agenda building should be viewed and how agendas emerge, this may be a time and there may be an opportunity for a coming together of the problem stream and the political stream (in conjunction with an outpouring of public and voter concern) about the condition of the United States economy and the "fiscal cliff" in a changed and changing global setting. There is a pressing need to devise ways to bridge the academic and policy divide in the nation.

It is a big proposition, but I hope advantage can be taken of the current window of opportunity to create a constituency for raising both the standards and the awareness of the importance of sound public finances and budget practices. In the U.S. domestic public sector, such a movement is clearly needed to clarify, explain, and rationalize the role and finances of the state-local public sector.

The essential problem is *not* that we don't have enough information, but that we have *too much* of it and it's too dispersed.

In the rest of this chapter, I suggest institution building for domestic public finance that takes account of available data and existing organizations and interests.[30] The greatest problems the Advisory Commission on Intergovernmental Relations (ACIR) had in carrying out its mission were that it was small and obscure and that its structure permitted too many interests to advance their multiple and diverse agendas.

Many organizations provide solid data and analyze them wisely to highlight state-local financial trends and conditions. For example, the Center on Budget and Policy Priorities (CBPP), the Pew Center on the States, and the Tax Foundation have capable, good-sized staffs, and high standards of analysis, yet they each are pursuing their own domestic policy goals. Research centers that study domestic issues and finances include the Urban Institute, the Brookings Institution, the American Enterprise Institute, the Heritage Foundation, and the Cato Institute. A financial oversight role is also played by public-interest organizations that represent states and localities (governors, legislators, mayors, counties, budget officials) or are active in particular functional areas of public affairs. This group also includes the Nelson A. Rockefeller Institute of Government, the Ravitch-Volcker Task Force on the State Fiscal Crisis, and many universities that sponsor and support public finance research centers, as in the case of the University of Illinois at Chicago, the host for the UIC Urban Forum. But candor requires that I point out that most of these organizations and the studies involved are limited in staffing or specialized in their activities. Their revenue sources are often sporadic and tied to specific time-sensitive projects and issues.

In my view, one national organization best represents what is needed and should originate institution and agenda building that raises the standards and awareness of government budgeting and public finance: the Congressional Budget Office.

Of all of the agencies and actors in what Kingdon in broad terms calls the "policy primeval soup," the CBO has emerged since its establishment in 1974 as the principal nonpartisan scorekeeper on the costs and consequences of new public policies and the setting in which they operate.[31]

I would like to put on the table ideas for creating a CBO-led consortium on state-local public budgeting and financial conditions. The money at stake for the U.S. economy is surely important enough to warrant investment in institution building for this purpose. It shouldn't be a peanut-sized public entity like the ACIR or even an up-sized ACIR. In the scheme of things in government, a system that fulfills the function envisioned here would not (at least by my standards) be expensive in relation to the need.

So, here is food for thought: Create a new deputy directorship and office at CBO for state and local finance that would be the center point for a consortium of federal offices and agencies that disseminate the types of data, research, and analysis to be input into a system of regular, online, user-friendly reports and studies on state-local finance. This consortium would include designated representatives from the Governments Division of the Bureau of the Census, which has had a historic role in this field for sixty years; the Department of Commerce's closely related Bureau of Economic Analysis; the Department of Labor's Bureau of Labor Statistics; the Government Accountability Office, which has an excellent track record for conducting in-depth state and local field studies; and the Congressional Research Service, which covers many important subjects in this territory—an alphabet soup of federal organizations and agencies that do work that should be pulled together under this proposed system for regularly reporting on state-local finances. The consortium would not have a policy agenda but would instead *provide regular information in digestible form.*

However this new office is composed, its main output should be regular reports, along with special state-local finance studies, on state and local government financial trends, conditions, and processes. In essence, this would involve *putting in time* (yes, time) the commitments and revenues of U.S. state and local governments. In addition, there should be special studies that focus on key aspects of state and local budgeting (both operating and capital) and the roles, structure, and finances of state and local governments, not all 89,000 of them, but the larger ones.

The Congressional Budget Office's convener role, working with other federal research and data-collection offices and agencies, should not be to produce large books like the ACIR's annual volumes, *Significant Features of Fiscal Federalism*. The work of the new consortium should be posted online. Printable, yes, but that's the individual's decision. Make your own bookshelf.

Among the steps involved in establishing such a consortium would be to decide what summarized regular indicators of state-local finance should be highlighted. Setting up such a system, for example, would provide an excellent opportunity to revive and revise the representative revenue and expenditure indices developed by the ACIR. These measures, which no longer exist, allowed the public and public officials to compare state and local taxes and expenditures on a basis that controlled for difference in their political structure, economic conditions, and public needs.[32] There are also lacunae of federal sources of information on grants-in-aid to state and localities; data sources that previously performed this role should be revived.

The consortium should lead in these ways and others to provide comparative across-the-board data and analysis. It should also conduct and sponsor special studies in major functional areas of government.

Its website should be a regular, must-open source nationally, regionally, and locally, providing explanations of local government finances, conditions, and trends in understandable form for the general public.

In addition, the consortium should issue quarterly reports on conditions and trends and an annual that includes pull-out reports for each state. All of its reports should have online guides so ordinary personal-computer users can access input data used in the consortium's reporting and analysis functions.

In sum, my experiences as a member of the Ravitch-Volcker Task Force, which at some point will go out of existence, in the conduct of state-local financial studies at the Brookings Institution, as a member of the late-lamented ACIR, and at the Rockefeller Institute of Government lead me to this conclusion: *There is a critical need for a centralized, well positioned, independent oversight capacity on state and local finances on a continuing, prominent basis that securely institutionalizes this function.*

Notes

1. John W. Kingdon, *Agendas, Alternatives, and Public Policies*, 2nd ed. (New York: Longman, 1995). As a teacher, I am indebted to Kingdon for the effective way this book works in the classroom.

2. Kingdon, *Agendas*, 1.

3. State Budget Crisis Task Force, *Report of the State Budget Crisis Task Force: Illinois Report*, October 2012, http://www.statebudgetcrisis.org/wpcms/report-1/, accessed May 15, 2013.

4. Ibid., 9–11.

5. Ibid., 7. I am indebted to David Merriman, associate director of the University of Illinois Institute of Government and Public Affairs, for his assistance and research on Illinois state pension issues.

6. Donald J. Boyd, *Fiscal Challenges of Public Sector Pensions*, Forum of the TIAA-CREF Institute and the Rockefeller Institute of Government, New York City, December 7, 2012, 4.

7. State governments cannot declare bankruptcy; although local governments can do so, they rarely take advantage of this bombshell option. I discuss rare exceptions later in the chapter.

8. Alicia H. Munnell, *State and Local Pensions: What Now?* (Washington, D.C.: Brookings Institution Press, 2012).

9. State Budget Crisis Task Force, *Report*, 3.

10. Pew Center on the States, *The Widening Gap Update*, issue brief, June 2012, http://www.pewstates.org/uploadedFiles/PCS_Assets/2012/Pew_Pensions_Update.pdf, accessed May 15, 2013.

11. John E. Petersen, "Stockton, California's Debt Problems May Set Precedent," Governing the States and Localities, May 2012, http://www.governing.com/columns/public-finance/col-stockton-californias-debt-problems-may-set-precedent.html, accessed May 15, 2013. Petersen passed away shortly before this final column appeared in Governing.

12. Petersen, "Stockton." See also Peter Henderson, "Assured Says Stockton Bankruptcy Plan Unfair, Favors CALPERS," Reuters, August 1, 2012.

13. Michael A. Pagano, *Funding and Investing in Infrastructure*, Urban Institute, December 2011, 2. He cites Utah for its model for five-year capital planning systems, urging its adoption by other states.

14. Pagano, *Funding*, 12.

15. Richard Gazarik, "Debt Mounts from State School Spending Boom," Trib-Live News, July 23, 2012, http://triblive.com/news/2055351–74/state-system-million-building-debt-university-projects-rating-california-convocation, accessed February 11, 2012. Pennsylvania's fourteen state-owned universities were accused of having accrued a nearly $1 billion debt that reflected unwise decisions to build "luxurious dormitories and elaborate academic facilities." State higher education agency officials

said in their defense that they were caught in a "campus arms race." But critics called it a "never ending spending merry-go-round."

16. "Race to the Bottom," editorial, *New York Times*, December 5, 2012, http://www.nytimes.com/2012/12/06/opinion/race-to-the-bottom.html?_r=0, accessed February 11, 2013.

17. William Selway, "Jefferson County's Journey from Sewer-Bond Scandal to Settlement: Timeline," *Bloomberg News*, September 16, 2011.

18. Floyd Norris, "Schools Pass Debt to the Next Generation," *New York Times*, August 17, 2012.

19. Ibid.

20. For an illuminating treatment of infrastructure privatization, see Philip Ashton, Marc Doussard, and Rachel Weber, "The Financial Engineering of Infrastructure Privatization," *Journal of the American Planning Association* 78:3 (2012): 300–312. The article warns "against leaving money on the table" when entering into such transactions and describes factors to consider to prevent doing so.

21. Catherine H. Lovell, Max Neiman, Robert Kneisel, Adam Rose, and Charles Tobin, *Federal and State Mandating on Local Governments Report to the National Science Foundation* (Riverside: University of California, 1979), 32. For this citation and generally for this section, I found the Wikipedia entry on "Unfunded Mandate" most helpful: http://en.wikipedia.org/wiki/Unfunded_mandate, accessed December 10, 2012.

22. Correspondence with Forrest Claypool, president, Chicago Transit Authority.

23. The Congressional Budget Office (CBO) is required under this law to report annually above a cost of $71 million. Twenty such reports were issued from 2007 to 2011 according to the Congressional Budget Office, "A Review of CBO's Activities in 2011 Under the Unfunded Mandates Reform Act," March 2012. See my discussion later in this chapter regarding the mandate-reporting requirement.

24. State Budget Crisis Task Force, *Report*, 15–22.

25. Ibid.

26. CAFRs are crucial and at the same time typically varied in their form and terminology; very often they are hard to decipher and work with even for the best-intentioned observers.

27. Proponents of the public-choice theory of local government argue that there are different service sheds for different local public services such that the way these units are configured in varied sizes and on an overlapping basis is often rational.

28. Richard P. Nathan, "Reinventing Government: What Does It Mean?" *Public Administration Review*, March–April 1995, 213–15.

29. I am indebted to Rudy Penner, who called this to my attention.

30. I herewith express my appreciation to my Rockefeller Institute colleague Donald J. Boyd and G. Edward DeSeve for their assistance on this section. I take full responsibility for the conclusions reached and proposals advanced.

31. Kingdon, *Agendas*, 1. "Policy primeval soup" is his term for the many political settings for policy decision making.

32. Yesim Yilmaz, Sonya Hoo, Matthew Nagowski, Kim Rueben, and Robert Tannenwald, *Measuring Fiscal Disparities across the U.S. States: A Representative Revenue System/Representative Expenditure System Approach* Fiscal 2002, Urban Institute, November 2006. See also Yesim Yilmaz, Sonya Hoo, Matthew Nagowski, Kim Rueben, and Robert Tannenwald, *Fiscal Capacity Across States, FY 2002*, Urban–Brookings Tax Policy Center, no. 16, January 2007, for state-by-state findings. Table 2 shows per capita, index, and rank scores for each state for revenue capacity, revenue effort, expenditure need, expenditure effort, and fiscal capacity. If a successor to these studies is considered, a principal challenge would be to translate and express the findings so they could be understandable by and accessible to a general audience.

Legacy Infrastructure Costs

Is the Cure Worse than the Disease?

DISCUSSANT: PHILIP ASHTON,
UNIVERSITY OF ILLINOIS AT CHICAGO

In this response to Richard Nathan's analysis of legacy costs, I focus more closely on the practices of managing legacy costs. Nathan's prescriptions for managing those costs are mostly *procedural*—he advocates more transparent decision making, greater scope for expert analysis, and tighter controls on the budgetary process. As the problems facing U.S. states and local governments in the wake of the 2008 financial crisis and Great Recession have become more compelling, I argue we need to assess the *content* of a short list of commonsense "fixes" that have emerged within policy communities and public discourse. These include, on the employment side, the privatization of government services and the restructuring of public-sector compensation packages along with changes in the right of public unions to bargain. My general concern is that these short-term fixes could do substantial harm over the long run by shaping a new set of legacy costs. I elaborate this concern from the perspective of infrastructure, where attempts to address legacy costs have increasingly involved public-private partnerships (also known as P3s).

The range of P3s can be quite broad and involve a variety of public-private configurations to deal with aging infrastructure or facilitate new investment.[1] From the 1980s onward, U.S. states and localities increasingly turned to private investors to design, build, finance, or operate new toll roads, bridges, and other key pieces of infrastructure, using long-term leases or other means to convey operating rights to private-sector operators.[2] In the 2000s, Chicago was an early innovator in extending this model to "brownfield," or existing, assets; long-term leases on the Chicago Skyway Bridge in 2004 and subsequent deals for the underground parking system, metered street parking, and the attempted privatization of Chicago Midway International Airport in 2008 all helped shape the U.S. market for brownfield infrastructure.[3] These deals often included controversial provisions—including long-lease terms (up to ninety-nine years in many cases), aggressive tolls, and noncompete clauses that limit the ability of the public sector to approve new infrastructure that might draw users (and revenues) away—that are now considered standard for U.S. deals.[4]

Since the onset of the Great Recession, there has been no lag in these deals.[5] Instead, there has been a supply push as cash-strapped localities have looked to reduce legacy costs or transform long-term revenue streams into up-front payments to fill deficits or raise cash. In extreme circumstances—for example, in Michigan, Pennsylvania, and New Jersey—asset privatization has been promoted as an emergency measure to deal with the imminent insolvency of local governments.

These moves are attractive for obvious reasons. They provide immediate cash infusions to localities, allowing the retiring of debt to improve municipal credit ratings. They reduce long-term operating-expense commitments, addressing looming legacy costs by shifting the risks (and rewards) to private-sector operators. They seem to protect the integrity of the asset, often mandating a maintenance schedule and requiring that the private concessionaire pay for capital improvements. Used creatively, they can also be used to leverage new investment and improved efficiency—for instance, through the adoption of electronic tolling on roads.[6]

However, there are several causes for concern in the recent wave of infrastructure deals. First, many of these deals have been criticized for their lack of transparency in decision making. Deals are often developed and approved without substantial public input or oversight or are accomplished on crash timetables—often only a matter of days.[7] Related to Nathan's concern over the adequacy of information is a concern over the lack of analysis used to justify the deals; none of the major Chicago infrastructure leases appears to have been vetted by analyses that address the long-term loss of planning capability through noncompete clauses or private control of rate setting. Privatization raises the concern that the deals may result in greater congestion or gridlock because critical transportation functions are handed over to the private sector.[8]

Second, the development of the market for brownfield infrastructure also raises a number of concerns over whether the deals are as good as they seem or whether the public sector can be an equal partner in its bargaining with investors. High bid prices paid to states and localities have been accompanied by contractual terms that either seem overly generous to bidders or expose the city to long-term risks. For instance, U.S. infrastructure deals have tended to have much longer terms than those in jurisdictions with experience in asset privatization, such as South America or Europe.[9] In a recent analysis conducted with UIC colleagues, I found the cash proceeds of offering a fifty-year over a ninety-nine-year deal to be not substantially different, raising the value of the bid price by only 15 percent.[10] In effect, by offering forty-nine extra years for only a marginal increase in up-front payment, the public sector is handing over long-term revenue opportunities for free.

It's also clear that the new generation of buyers—consisting primarily of investment banks or infrastructure funds specializing in capital market access, as opposed to the engineering conglomerates that specialize in building and operating infrastructure—are attracted not to long-term ownership and management but rather to the extraction of maximum short-term payouts.[11] These are produced through aggressive fee increases that outpace inflation, noncompete or other clauses that protect the investment's value or that require compensation for lost revenue, or high levels of leverage combined with the use of financial engineering—interest rate swaps and other structured debt techniques—that manipulate cash flow to speed payments to investors.[12] Whereas these provisions help to increase the value of the concession for investors (and payouts to localities), they also expose the deals to much higher levels of risk—risks that revenue projections will not be sufficient to support debt service, or that lenders and counterparties will refuse to roll over credit. The concession contracts supposedly protect the public sector's interest in the case of default, but under such circumstances the city would face a limited menu of options, including: reassuming financial responsibility by taking the asset (and its debt) back onto its books; wiping out creditors and cancelling the deal; or renegotiating the deal to produce conditions for renewed profitability.[13] As such, the idea that these deals shift costs and risks from the public sector is somewhat illusory, and recent defaulted deals in places like Denver or San Diego highlight the capacity of failed deals to produce new legacy costs for states and localities.

Third, as infrastructure privatization increasingly becomes part of the solution set for cash-strapped localities, I would argue that we have few means to evaluate the long-term planning and fiscal consequences. That is, as asset privatization ceases to be a one-off response to specific infrastructure needs and instead becomes a broad strategy for managing legacy costs, it produces a set of uncertainties that states and localities are poorly equipped to address. An analogue here would be tax increment financing (TIF). The diversion of property tax revenues to pay for site-specific redevelopment might seem straightforward for a single deal, but there are unexpected consequences when this is implemented across one-fifth of the city's property tax base.[14] In the case of infrastructure privatization, does the city's revenue base become less resilient as it hands over multiple long-term revenue sources (toll fares, parking meter revenue, and landing fees) for up-front payments? Similarly, it is reasonable to ask if there is a saturation point to the use of higher user fees on multiple and successive concession contracts. Does the proliferation of user fees that comes with *widespread* privatization have the same effect as general tax increases would, shifting consumers' and business' incentives in ways that harm economic development? To return to the question posed by Nathan, do we have adequate decision-making tools to answer these questions in advance? Or are we blindly swapping one set of legacy costs for another?

This raises the question of what can responsibly be done to manage legacy infrastructure costs. I would argue that, whereas there is great scope for localities to define new innovative models for P3s, there is a pressing need for higher-level solutions. These should include implementing or reforming state P3 legislation to structures the infrastructure market to make it more rational. The supply push produced by fiscal distress is real, but we can avoid creating new kinds of legacy costs if the terms of concession agreements are subjected to due-process requirements, oversight, and regulation.[15] There are examples in this area; the earliest P3 legislation in Virginia in 1988 and the subsequent concession contract for the Dulles Greenway (opened in 1995) are notable for limiting the lease term to 42.5 years and for subjecting the toll road to public utility commission–style regulation of toll rates.[16] Alternately, federal programs such as the Obama's administration's proposed infrastructure bank could alter the decision context for cash-strapped localities by allowing them to raise least-cost funds to refinance debt or pay for new capital investments. These may not alter the fiscal pressures surrounding infrastructure investment and upkeep, but they may put localities in a better bargaining position with private investors and help localities avoid a situation in which short-term fixes shape future legacy costs.

Notes

1. Sasha Page, William Ankner, Cheryl Jones, and Robert Fetterman, "The Risks and Rewards of Private Equity in Infrastructure," *Public Works Management and Policy* 13:2 (2008): 100–113.

2. Jaime Rall, James Reed, and Nicholas Farber, *Public-Private Partnerships for Transportation: A Toolkit for Legislators* (Washington, D.C.: National Conference of State Legislators, 2010).

3. Phineas Baxandall, *Road Privatization: Explaining the Trend, Assessing the Facts and Protecting the Public* (Boston, Mass.: U.S. PIRG Education Fund, 2007).

4. Ellen Dannin, "Infrastructure Privatization Contracts and Their Effect on Governance," Legal Studies Research Paper No. 19–2009, Dickinson School of Law, Pennsylvania State University, 2009.

5. Harris Kenny and Adam Summers, *Annual Privatization Report 2011: Local Government Privatization* (Washington, D.C.: Reason Foundation, 2012).

6. Kenny and Summers, *Annual*, 5; Michael Pagano and David Perry, "Financing Infrastructure in the 21st Century City," *Public Works Management and Policy* 13:1 (2008): 22–38.

7. Office of the Inspector General, *Report of Inspector General's Findings and Recommendations: An Analysis of the Lease of the City's Parking Meters* (Chicago: Office of the Inspector General, City of Chicago, 2009).

8. Ibid.; Baxandall, *Road*, 3.

9. Germa Bel and John Foote, "Tolls, Terms, and Public Interest in Road Concessions Privatization: A Comparative Analysis of Recent Transactions in the U.S. and France," *Transport Reviews* 29:3 (2009): 397–413.

10. Philip Ashton, Marc Doussard, and Rachel Weber, "The Financial Engineering of Infrastructure Privatization: What Are Public Assets Worth to Private Investors?," *Journal of the American Planning Association* 78:3 (2012): 300–312.

11. Martin Lawrence and Geofrey Stapledon, "Infrastructure Funds: Creative Use of Corporate Structure and Law—But in Whose Interests?," unpublished manuscript, 2008, available at http://ssrn.com/abstract=1092689, accessed September 19, 2010.

12. Ashton et al., "Financial," 309; Page et al., "Risks," 100.

13. Dannin, "Infrastructure."

14. Rachel Weber, "Selling City Futures: The Financialization of Urban Redevelopment Policy," *Economic Geography* 86:3 (2010): 251–74.

15. Rall et al., *Public-Private*, 2.

16. Ibid.

Pension Costs and Durable Public Infrastructure

DISCUSSANT: DAVID MERRIMAN,
UNIVERSITY OF ILLINOIS AT CHICAGO

Richard Nathan has written an engaging and accessible general overview of issues related to "legacy costs" of government actions. His essay is dotted with colorful historical anecdotes and engaging facts. Nathan's sharp writing style, wit, wealth of knowledge, and historical experience stimulate thinking about many issues.

Nathan focuses on financial strategies that involve acting now and paying over time. He reminds us that "there is nothing intrinsically wrong with funding pension systems over time and amortizing revenue-producing capital assets" but notes that this may not work "so well in practice when the financial arrangements needed to accumulate pension-system investment income or pay the interest on municipal bonds are not in place and soundly structured."

No doubt state and local governments have gotten themselves into fiscal difficulties in many cases because of pensions and in rare cases because of public debt. I am less certain than Nathan that entitlements or mandates are a major cause of legacy (act-now pay-later) costs for state and local governments—Medicaid, the most important cost-sharing entitlement, is a strictly pay-as-you-go system. In my view, Medicaid-related financial problems stem from rapidly rising health care costs and concentrated poverty and have little to do with government officials' alleged short-sightedness.

When thinking about legacy costs, it is helpful to focus on a narrower range of issues than Nathan discusses. In particular, we should scrutinize underfunding of public pensions and mismanagement of investment in durable public infrastructure such as roads, bridges, and airports.

PUBLIC PENSIONS

There is widespread underfunding of public pensions, often (but not always) because governments have acted badly in the sense that they have not made sufficient contributions to fund the promised benefits. This observation should not be interpreted to let employee representatives—generally unions—off the hook. The amounts of government contributions are public knowledge, and the employee representatives (and the general electorate) bear responsibility for not objecting loudly enough or effectively enough to unsustainable policies.

Nathan sometimes falls into the trap of believing that this lack of foresightedness is intrinsically a public-sector problem (e.g., "Elected officials live in the present. They care about getting elected (or reelected) now. There are any number of ways they can satisfy desires now and pay later.") It is important to remember that the very term "legacy cost" apparently originated with the discussion of General Motors' competitive disadvantage vis-à-vis Japanese auto companies. The problem, it seems, was that GM steadily increased worker benefits (pension and health care) without putting aside sufficient funds to pay for them.[1] GM was not an isolated instance, and indeed many private-sector companies still underfund their pensions.[2] Of course, we might hope that competition in the private sector would eliminate such misbehavior, but this is not what happened in the case of GM or other large firms. Instead, the U.S. government formed the quasi-public Pension Benefit Guarantee Corporation (PBGC), which annually pays substantial benefits to participants in failed pension plans. PBGC is funded by insurance premiums paid by private-sector employers who have defined-benefit pension plans. As of this writing, public-sector employers are still not protected under the PBGC umbrella, perhaps because such employers have in the past rarely gone bankrupt or defaulted on pension obligations. Unfortunately, government fiscal problems are nearing a crisis stage and additional institutional protections are now necessary.

My main point here is that our society has developed private-sector institutions to deal with what seems to be our inherent tendency to, as Nathan puts it, "promise now, pay later." To date we have not developed good institutions to deal with this sort of behavior in the public sector. Nathan's policy proposal (a new CBO directorship), while constructive, is too timid on this point. Admittedly, constitutional restrictions specifically regarding sovereignty of states may make it more difficult for the federal government to impose fiscal discipline on states than it is to impose fiscal discipline on private-sector actors. Nevertheless, as Nathan points out, the federal government is quite good at getting state and local governments to do what it wants through mandates, matching funds, and the like. It seems likely that clever federal government lawyers could craft legislation that would essentially require state and local governments to fund public pensions responsibly (perhaps in exchange for some federal government perk) if the political will were there. Representatives of public employees would have a strong incentive to bring such legislation before the U.S. Congress. It is in the national interest to have fiscally sound public pension programs, and the federal government could, and should, do more.

INVESTMENT IN DURABLE PUBLIC INFRASTRUCTURE

In telling the sensational anecdote about the default by Jefferson County, Alabama, Nathan argues that "fiscally tight times can be an incentive for entering into questionable long-term financial deals, pushing payments way out into the future." It seems clear, however, that defaults on general-obligation bonds (those backed by the full faith and credit of a government) are rare and essentially unrelated to fiscal conditions.[3] This is unsurprising because lenders have just as much incentive to monitor the creditworthiness of municipal borrowers as do private borrowers. While unsophisticated municipal borrowers or investors sometimes are taken advantage of by unscrupulous people in the finance industry, this has little to do with legacy issues. As a country, we seem to want more and better regulation of the private-sector finance industry, which the Consumer Financial Protection Bureau was created in 2011 to address. It seems reasonable to ask for similar regulatory agencies to protect unsophisticated borrowers and investors in business and government.

Nathan argues that in "the political arena, seemingly essential or hurry-up needs can cause questionable infrastructure investments as, for example, for economic development and job creation purposes. Such attitudes can result in fast-tracking pressured decisions on deals that do not (and maybe never could) produce economic benefits."

While I agree with Nathan that infrastructure is "the hardest [legacy problem] to assess . . . [because] [t]here are . . . no government-provided statistical sources that enable analysts to compare jurisdictions on the size and character of their capital needs or on the soundness of their infrastructure expenditures," I think it unlikely that legacy problems are causing U.S. overinvestment in public infrastructure, and indeed the United States is certainly not known for overinvesting in public infrastructure. The U.S. Organization for Economic Cooperation and Development (OECD) figures suggest public investment in the United States is typical of OECD countries—slightly more than the EU average but considerably less than Korea, New Zealand, or Japan (see fig. 1).[4] Moreover, the State Budget Crisis Task Force concluded that "America's aging infrastructure faces growing capital needs, most of which are funded by state and local governments. However, these critical needs suffer from low budgetary priority."[5]

Thus, the tendency toward government short-sightedness that Nathan rightly highlights is more likely to lead to under- (rather than over-) investment. In my view, underinvestment in public infrastructure is only partly the result of government short-sightedness. Perhaps just as important is the fact that much infrastructure is, to some extent, a public good from the point of view of the state or local government. For example, a highway that allows transport of goods across the state of Illinois benefits the shippers and the consumers, but not necessarily Illinois residents. Thinking only of their own benefit, Illinoisans will underinvest in these goods. Traditionally, we have used two strategies to compensate. When possible, we have employed user fees, such as tolls and gas taxes, to shift costs from the general taxpayer to the users who benefit from the infrastructure. Traditionally, user fees have

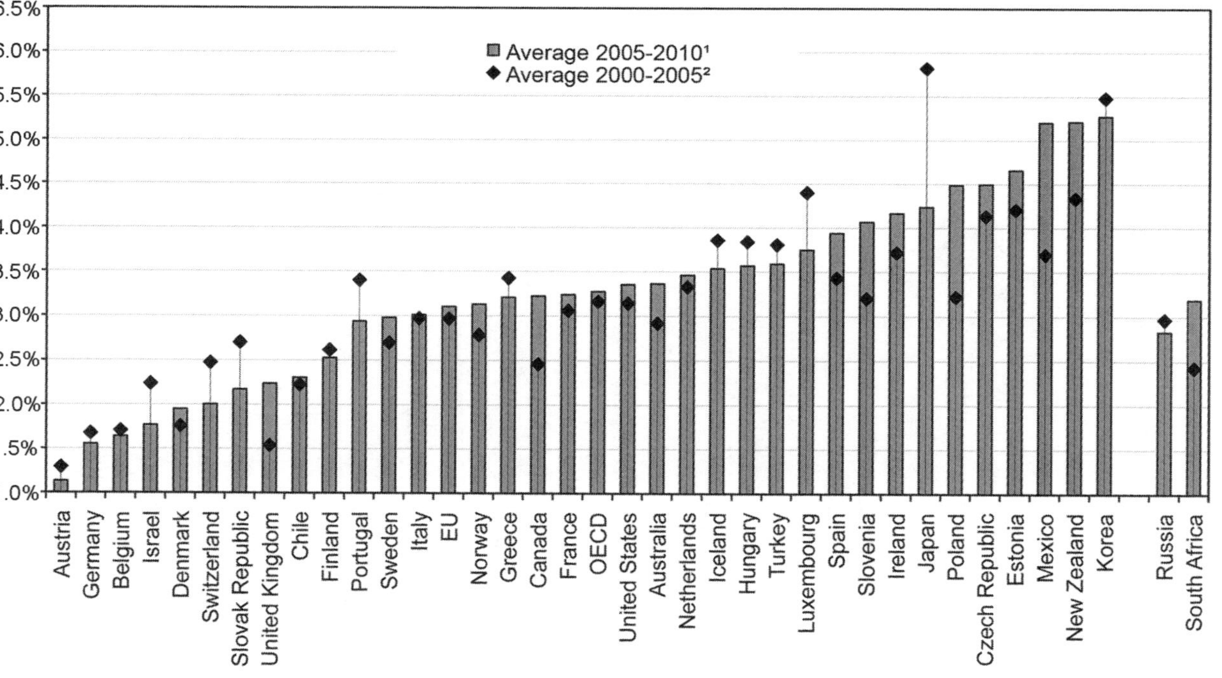

Note: Users of the data must be aware that they may no longer fully reflect the current situation in fast reforming countries.
1. Average 2005-2009 for Chile and Russia.
2. Average 2002-2005 for Russia.
Source: OECD (2011), OECD *Economic Outlook*, No. 90.

Figure 1. Public Investment as Percentage of GDP.

faced technological limitations (e.g., slow traffic through tollbooths), but technological advances (e.g., open-road tolling) make such user fees a more appealing option.

User fees are a good option and have great potential to be expanded, but they face political obstacles. For example, despite the fact that the federal gas tax is widely viewed by experts as a user fee that is too low, it has not been significantly increased in many years. The major reason for the resistance to an increase in the gas tax seems to be that Congress, and perhaps the general public, argue that the additional revenues a tax increase would generate would not bring sufficient additional benefits to compensate for the higher payment. This attitude is disturbing because this user fee is earmarked to support clearly identifiable and visible public goods. If political opposition to earmarked user fee increases is so strong when it is wrongheaded, it is hard to see how any general-purpose tax can gain widespread support. In this environment, it seems we might accept the conclusion that the general public is unwilling to pay for a high level of government services, which would then encourage us to figure out how to reduce both government spending and service provision. Alternatively, we might conclude that significantly increased educational efforts are necessary to help decision makers understand the link between tax revenues and public goods and services.

When it's not feasible to assess user fees, we have had matching federal government grants to state and local governments. In many cases, matching grants have been poorly designed and targeted. Sometimes indeed these matching grants have reduced state and local governments' costs so much that there has been overbuilding of public infrastructure in some places (e.g., major highways in rural areas with little potential for high traffic flows). However, at other times, the matching grants have probably underfunded important public infrastructure (e.g., highways and highway repair around dense urban areas).

Richard Nathan's suggestion of a new deputy directorship and office at CBO could be highly constructive in identifying areas where more spending is needed, as well as areas where less spending is needed, and in identifying looming but not yet evident fiscal crises. I agree with Nathan that the task is daunting and that simply providing more and better information in itself is important, possibly the most politically feasible and potentially constructive course of action at this moment in history. Policy analysts need to challenge themselves to design constructive and politically feasible policies to bring greater balance between current spending and current benefits.

I should note that the kind of policies I am thinking of would, if successful, discourage future missteps but would not reduce the legacy of unfunded liabilities that state and local governments currently face. Dealing with these legacy costs will require patience and shared sacrifice—tax payments will have to exceed current benefits for many years to come. In the final analysis, perhaps the most important legacy of our past flawed fiscal behavior will be the realization that we must place a high priority on developing political and fiscal institutions that constrain our capacity to make short-sighted and irresponsible decisions. This is a joint challenge for scholars and for political leaders.

Notes

1. Roger Lowenstein, "Siphoning G.M.'s Future," *New York Times*, July 10, 2008, http://www.nytimes.com/2008/07/10/opinion/10lowenstein.html?_r=0, accessed November 25, 2012.

2. Floyd Norris, "Private Pension Plans, Even at Big Companies, May Be Underfunded," *New York Times*, July 21, 2012, http://www.nytimes.com/2012/07/21/business/pension-plans-increasingly-underfunded-at-largest-companies.html, accessed November 25, 2012.

3. Jason Appleson, Eric Parsons, and Andrew Haughwout, *The Untold Story of Municipal Bond Defaults*, Federal Reserve, August 15, 2012, http://libertystreeteconomics.newyorkfed.org/2012/08/the-untold-story-of-municipal-bond-defaults.html, accessed December 27, 2012.

4. U.S. Council of Economic Advisors, *Economic Report of the President, 2012*, table B21 (Washington, D.C.: U.S. Government Printing Office, 2012), http://www.gpo.gov, accessed December 27, 2012.

5. State Budget Crisis Task Force, *Report of the State Budget Crisis Task Force: Illinois Report*, October 2012, 7, http://www.statebudgetcrisis.org/wpcms/report-1/, accessed May 15, 2013.

PART THREE
SUMMARY

Conversations with Local Policy Officials

A Synthesis

BREEZE RICHARDSON

WBEZ

The 2012 UIC Urban Forum began with opening remarks from Chancellor Paula Allen-Meares, who welcomed the audience and restated the commitment of the University of Chicago at Illinois to "a national discussion of the vital issues facing urban areas."

It has now been four years since it was recognized that, "for the first time in human history, more than half of the world's population live[s] in cities." That same year, 2008, also marked the start of the Great Recession, understood to be the worst economic downturn since the 1930s, which placed significant economic pressures on urban centers. And so it seems that the quality of urban life as we move forward will depend on "the capacity of metropolitan areas to respond to the challenges of this global era." However, perhaps unlike before, there appears to be a focus on cooperation within metropolitan regions: among sectors of the government, and between government and the corporate sector, civic sector, the community, and the academy to work collaboratively to make our cities grow and prosper.

Taking the podium at the forum, University of Illinois Board Chair Christopher Kennedy reflected on how undeniably intertwined the success of this metropolitan region is to the success of the state, noting that "75 percent of Illinois's population [reside in Chicago] and generate nearly 80 percent of the state's economic output."

The role of our metropolitan region in the global economy remains less certain, however. Fifty years ago, Chicago was one of the ten largest cities in the world. Today it is struggling to remain in the top thirty, and has fallen from 115th to 127th on the list of fastest-growing large metropolitan communities in the world. To remain competitive and attract economic assets to this region, Chicago will have to reverse this trend and demonstrate strong population growth rates and greater economic activity.

CHICAGO METROPOLITAN RESILIENCE: REDEFINING THE NEW NORMAL

To explore how we are proceeding in this new economic climate, WBEZ's Niala Boodhoo moderated a panel with Steven Koch, deputy mayor of Chicago; Neil Khare, deputy chief of staff to Cook County Board president Toni Preckwinkle; and Cristal Thomas, deputy governor for the state of Illinois. Boodhoo began the conversation with an illustration of "Chicago's new normal" from a numerical perspective: for the first time in history, there are more than half a million people living in poverty in Chicago suburbs, more than within the city limits. The city budget deficit is around $300 million, while the Cook County budget deficit is around $260 million. The state of Illinois has an appalling credit rating, in no small part due to the unfunded pension liability, which is also the worst in the nation.

Nevertheless, the past two years have seen good job growth across the region, the city budget deficit has been cut nearly in half, there has been "an unprecedented partnership between the city and the county" that has identified at least $66 million of potential savings from collaboration between these agencies, and a solution to the state's pension crisis appears to be on the horizon.

How Does Each Government Level Perceive the New Normal?

Cristal Thomas, deputy governor for the state of Illinois, began this discussion. The new normal at the state level consists of a) a new level of need, and in new places, which is leading to a needed change in how the state does business, and b) the reality of the budget itself: budget reductions, budget challenges, and continuing to do more with less.

For Steven Koch, deputy mayor of Chicago, the new normal is not without hope, given the resurgence of central cities in U.S. life. However, after decades of not recognizing the true cost of the public sector, we now face "the absolute full force and brunt" of deferred costs, as well as structural deficits existing at all levels of government. Although some may wish otherwise, it couldn't be clearer to Koch that "business as usual" is over; we can't afford it, and the financial markets that support government in the modern era simply won't tolerate it.

Unlike the leadership of the past, the leadership of today has adopted a consistent "lens of fiscal responsibility," according to Neil Khare, deputy chief of staff to Cook County board president Toni Preckwinkle. This is in part because of the electorate's attention to economic issues such as pensions. Khare feels that today's citizenry has a deeper understanding that allocating today's dollars toward borrowing means creating debt for the future, taking dollars away from critical services. When the new county administration took office in December 2010, it faced a $500 million budget gap, out of a $3 billion budget, which necessitated tough and immediate decisions. So, in collaboration with informed labor leaders and communities, with a lens of fiscal responsibility, the county has made decisions that Khare believes will lead to more sustainability in the future.

What Do a Commitment to Fiscal Responsibility and an Understanding of Deferred Costs Mean for Today's Pension Crisis?

Achieving a better understanding by taxpayers of the challenges government faces today, and of what the cost of government truly is, has been an important early goal for Governor Quinn and his staff as they work to address the $95 billion unfunded liability of the state's five pension systems.

For the city of Chicago, this is an issue of major concern given that the city's pension obligations could reach $1.2 billion by 2015. The panel agreed on that point, as well as on the observation that for something like twenty or thirty years, both state and city pension funds have been a convenient place to borrow from. This inadequate funding has led to where we find ourselves today: wrestling a structural deficit that exists in terms of current cost versus current revenue alongside a long-term commitment that has been avoided.

However, it's taken more than just inadequate funding to get us into the state we are now. Over the past several decades, contract negotiations have been mismanaged, extending benefits in lieu of raising wages when the latter lacked political support. Actions such as lowering the retirement age, or decreasing the accrual rate, were made without taking responsibility for the "enormous financial consequences" that commitment would leave future taxpayers. Today, the state of Illinois has over $100 billion of liability, and the city of Chicago has over $25 billion of liability. Things are now so critical that even if a decision were made to contribute the necessary funds at the city, county, and state levels so that the unfunded liability would at least stop growing, "it would bankrupt all three levels of government instantly."

It appears to Steve Koch that this leaves us with no choice other than to have the difficult conversation to determine how we can reduce benefits to a level that is actually payable. Recognizing that Illinois's state legal system is "amongst the most restrictive in the country" in terms of how contract rights intersect with the state constitution pension clause, and the reality that all three levels of government go to financial markets multiple times a year in order to refinance existing obligations, this process will be arduous but one we can no longer avoid. If the bond markets decide to stop lending money to the state of Illinois, it will "face meaningful financial constraints going forward."

For Neil Khare, the inability for everyone to see just how massive this problem is has been fascinating. While Cook County may be in the best position, with pensions currently funded at 58 percent, it is clear the county will go bankrupt if changes aren't made. Looking forward, there is the possibility that the proposed House Bill 6258 will lead to continued discussion within the state legislature and to a clear way forward before the new legislature is sworn in on January 9, 2013. [*Editor's note: the last action taken by the legislature on this bill was on January 8, 2013.*] If left unaddressed, significant property tax increases or cutbacks to critical services will be required—an outcome everyone agreed should be avoided.

But how unique is this problem to Illinois? According to Steve Koch, it's not at all unique; many municipalities around the county are facing this "disease." The desires to defer the cost, defer the question, defer the discomfort of addressing the true cost of providing the level of service governments had committed to providing, at all three levels of government, have led us to where we are today. Which means that now there has to be a different conversation: one that is focused on rethinking and austerity, living on less and being smarter, restructuring budgets, and working to eliminate the structural operating deficit. And that conversation has to take place within the context of remaining thoughtful about how to provide critically needed services in a way that doesn't burden future generations.

It is Koch's hope that we will be able to address this issue head-on, and then work toward making our region "the best place in the world for people to come and live, to make a life, to earn a living, and to realize their aspirations."

Cristal Thomas is also quick to acknowledge the severity if changes are not made. Every year Illinois's mandated pension payment goes up. Five years ago the pension payment was $1.8 billion. In 2012 it was $5.2 billion, in 2013 it'll be $6 billion, and the increases will continue from there. This challenges the state's ability to fund other parts of its budget, including funding for municipalities. With the state's ability to borrow and to fund future infrastructure investments or even current debt also in jeopardy, it remains clear: nothing in state government is more pressing than pension funding.

How Can we Prevent Future Legacy Costs?

The panel agrees that strong leadership is essential to accomplishing structural change, and structural change must be the focus. Whether it's on the expense side or the revenue side, providing the executive team with a clear framework can allow for a budgeting process that identifies real cuts. But for Neil Khare, while there is an opportunity to find efficiencies and lower costs in areas such as health care, there is also a need to align policy with the idea of fiscal responsibility.

For example, Khare outlined an opportunity the county has to work with policy makers in just this way: the Cook County Jail is a major county expense, costing $143 a day to house someone. Therefore, lowering the jail population is an agency goal. Electronic monitoring for detainees identified as low-level, nonviolent offenders would reduce that cost by almost half.

However, finding basic efficiencies still needs to be a higher priority, according to Steve Koch. Noting it to be an interesting difference between the public and private sectors, Koch believes there isn't enough communication between government and taxpayers about how money is spent. In Koch's opinion, a majority of taxpayers think the government is inefficient, noting that he himself would most likely answer "no" if asked whether tax dollars are well-spent by government. This is therefore a critical issue, where strong leadership should demand the ability to represent itself to taxpayers as "good stewards." Koch proposed: When the electorate understands and believes their money is well-spent, and they are getting what they should for dollars paid, it will be because the "hard work [was done to make] a huge organization efficient and effective."

How Can City-County Collaboration Reduce Legacy Costs and Create Structural Change?

The elected leadership of Chicago and Cook County shares a vision of fiscal responsibility, which led to a process that identified between $66 and $140 million worth of savings from 2010 to 2014 . Neil Khare confirmed that, in the first year alone, there was $39 million in savings, with $34 million of that being annual.

As large organizations, with budgets ranging from $3 to $6 billion and a combined 50,000 people employed, these are large metropolitan governments that share several similar functions: both have revenue departments that collect taxes, both have large technology divisions that support government functions, and both have procurement organizations that buy goods and services. Therefore, there has been an opportunity to not only share best practices, but also issue joint request for proposals (RFPs) and consolidate staff.

Illinois has more units of government than in any other state. It seems that now might be the time for an assessment to finally be made of how much of that is really necessary. Steve Koch addressed the city's decision to hand health care service provision to the county. While Chicago retained public health and epidemiological responsibilities, establishing a strong partnership with the county allowed for the change to take place, eliminating costs.

But operating more efficiently will mean cutting jobs. For Chicago, where 70 to 80 percent of the city budget is labor, addressing the economic impact created by such structural changes is challenging. But if the enormous overlap between the city, county, and state is to be addressed, this hard work is unavoidable.

This question of how to operate more efficiently has led the state to close some facilities. Governor Quinn has championed the closing of prisons, developmental disability centers, and hospitals—acknowledging these as legacy costs. Built decades ago, they "have hundreds of millions of dollars of deferred maintenance" and are expensive to operate. Today, especially in health care, Cristal Thomas explained how community-based services have been identified as the best-practice model, but transitioning in that direction has become an economic development issue for many affected communities. The state is working to play an active role in leading conversations that aim to restructure local economies, while identifying where collaboration or a new model can create efficiency and better service.

How Much Intraregional Competition Is There?

According to Steve Koch, in today's global marketplace, competition is less between two suburbs of Chicago than it is between this region and every other metropolitan region in the world. However, easier mobility by both the private sector and its potential workforce means it is now more important than ever to consider what economic opportunities should be pursued by the region and what will burden the tax base for an extended period of time without delivering clear long-term benefits. Economic incentives play a crucial role.

Therefore, the city and state often work together to author packages, which include both city and state financing components, to bring economic development opportunities to the region. There is also collaboration across the Midwest to position the region as a whole to be more competitive against foreign markets.

Other leadership in the region has supported this approach. The Organisation for Economic Cooperation and Development (OECD), Chicago Metropolitan Agency for Planning (CMAP), and World Business Chicago have all released reports in recent years focused on regional economic development. The competition the Chicago region faces from regions around the globe that have incredible assets and institutions as well as populations of ten million or more, means Chicago must take a regional approach.

Neil Khare did the math: with only 2.7 million people in Chicago, or 5.2 million people in Cook County, the region's leadership must start thinking about a six-county region or ten-county region in order to be viable in the global marketplace. In the future, coordinating a fourteen-county region that includes Milwaukee, southeastern Wisconsin, and parts of northwestern Indiana may even be required.

And so with an eye toward even greater collaboration in the future, making the metropolitan region of Chicago, and Illinois as a whole, an attractive place to invest and locate will require sustained effort by all agencies to break down the silos that have been created around local economic development. Cristal Thomas is quick to recognize that offering funding to local communities is a big part of the state's role. But there also needs to be a strong commitment toward addressing other factors, such as education and crime. Infrastructure is also an important responsibility—targeting an increasingly shrinking amount of resources toward the areas of highest need and highest priority. And it will only be through a collaborative approach that need and priority can be identified and resources pooled. For example, in some of the neighborhoods of Chicago, the city and state are collaborating on violence prevention efforts. And the state has worked with the county to help leverage federal dollars to assist with meeting the health care needs of county residents.

For the county, economic development has only recently been identified as a priority. With two-thirds of the budget focused on health care and public safety, economic opportunity is recognized as a lead factor in people's lives, impacting both health and crime. While the county doesn't have the same financial resources to address the economy as the state might, Khare shared the county's interest in playing a bigger role in convening various governments so that educational institutions and other resources can be coordinated to "make a measurable and meaningful impact on growing jobs in this region."

How Is the Region Acknowledging Its Growing Reality of Suburban Poverty?

Neil Khare began by pointing out the disturbing absence of a social safety net in many south suburban communities, which lack the nonprofits and support services that are common in urban areas. New community development programs, funded by the state and federal governments, have allowed for the county to focus on "tangible projects that create jobs" as one way to address this.

There has also been a clear impact on both the quality of care and financing to the Cook County health care system. In 2012, over 50 percent of those seeking services "self-pay" (meaning they are uninsured). Cristal Thomas addressed the possibility of the Affordable Care Act ushering in health care reform—and more federal dollars—which both the state and county aim to leverage.

For the state, addressing suburban poverty has created greater demand in its suburban offices. Adding staff and increasing access in these regions has been a challenge given the lack of nimbleness traditional to government. The number of people enrolled in the state Medicaid program has increased, and the rate of uncompensated care continues to rise, raising serious concerns for doctors and nurses throughout the region and the ability of our health care system to stay viable. As food pantries and food banks see increased demand, the state is working to do more outreach around programs like the supplemental nutrition program, though Thomas is quick to admit there are fewer resources available to respond to a greater need.

What Will Continued Collaboration Require?

Acknowledging the need for strong communication, Cristal Thomas began discussing this question by saying the state will benefit from better understanding the direction the city and county are working in so that state policy can be best aligned. For Steve Koch, it seems clear that for the state to prosper, the city and county need to be doing well and the real opportunity for efficiency will be gained through both independent and collective efforts. And although there are political differences across the three levels of government,

Neil Khare believes that the "fiefdoms" of the past are gone. He would like to see the collaborative spirit present between governments turn outward, leading to more cooperation with community foundations, organizations, and faith-based groups—to better involve them when making critical decisions across policy areas, from public safety and health care to education, economic development, and job creation.

As the region's institutions continue to grow and adapt to the new economic reality, there is an incredible opportunity for a more responsive kind of government, says Steve Koch. Education reform has occurred at all levels, health care is transforming, and these changes will continue to have an impact over the long term. For the state's part, Cristal Thomas reiterated the commitment of Governor Quinn to examine how services are being delivered across systems and work to make them as resilient as the people of the region.

EMERGING FROM THE GREAT RECESSION: HOW CITIES RESPOND TO AND THRIVE DURING CHALLENGING ECONOMIC TIMES

In the forum's second hour, WBEZ's Natalie Moore moderated a panel with the Honorable Michael Coleman, mayor of Columbus, Ohio; Betsy Fretwell, city manager of Las Vegas, Nevada; and the Honorable Luke Ravenstahl, mayor of Pittsburgh, Pennsylvania. Moore began by asking each to share a "snapshot" of their city and to speak to the economic turmoil and other challenges faced by each.

Mayor Michael Coleman of Columbus spoke first. Although Columbus is now the largest city in Ohio, followed by Cleveland (with half the population of Columbus) and Cincinnati (with one third the population of Columbus), this wasn't always the case. Indeed, Columbus now successfully drives the state economy as a result of people immigrating to Columbus from around the world, and a dramatically growing business sector.

Not long ago, however, Columbus faced its own substantial fiscal cliff. Beginning in 2008, a process began in the face of crisis to examine what changes needed to be made in order to make the city prosperous into the future. Facing high pension costs and high labor costs—the economic reality Chicago faces today—Columbus "took a look in the mirror" and evaluated things. Today, Columbus is financially stronger, with a triple-A credit rating, the highest of all cities of its size in the nation. This turnaround was achieved after a "laser-like focus on job creation" to grow the city's tax base, which is funded through a municipal income tax as opposed to a property tax. A *New York Times* article credits Mayor Coleman with Columbus's success—though he is quick to say there were many people behind the transformation—pointing to job development and business growth as a winning strategy for the state.[1] Today Columbus sees itself as a global city.

Betsy Fretwell next addressed the audience about Las Vegas, where she is city manager. With a metropolitan area of around two million people, the city proper has a population of 600,000 people, and budget of $1.5 billion. For nearly two decades, Las Vegas led nearly every growth chart: fastest growing city, building between fifteen and seventeen new schools each year, with 8 to 10 percent growth in personal income per year, and a booming housing market with new construction 6 to 7 percent above the national average.

Then, in 2008, Las Vegas—along with the rest of the country—hit a wall. While the city's previous reputation had been "last one in, first one out," this recession was different. Personal income growth fell by 8 percent by 2009, unemployment rose to 14 percent, and the city faced a growing deficit. Revenues dropped to 2004 levels, resulting in a lost of over $80 million in general-fund revenues. Approximately $115 million in cuts were made, including negotiations to existing labor agreements where past promises simply couldn't be met. It took nearly two years to convince labor leaders and city workers that the decades of previous prosperity were gone and not returning.

Today Las Vegas is adapting, working to build a new economy on the strength of the city's hospitality and leisure industries. However it continues to struggle with a foreclosure crisis—20 percent of homes in the region are grappling with foreclosure, affecting over 130,000 homes. But Fretwell was quick to acknowledge the city's resiliency, noting, "Who can build a gaming mecca out of a desert? If we can do that, we certainly can come back from this."

Among the city's new priorities are entrepreneurs, with Las Vegas now ranked second in the nation for the number of start-ups, and over $400 million has been invested in the downtown area, including a new state-of-the-art performing arts center, a new city hall, three new museums, and the arrival of the city's first Fortune 200 company—Zappos.com—which is relocating its headquarters to the former city hall building. There is also $350 million in private funds earmarked for education, start-up funds, and downtown redevelopment, which is supporting the city's efforts. All this acknowledged, Fretwell was quick to conclude: there remains a lot to learn.

The mayor of Pittsburgh, Luke Ravenstahl, shared the story of his city, where thirty years ago—in 1983—the city experienced an economic crisis. The unemployment rate was approaching 19 percent, following a collapse in the steel industry. This ushered in a "rebirth" for Pittsburgh, which had previously relied on steel and heavy manufacturing, but now had to accept—much like Las Vegas—that those jobs were not coming back.

The story of Pittsburgh today is a successful one, hosting a diversified economy, with a strong presence by education and health care industries, a strong financial-services sector, home to 1,500 high-tech companies, 600 life sciences companies, and with a substantial opportunity to grow jobs in the energy sector. Unemployment today is just over 7 percent, which is well below both the state of Pennsylvania and the national average. Home ownership is up, housing values are up, and Ravenstahl is quick to proclaim Pittsburgh to be a good place to live and do business.

Many leading publications have echoed his sentiment. Pittsburgh has been called "America's most livable city" and a great place to raise a family, start a business, retire, and visit. Ravenstahl points to President Obama's decision in 2009 to have Pittsburgh host the G-20 Summit as a major factor in the city's turnaround. The event was one of the safest of any summit of its kind, held anywhere in the world, and the global stage it created was a remarkable opportunity for Pittsburgh to tell its story. The image problem that the city once had, of being an old, dirty, smoky town, became history. Today, Pittsburgh stands as a green city, with clean water, and a beautiful skyline.

How Have Legacy Costs Been Addressed?

For Pittsburgh, legacy costs remain one of the biggest challenges facing the city. In 2004, the year Luke Ravenstahl became a member of the Pittsburgh City Council, the city was declared "financially distressed." This led to a restructuring of the city government, by mandate of the state under Act 47. At that time, the city employed four thousand people. Following attrition and layoffs, there were just three thousand city employees in 2012. Other difficult decisions included closing neighborhood swimming pools, recreation centers, and firehouses. But taxes were never raised, and the city of 300,000 is now beginning to grow again (although today's population is half of what it had been at the height of Pittsburgh's manufacturing era), following reforms to align the government and delivery of government services to better reflect a smaller city.

However, pension obligations were then, and remain now, one the city's largest legacy costs. Though pension fund restructuring has taken place, benefits have been changed, and an effort has been made to contribute more, pensions are still only around 35 percent funded. Ravenstahl's administration advocates for changes to state law to relieve the pension fund situation in Pittsburgh. However there may be hope. Pennsylvania Governor Tom

Corbett announced in 2012 that addressing the pension crisis facing the state and its municipalities would be a top priority in 2013.

In addition to pension costs, Pittsburgh was struggling with substantial debt. When Ravenstahl took office as mayor, the debt burden was approximately $900 million. With an agreed-upon debt payment of 10 percent each year, the city spent $90 million of its $400 million budget—nearly 25 percent—in debt repayment. To address the issue, a five-year hold on any new debt was approved and the city instituted a pay-as-you-go capital budget using operating funds to survive. It was a difficult period for the city, but the efforts were successful. Just five years later, the debt burden is down to $600 million. Last year the city decided to take on new debt for the first time, and was able to do so in a responsible way, in part because the city's credit rating is better than ever before, having been upgraded nine times since 2006.

Currently in his second term as mayor, Ravenstahl is just thirty-two years old and continues to hold the distinction as the youngest mayor of any major U.S. city. As a younger mayor, Ravenstahl believes he has a vision for the future and is addressing his city's legacy costs with an awareness of what long-term impact those commitments will have for the city's future.

In Las Vegas, many of the same things have taken place. Here too, legacy costs are present and burdensome. Approximately $50 to $60 million a year is spent on pension costs, which are somewhere between 65 and 75 percent funded. In Betsy Fretwell's opinion, the state system is well-managed, and the state legislature has tightened several rules that should have a positive long-term impact on the governance of state pensions, but this expense is still a significant one for the city.

In 2008, when this crisis was hitting Las Vegas hard, the city government realized it had been "going so hard, so fast, for so long" that there wasn't a relationship between the city and its citizens in the way the government now needed. Thirteen community meetings were scheduled to gather constructive feedback and discuss where cuts could be made. More often than not, over half the audience would be made up of firefighters or city employees, worried they would lose their jobs—a challenge Pittsburgh also faced. Swimming pools and community centers were closed, work was shifted to the nonprofit sector, there was some privatization, and all the city's compensation systems were rescaled.

Fretwell feels the citizens were remarkably tolerant throughout the process, and believes they were appreciative of the transparency, strong communication, and inclusiveness. In addition to conducting surveys and focus groups, the city held participatory budgeting sessions and the strategic plan was publicly rewritten through city council sessions. Rebuilding confidence in government was absolutely critical, and Las Vegas's business community was joined by citizen committees to assist with the restructuring process. This seems to have helped restore faith in government and allowed for many to better understand the limitations of government in this new era.

Michael Coleman has experienced two major recessions as mayor of Columbus. The first was in 2001, following the 9/11 terrorist attacks, which sparked a national recession felt deeply by many U.S. cities. The second was worse; beginning in 2008, it was the longest and deepest recession many cities, including Columbus, had faced in nearly eighty years. Particularly disadvantaged neighborhoods in Columbus faced unemployment numbers that rivaled those of the Great Depression.

The impact was felt immediately. Within a month of the city government passing a balanced budget—a mandated requirement of the city's charter—Coleman found himself required to make cuts totaling more than $100 million. There were massive layoffs, including upwards of 540 police and firefighters; closed public facilities; and cutbacks to other government services. The city realized it faced a decision: what kind of city did Columbus want to be?

The quality of life in Columbus appeared to be in serious jeopardy, which led to the first tax increase in nearly thirty years. The city launched a public campaign to advocate for the increase, working closely with the business community, which supported the decision so strongly they funded the effort. An increase of 0.5 percent was approved, with the promise by Coleman that reform would continue and pension costs would be addressed.

In Columbus, historic commitments made by previous mayors to cover pension and health care costs, in addition to raises, had led to 100 percent of pension contributions being made by the city for nearly all its employees. Coleman understood this needed to change. He pledged to save the city $100 million in pension costs. Through his efforts, as of today over $210 million of pension costs have ultimately been cut back.

Today, Coleman clearly sees the impact these adjustments have had on his city. A combination of reduced costs and expenses, greater efficiency, and increased revenue has transformed Columbus into the strongest economy in the state of Ohio. Unemployment has remained low, and over 92,000 new jobs have been attracted to, and retained by, the city. Ohio State University, located in Columbus, is among the largest universities in the nation, with 56,000 students, and it—alongside other businesses and institutions—successfully collaborated with government leadership to make this economic growth possible. The city is now operating a diverse economy, including a strong research base and growing high-tech sector, and a new strategic plan for the region aims for an additional 180,000 jobs by 2020 alongside a 33 percent increase in per capita income for Columbus residents. With these commitments, the city remains aggressive in addressing economic development for the city.

How Has Pittsburgh Attracted New Investment?

Under Mayor Ravenstahl's leadership, Pittsburgh is said to be experiencing its third renaissance, a revitalization marked by population growth, job creation, and $5 billion in investment in the downtown district alone. This investment has unequivocally occurred in partnership with the business community, where, as an example, PNC Bank has constructed two high-rise buildings—the second being noted as world's tallest and greenest building, constructed without government subsidy. The city did support the construction of the first building, funded through a TIF, which Ravenstahl believes helped start the economic development in downtown.

But the future of Pittsburgh's economy is linked to the ability of research institutions, such as Carnegie-Mellon University (CMU) and the University of Pittsburgh, to create it. Another example of business investment and innovation in Pittsburgh is the story of Google: after moving downtown, its expansion has been amazing. Today, Google employs over two hundred people in East Liberty (a neighborhood of Pittsburgh) at the site of a former Nabisco bakery, which had stood abandoned for nearly fifteen years. With the aid of state funding, the city government rehabilitated the building and Google moved in. Google has now acquired additional space across the street to erect a second building.

For Ravenstahl, the city's commitment to strong public transportation, bike lanes, and bike-sharing programs has created an environment where young people want to live and work. The city's focus is now to keep the best and brightest minds in Pittsburgh. The second largest city in Pennsylvania, after Philadelphia, Pittsburgh enjoys both the second and third largest economic hubs, located just miles apart in downtown Pittsburgh and the Pittsburgh neighborhood of Oakland, home to both the University of Pittsburgh and Carnegie Mellon University. Strongly linking these two economic engines will allow for the use of the tremendous intellectual capital of these universities to fuel continued economic development for the region.

What Is the Role of Gaming Revenue for the City of Las Vegas?

City Manager Betsy Fretwell is confident that the city's hospitality and leisure industry has almost recovered, remaining only 2 or 3 percent down from the industry's peak. And it has been extremely important that employment in this sector recover. In Las Vegas, gaming revenue is mostly received by the state and county, though the city sees revenue through retail sales and property value increases.

Today, the city is focused on diversifying the downtown economy, which was the original casino core in the Las Vegas Valley. There is a renewed effort to reinvest in infrastructure along this historic corridor, which is bounded by several freeways. The city of Las Vegas leads the state's economic development efforts, operating a $20 million redevelopment agency. Working to establish a regional approach, Fretwell had been serving as the executive director of the Las Vegas Redevelopment Agency, where state-mandated restructuring has benefited the city's efforts. Throughout restructuring, no cuts were made to economic development efforts, additional staff was hired, and creating a business-friendly environment across the region has been a priority.

In part, this has meant a simple focus on speed: streamlining ordinances and reducing turnaround time for things like a business license (where a thirty-day waiting period has been reduced to just five days). The city is more committed than ever to helping businesses grow, whether or not they are gaming related. For example, Take-Two Interactive is bringing two hundred new jobs to downtown Las Vegas. This underscores how Fretwell sees the need for expectations in Las Vegas to adjust. Celebrating the arrival of two hundred jobs—in comparison to a new casino opening, which would mean two thousand jobs—represents a change in itself. But smaller investment adds up. Start-up companies that begin with two employees are within three or four months up to ten employees. Multiply that by twenty, which is what has happened in Las Vegas over the past six months, and it is clear just how much small business growth is making an impact on the future of this city.

What Creates Economic Opportunity in Today's Cities?

For Mayor Coleman, the key to economic vitality in a city is a strong downtown, including a strong sense of "livability." When he took office in 2000, the downtown of Columbus was not what you see today. Reflecting on the stories of Pittsburgh and Las Vegas, he sees the strength of a city's downtown transform what's possible for Columbus—making downtown a good place to work and a great place to live. From condominiums and apartments to bike lanes, downtown investment has revitalized the city center. Today the average Columbus resident is thirty-one years old, and this youthfulness has contributed to the vitality you see today, with millions of dollars invested in a riverfront district with public parks, art, and restaurants.

Mayor Ravenstahl was quick to agree: Public space creates a valuable sense of community and can be a tremendous economic driver to a city's downtown.

City Manager Fretwell acknowledged the importance of redefining a city's downtown, if required. In Las Vegas, what was previously approximately an eight-block downtown area is now over a mile in diameter. Both Ravenstahl and Coleman agreed. In Pittsburgh, the rivers that historically created geographic limitations have been crossed and new development has reinforced the desire by the community to occupy these spaces. In Columbus, a previously spread-out downtown has become much more densely occupied, contributing to a vastly different experience for those who live and work there.

What Is the Role of City Neighborhoods?

Mayor Coleman confirmed: you have to balance the bright lights of downtown with economic development planning that benefits a city's neighborhoods. You can often work with businesses to leverage the efforts being made in downtown as an incentive for needed development in neighborhoods.

In Las Vegas, there was a concerted effort to get the city's residents to care about downtown, which had been neglected. After twelve years of working to address downtown, many neighborhoods started to voice their desire for more economic development in the neighborhoods. Infrastructure investments to sidewalks, streets, and parks have been celebrated, aiming to strike a balance—as Coleman stated—so that strong economic development downtown could create the revenue necessary for neighborhood improvements to continue.

It's the same story in Pittsburgh, according to Ravenstahl. A strong city requires both a strong downtown and strong neighborhoods, and the success of downtown can be leveraged to enhance neighborhood development. For example, the creation of a Neighborhood Renaissance Fund was instigated by Pittsburgh's Urban Redevelopment Authority, following the sale of downtown real estate to PNC Bank for their previously mentioned expansion. These proceeds are now being used to fund neighborhood development projects. The first ten recipients were recently awarded with grants ranging between $10,000 and $100,000, which the city anticipates will impact neighborhoods in a meaningful way.

In conclusion, to reiterate University of Illinois at Chicago Chancellor Paula Allen-Meares's opening remarks, "for the first time in human history, more than half of the world's population lives in cities. . . . and so it seems that the quality of urban life as we move forward will depend on the capacity of metropolitan areas to respond to the challenges of this global era." With a new focus on cooperation within metropolitan regions—among sectors of the government, and between government and the corporate sector, civic sector, the community, and the academy—we have the capacity to make our cities grow and prosper. While the role of our metropolitan region in the global economy remains uncertain, in order to remain competitive, we will have to demonstrate strong population growth rates and greater economic activity. Learning from the experiences of other metropolitan regions allows for Illinois to explore new ideas and consider solutions that have proven successful.

Note

1. "Did Barack Obama Save Ohio?," *New York Times Magazine*, September 5, 2012.

PART FOUR
POLICY EXPERIMENTS

What Now?

The authors of the white papers (and the chapters in this book), the discussants at the UIC Urban Forum panels, and the moderators identified, debated, and discussed a broad range of possible policy experiments for the future resilience of the metropolitan region. Drawing on suggestions and recommendations, we offer the following synopsis of possible policy experiments

Determine How to Build the Local Social Safety Net in an Era of Fiscal Constraint

- Strategies for strengthening the social safety net include improving take-up of federal social benefits, especially in immigrant communities;
  - building coherent regional systems for delivering services;
  - strengthening the role of metropolitan planning organizations and community development financial institutions in creating regional systems for services;
  - devising new federal programs to work with regional nonprofits and philanthropy to address the special problems of highly distressed suburbs and cities;
  - reengaging local governments as advocates for federal programs that support low-income residents, such as the TANF Emergency Fund, which allowed states to create subsidized jobs for TANF recipients.
- Enhance data collection on municipal activities that can be analyzed and shared with others.

- Support "family-supporting wages" or livable wages.
- States should invest more in workforce development, social services, better safety nets.

Determine What Constitutes Resilient Economic Development: Challenges and Opportunities

- Identify and devote resources to develop a sober assessment of the prevailing landscape, with a focus on weaknesses and opportunities.
- Establish a small committee of leaders tasked with identifying organizations with adequate capacity to take a leadership role in the execution of the on-going economic development strategy.
- Encourage regular bilateral and multilateral meetings between "unnatural" bedfellows.
- Cities can be leaders of a region's renaissance.
- Reduce municipal reliance on business incentives.
- Invest in basic infrastructure that benefits the entire community today and in the future.
- Better design community college and high school curricula to target opportunities for employment.
- Economic investment activities must be created with the understanding that the city and region are connected to the broader global economy.

Identify How Cities Collaborate While Competing in the New Economy

- Local government officials need to be sensitive not just to economies of scale, but also to possible positive and negative spillovers across governments and functional areas that may first appear to be unrelated to each other.
- The choices for addressing regional governance issues go beyond conventional comparisons of political markets and regional institutions.
- Local actors design collaborative mechanisms to reduce collaboration risks and to make commitments more credible and binding.
- Local policy makers and administrators need to create new venues and take advantage of existing venues that provide opportunities for face-to-face interactions with both competitors and collaborators in order to build knowledge and social capital that can advance their collective interest.

- Decision makers need to be aware that the efficiency advantages of self-organizing mechanisms may come at the cost of increased service inequality across jurisdictions.
- City size matters in creating partnerships, and formal or informal arrangements may be pursued, depending on city size.
- Some issues cannot be resolved by bilateral negotiations; instead, regional solutions to intractable issues (e.g., sprawl) are warranted.

Determine the Legacy Costs of Earlier Decisions

- Create a new deputy directorship and office at CBO for state and local finance that would be the center point for a consortium of federal offices and agencies that disseminate the types of data, research, and analysis that are needed as inputs to a system of regular online, user-friendly reports and studies on state-local finance.
- The consortium should lead in these ways and others to provide comparative across-the-board data and analysis. It should also conduct and sponsor special studies in major functional areas of government.
- Any public-private partnership to support infrastructure development must be transparent and subject to public debate and consideration; there must be adequate oversight; and the regulation of the private partner must be in the public's interest.
- Design better means for assessing the long-term planning and fiscal implications of public-private partnerships.
- Consider developing a national infrastructure bank.
- Infrastructure may be overbuilt due to the opportunity to postpone payments for repair to another generation of users and payers, which may require downsizing.
- Better design and target federal and state grants for infrastructure such that overbuilding is not stimulated but right-size building is.
- Responsibly fund state and local pensions.

Each city and metropolitan region is unique. Its demographics, employment structure, the investment in its social and physical capital, the quality of life of its residents, the vibrancy and dynamism of its neighborhoods, its sustainability with respect to energy consumption, and a host of other characteristics makes cities similar along some dimensions and quite different along others. The selection of policy tools to address concerns will have a profound and lasting impact on the city, its design, and its future. Cities learn from the effects and impacts of decisions of earlier generations. And they reexamine their current situation and future potential. Their resilience is a function of their learning, adapting, and strategizing about their future. The challenges for cities and metropolitan regions are and will be addressed because the people in those cities and metropolitan regions are motivated to enhance their quality of life, the human condition, and the opportunities and possibilities for their progeny.

Contributors

PHILIP ASHTON joined the Urban Planning and Policy Program at the University of Illinois at Chicago (UIC) in August 2005. Initially trained as a political scientist and an urban planner, he worked as a technical assistance provider for existing and startup consumer cooperatives in Canada and the United States. For six years, he was a research associate at the Center for Urban Policy Research at Rutgers University, investigating neighborhood change in Newark, New Jersey, and large-scale urban redevelopment in Camden, New Jersey. He has also been a research consultant for the Fannie Mae Foundation.

Currently, Ashton's research focuses on three interrelated areas. His primary scholarly focus is the restructuring of U.S. retail finance and its relationship to U.S. central cities. He has published several analyses of the subprime mortgage market that critique conventional interpretations of how minority borrowers and neighborhoods will fare in the "new financial marketplace." With Rachel Weber and Marc Doussard, he is investigating the role of investment banks and infrastructure funds in producing the growing market for urban infrastructure assets, including long-term leases for Chicago's Skyway and parking meters.

A second line of research examines the neighborhood effects of broad changes in financial markets and urban policy, attempting to distinguish the different paths to neighborhood change that have accompanied the marketization of urban redevelopment. With Kathe Newman at Rutgers, Ashton conducted a detailed neighborhood study of real-estate development in Newark. He was part of a team conducting a study of neighborhood changes produced by concentrated subprime lending in Chicago. A project he is involved in evaluates the progress of Chicago's Neighborhood Stabilization Program in addressing the growing problems of concentrated foreclosures across the city.

Third, Ashton is interested in the regulatory regime governing the U.S. financial system, and in the modes of credit market regulation capable of shaping a progressive path within financial sector reform. He has written on the Community Reinvestment Act and on the tensions in various civil rights frameworks as they have been applied to questions of credit access. In 2008–9, Ashton was a faculty scholar at the Great Cities Institute at UIC, beginning a research project on financial citizenship and the reconfiguration of credit risk within recent financial crises.

Ashton has a bachelor of arts (Honours) from the University of Winnipeg, a master in urban planning from McGill University, and a doctorate from Rutgers University.

RAPHAEL W. BOSTIC is the Judith and John Bedrosian Chair in Governance and the Public Enterprise at the Sol Price School of Public Policy at the University of Southern California (USC). He directs the Bedrosian Center on Governance and the Public Enterprise.

He recently returned to USC after serving three years in the Obama Administration as the assistant secretary for policy development and research (PD&R) at the U.S. Department of Housing and Urban Development (HUD). In that Senate-confirmed position, Bostic was a principal advisor to the secretary on policy and research, with the goal of helping the secretary and other principal staff make informed decisions on HUD policies and programs as well as budget and legislative proposals. Bostic led an interdisciplinary team of 150, which had expertise in all policy areas of importance to the department, including housing, housing finance, rental assistance, community development, economic development, sustainability, and homelessness. During his tenure and with his leadership, PD&R funded more than $150 million in new research, became an important advisory voice on departmental budget and prioritization decisions, and reestablished its position as a leader on developing policies associated with housing and urban development.

Bostic became a professor in the USC School of Policy, Planning, and Development in 2001. His work spans many fields, including home ownership, housing finance, neighborhood change, and the role of institutions in shaping policy effectiveness. A particular emphasis has been on how the private, public, and nonprofit sectors interact to influence household access to economic and social amenities. His work has appeared in the leading economics, public policy, and planning journals. He was director of the master of real estate development degree program at USC and founding director of the Casden Real Estate Economics Forecast. Prior to that, he worked at the Federal Reserve Board of Governors, where his work on the Community Reinvestment Act earned him a special achievement award.

In an earlier stint at HUD, Bostic served as a special assistant to Susan Wachter, the assistant secretary for PD&R. He earned his PhD in economics from Stanford University and his BA from Harvard University.

RICHARD C. FEIOCK is internationally recognized for his expertise in local government and local democratic institutions. He holds the Jerry Collins Eminent Scholar Chair and is the Augustus B. Turnbull Professor of Public Administration and Policy in the Askew School at Florida State University (FSU). He is the founding director of the FSU Local Governance Research Laboratory and served as doctoral program director for the Askew School from 1999 to 2004. He also directs the Sustainable Energy and Governance unit of the FSU Institute for Energy Systems, Economics and Sustainability.

Feiock received his BA degree from Pennsylvania State University, and his MPA and PhD from the University of Kansas. He is a recipient of the Herbert Kaufman Best Paper Award from the section on public administration, American Political Science Association, the 2008 William E. and Frederick C. Mosher Award for the best article published in *Public Administration Review*, the 2009 Manning J. Dauer Award for research and service from the Florida Political Science Association, the 2010 Donald C. Stone Award for career contributions to the field of intergovernmental management from the American Society for Public Administration, and the 2011 Marshall Dimock Award for the best lead article published in *Public Administration Review*.

Feiock has been principal investigator on four National Science Foundation research grants as well as grant awards from the Lincoln Institute for Land Policy, the Aspen Institute, the IBM Center for the Business of Government, and the Fulbright Scholar Program. He has published five books and more than a hundred refereed articles. His work appears in the leading scholarly journals of political science, public administration, planning, and urban affairs. His books include *Institutional Constraints and Local Government* (SUNY Press), *City-County Consolidation and Its Alternatives* (M. E. Sharpe), *Metropolitan Governance: Conflict, Competition, and Cooperation* (Georgetown University Press), and *Self-organizing Federalism* (Cambridge University Press).

RACHEL A. GORDON is an associate professor of sociology and faculty fellow of the Honors College at the University of Illinois at Chicago and a faculty member of the Institute of Government and Public Affairs (IGPA) at the University of Illinois. She has a BS in psychology from Pennsylvania State University, an MPP and a PhD in public policy from the University of Chicago, and received predoctoral training in demography and postdoctoral training in work-family research at the NORC Research Centers. Gordon's research broadly aims to measure and model the contexts of children and families' lives, often using longitudinal data sets. She regularly engages with audiences beyond academia in order to both increase the relevance of her research for public decision making and to share the results of her own and her colleagues' research with policymakers, practitioners, journalists, and the public.

Gordon has served seven terms on the editorial board of the *Journal of Marriage and Family*, as a council member for the Section on Children and Youth of the American Sociological Association (2009–12 term), and as a steering committee member of the University-Based Child and Family Policy Consortium (2010–12). She also served three terms as cochair of the Committee on Research, Policy and Public Information of the Society for Research on Adolescence (SRA); was review panel chair for Applied Research, Program Evaluation and Public Policy for the 2010 SRA Biennial Meeting; and was cochair of the Panel on Policy, Intervention, and Vulnerable Populations for the Society for Research in Child Development 2012 Themed Meeting on Transitions from Adolescence to Adulthood.

For her research and engagement activities, Gordon has received funding from a wide range of sources, including the National Institute of Child Health and Human Development, National Science Foundation, U.S. Department of Agriculture (Research and Innovation Development Grants in Economics [RIDGE] in the Economic Research Service), U.S. Department of Education (Institute of Education Sciences), U.S. Department of Health and Human Services (assistant secretary for planning and evaluation), and U.S. Department of Labor (evaluation contract through Jobs for Youth/Chicago). She has also received engagement-related grants from the Foundation for Child Development, the John D. and Catherine T. MacArthur Foundation, and the William T. Grant Foundation.

REBECCA HENDRICK received her PhD in political science from Michigan State University (1986) and is currently an associate professor in the Department of Public Administration at the University of Illinois at Chicago (UIC).

She was previously on the faculty of the University of Wisconsin–Milwaukee, where she directed the Master of Public Administration Program.

Her current research merges the four subject areas of financial management, organizational behavior, public finance, and governance, focusing on local governments in a regional context. She is the author of *Managing the Fiscal Metropolis: The Financial Polices, Practices and Health of Municipalities* (Georgetown University Press, 2011). The book examines how suburban municipal governments in the Chicago metropolitan area manage their finances during recessions and in response to a range of fiscal threats and opportunities. It pays particular attention to how these governments manage their finances within the fragmented system of local governance that exists in this region and the rules of local finance established by the Illinois state government. Since she came to UIC in 1998, much of her research has focused on local governments in the Chicago metropolitan region, which has more local governments than any other metropolitan region in the nation.

Hendrick's other research examines the nature and impact of local government tax competition in the state of Florida (*Public Finance Review*, 2009) and the effects of local government fragmentation on spending in metropolitan regions nationwide (*Urban Affairs Review*, 2011). She has also investigated the reaction of the city of Chicago to the Great Recession and its likely effects on the city's future finances (*Municipal Finance Review*, 2011). She is working on several projects that further examine the impact of government fragmentation and state-local relations on local government interaction and behavior toward each other. She is also engaged in research that expands on her prior research on the effects of fiscal structure on local government financial decisions.

GEOFFREY J. D. HEWINGS is director of the Regional Economics Applications Laboratory at the University of Illinois at Urbana-Champaign, as well as a professor in the departments of Geography, Economics, Agricultural and Consumer Economics, Urban and Regional Planning, and in the Institute of Government and Public Affairs. His undergraduate degree is from the University of Birmingham, England, and master's and doctoral degrees are from the University of Washington, Seattle. Prior to joining the University of Illinois, he served on the faculties of the University of Kent and the University of Toronto. He has served as a visiting professor at universities in Australia, Israel, Japan, Korea, and China. He received awards from the Fulbright Commission, the Woodrow Wilson Foundation and was designated a university scholar by the University of Illinois. He received a doctorate, *honoris* *causa*, from the University of Bourgogne. He has been elected a fellow of the Regional Science Association International, the Western Regional Science Association, and the International Input-Output Association.

Hewing's main research areas are in the fields of urban and regional analysis, with a strong emphasis on the development and application of large-scale models. His research activities are centered in the Regional Economics Applications Laboratory (REAL), a unit he cofounded in 1989. In Chicago he has conducted a variety of impacts analyses—on tourism, marathons, and art exhibitions—and has prepared an occupational information system for the Chicago City Colleges as well as a study examining interdependencies among subregions in the metropolitan economy. Other work focuses on the role of interstate trade among the states of the Midwest; the impacts of aging and in- and out-migration on the Chicago economy through 2050; and the impacts of port efficiency on the Brazilian economy. REAL maintains comprehensive impact and forecasting models for each Midwest state and for the Midwest as a whole; in addition, a monthly forecasting index for Chicago was featured in *Crain's Chicago Business* for many years. REAL's Chicago 2040 forecasts have been used by Chicago Metropolis 2020 and the Chicago Metropolitan Agency for Planning. In addition, REAL provides housing forecasts for Chicago and Illinois on a monthly basis for the Illinois Association of Realtors.

His publications include fourteen books, more than seventy book chapters, and 170 articles in major professional journals; he has supervised around fifty doctoral dissertations. Details are at www.real.illinois.edu.

DAVID MERRIMAN is professor and associate director at the Institute of Government and Public Affairs, and professor in the Department of Public Administration in the College of Urban Planning and Public Affairs at the University of Illinois at Chicago. He is also codirector of the University of Illinois Fiscal Futures Project, which monitors the fiscal condition of the state of Illinois. Merriman briefs the University of Illinois Board of Trustees and state legislators on fiscal conditions and policy in Illinois.

Merriman's scholarly work has included numerous papers on state fiscal responses to business cycles, differing rates of health care expenditure growth across states, cigarette tax evasion, tax increment financing, Cook County assessment caps, and Walmart's effect on local retail markets. Some of his recent work has been published in *Real Estate Economics*, *Journal of Housing Economics*, *Urban Affairs Review*, and *American Economic Journal: Economic Policy*.

Merriman also has been a senior research associate in the Urban Institute's Assessing the New Federalism project, where he studied the effect of changes in federal welfare funding on state finances. He holds a PhD in economics from the University of Wisconsin–Madison; his dissertation was awarded first prize for the outstanding doctoral dissertation in government spending and taxation by the National Tax Association.

RICHARD P. NATHAN directed the Rockefeller Institute of Government from 1989 to 2009. Prior to that he was a professor at Princeton University and a senior fellow at the Brookings Institution. Nathan served in government as an assistant director of the U.S. Office of Management and Budget, a member of the Advisory Commission on Intergovernmental Relations, and an associate director of the National Advisory Commission for Civil Disorders (the Kerner Commission).

Nathan is a graduate of Brown University and has a PhD from Harvard University in political economy and government. He is a member of the Richard Ravitch–Paul Volcker Task Force on the "State Fiscal Crisis." His fields of interest are state and local government and finance, American federalism, and possible policy and administrative responses to the challenge of rising U.S. health care costs.

MICHAEL A. PAGANO is dean of the College of Urban Planning and Public Affairs at the University of Illinois at Chicago, professor of public administration, fellow of the National Academy of Public Administration (which was chartered by Congress to assist federal, state, and local governments in improving their effectiveness, efficiency, and accountability), coeditor of *Urban Affairs Review*, and faculty fellow of UIC's Great Cities Institute. He has published four books, including *Cityscapes and Capital* and *The Dynamics of Federalism*, and over eighty articles on urban finance, capital budgeting, federalism, transportation policy, infrastructure, urban development, and fiscal policy. Since 1991 he has written the annual City Fiscal Conditions report for the National League of Cities, and between 2003 and 2008 he wrote a column called the Third Rail for State Tax Notes, which examined contemporary local government fiscal issues. He has delivered more than a hundred papers and speeches. He is principal investigator with Christopher Hoene of the National League of Cities and Richard Mattoon of the Federal Reserve Bank of Chicago on a three-year grant (2012–15) from the John D. and Catherine T. MacArthur Foundation to examine the constraints on cities' fiscal policy responses to changes in their financial environments.

BREEZE RICHARDSON is the director for Strategic Partnerships. She is responsible for working to ensure a coordinated and fully developed partnership program for Chicago Public Media. Through collaborations with institutions throughout the region, the program produces content for distribution on-air, online, and through live events. As a producer, Breeze manages *Chicago Amplified*, Chicago Public Media's gateway to community voices and ideas, as well as WBEZ's *Louder Than a Bomb* Series.

Breeze joined Chicago Public Media in September 2003 as an intern for *Worldview*, WBEZ's weekday global affairs program. She later became a producer for *Worldview*, then went on to produce StoryCorps-Chicago in 2005. From 2008 to 2012 Breeze served as the executive director of the *Off-Air Event Series*, producing over forty-five live events hosting nearly thirty thousand participants.

In December 2011, Breeze published "Measuring Community Engagement: A Case Study from Chicago Public Media" (Reynolds Journalism Institute, University of Missouri), and in 2012 she was interviewed for "Engaging Audiences: Measuring Interactions, Engagement and Conversions" (May) and "Dialogue and Deliberation for Civic Engagement in Chicago: Building A Community Of Practice" (December).

Prior to joining Chicago Public Media, Breeze hosted *Get Up, Stand Up* at WHPK at the University of Chicago, was a regular columnist for the *University Daily Kansan*, and produced the *Kaw Valley Independent* (a community newspaper in Lawrence, Kansas). Breeze has a MPP from the University of Chicago's Irving B. Harris Graduate School of Public Policy and a BA in economics and American studies from the University of Kansas.

Originally from Kansas, Breeze resides in the Northcenter neighborhood of Chicago with her husband, Kelsey, and their boys, Gus and Iggy.

ANNETTE STEINACKER is the director of the Urban Affairs and Public Policy Program at Loyola University Chicago. Her research primarily focuses on issues of urban economic development and metropolitan governance. She has done work on changes in the number and types of jobs available in central cities, factors that influence the location decisions of businesses, and the role of property tax abatements as part of a local economic development strategy. Extending work she did for local government agencies in the past, she has also worked on a project that identifies the skills gap between graduates of local higher education institutions and projected sectors of job growth in metropolitan areas. Mapping graduates' fields of study and types of degree to the expected labor demands in a metropolitan's growing economic sectors is used to determine likely deficiencies in the labor pool. The goal of the pilot study was to identify potential partnerships between a county economic development office and regional colleges in order to develop or expand programs to fill the specific labor market shortages.

Steinacker has also studied the impact local government organization has on public policy outcomes and the political feasibility of changing these structures, specifically the creation of metropolitan governments and special districts. Her approach to these topics combines quantitative analysis of national data sets as well as in-depth case studies of specific cities. Her research has been funded by the National Science Foundation and several private foundations.

Steinacker received her PhD in political science from the University of Rochester, a master's of Public Administration from Texas A&M University, and a BA from the University of Wisconsin–Madison. She previously taught at Columbia University, Texas A&M University, Georgetown University, University of Miami, and Claremont Graduate University. She was director of the public policy program at Claremont for ten years prior to joining Loyola University Chicago, and served as associate provost for faculty development at Claremont Graduate University.

NIK THEODORE is an associate professor in the University of Illinois at Chicago's Urban Planning and Policy Program and the former director of the Center for Urban Economic Development. His research spans urban political economy, labor markets, informal economy, policy mobilities, labor standards, neoliberal urbanism, and economic restructuring. He has conducted national studies of labor practices, working conditions, and compensation in low-wage industries employing largely immigrant workers, including day labor, domestic work, big-box retail, warehousing, and car washes.

RACHEL WEBER is an associate professor in the Urban Planning and Policy Program at the University of Illinois at Chicago (UIC), where she teaches and conducts research in the fields of economic development, real estate, and public finance. She is also the associate director of the UIC Great Cities Institute, where she coordinates university-wide research, teaching, and outreach initiatives that address issues facing the Chicago metropolitan area and other cities around the world. Recent work has focused on the design and effectiveness of property tax–based incentives for urban development; publications on this topic have appeared in such journals as *Economic Geography*, the *Journal of the American Planning Association*, and *Regional Science and*

Urban Economics. She is the coeditor of the *Oxford University Press Handbook of Urban Planning* (Oxford 2012), author of *Swords into Dow Shares: Governing the Decline of the Military Industrial Complex* (Westview, 2001), and author of the forthcoming book *Why We Overbuild* (under contract, University of Chicago Press).

In addition to her academic research agenda, Weber consults for local governments and community-based organizations on issues related to public spending, property taxes, and neighborhood revitalization. She was appointed by Chicago mayor Rahm Emanuel to the Tax Increment Financing Reform Task Force in 2011 to provide recommendations to the new administration for reforming this economic development tool and was a member of the Urban Policy Advisory Committee for then-presidential candidate Barack Obama. She received her undergraduate degree from Brown University and her master's and doctorate degrees in city and regional planning from Cornell University.

MARGARET WEIR is professor of sociology and political science at the University of California, Berkeley. Before coming to Berkeley, she taught in the Government Department at Harvard University and was a senior fellow at the Brookings Institution. Weir has been a member of the Institute for Advanced Study in Princeton, a visiting fellow at the Russell Sage Foundation, and a fellow at the Radcliffe Institute. She has received fellowships from the Ford Foundation, the Robert Wood Johnson Foundation, and the German Marshall Fund. She is a fellow of the American Academy of Arts and Sciences and the National Academy of Social Insurance. She chaired the MacArthur Foundation Research Network on Building Resilient Regions.

She is the author of several books, including *Schooling for All: Race, Class and the Decline of the Democratic Ideal* (coauthored with Ira Katznelson; Basic Books, 1985); and *Politics and Jobs: The Boundaries of Employment Policy in the United States* (Princeton University Press, 1992). She has also edited several books that examine the development of social policy in the United States, including *The Politics of Social Policy in the United States* (with Ann Shola Orloff and Theda Skocpol, Princeton University Press, 1988) and *The Social Divide* (Brookings and Russell Sage, 1998), the latter of which analyzed social policymaking during the Clinton administration. Most recently, she coedited *Building Resilient Regions*, vol. 4 of *Urban and Regional Policy and Its Effects* (with Nancy Pindus, Howard Wial, and Harold Wolman, Brookings Institution Press, 2012), which examines how metropolitan regions develop the capacity to bounce back from economic and demographic shocks.

New work includes a book titled *Out of Sight, Out of Mind: Marginalizing the Poor in Metropolitan America.* Drawing on evidence from Atlanta, Chicago, and Phoenix, the book analyzes strategies for adapting existing policies and building political alliances to fit the new, more variegated social geography of need in metropolitan America. The book examines institutional development and policy conflicts in the domains of social services, housing, and transportation. Articles from this research have been published in the *Urban Affairs Review*, *Regional Studies*, and *Studies in American Political Development.*

The University of Illinois Press
is a founding member of the
Association of American University Presses.

Composed in 10.5/13 Adobe Minion Pro
with ITC Franklin Gothic Std display
by Lisa Connery
at the University of Illinois Press
Manufactured by Sheridan Books, Inc.

University of Illinois Press
1325 South Oak Street
Champaign, IL 61820-6903
www.press.uillinois.edu